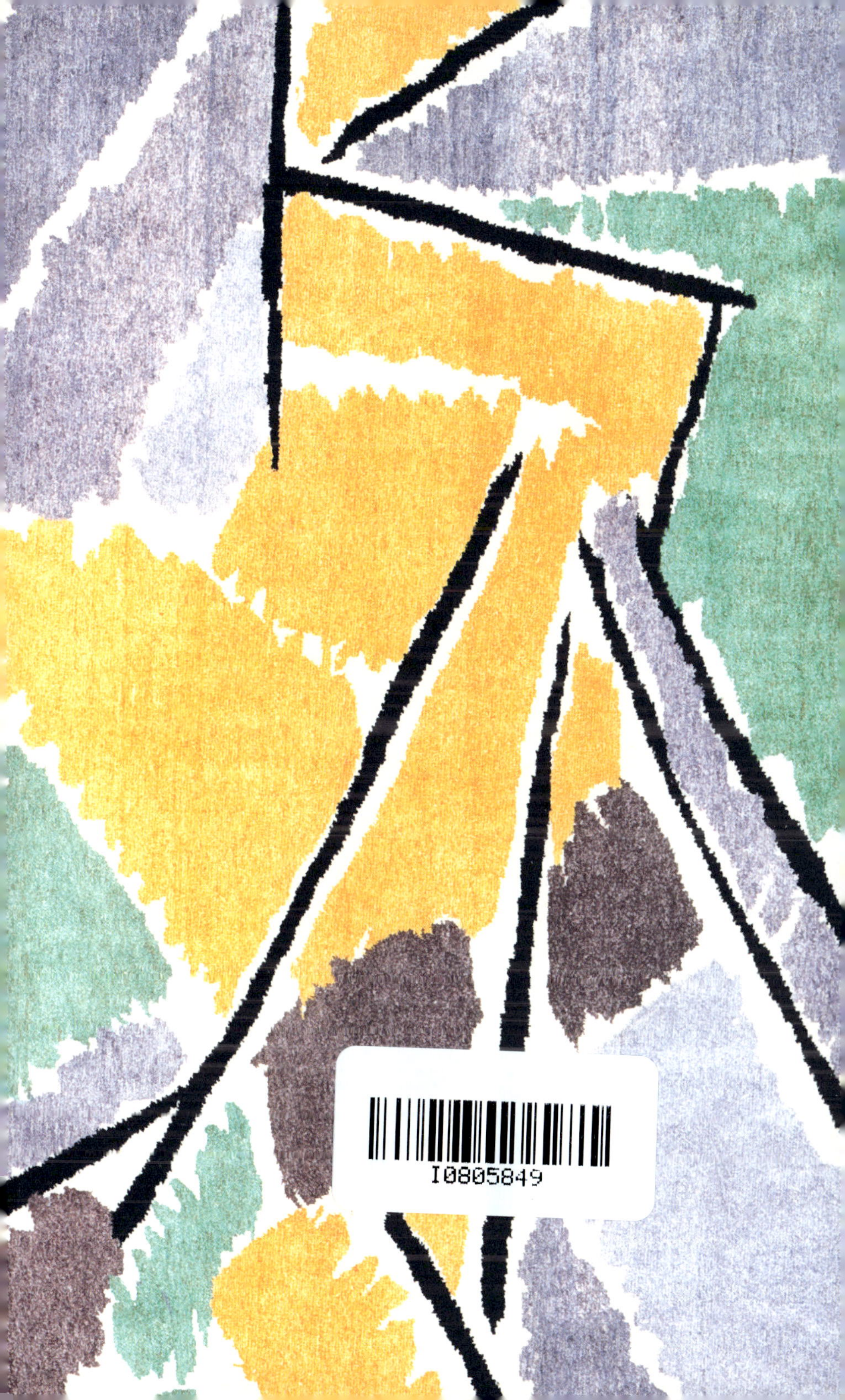

ROGER
FRY

ROGER FRY

Bloomsbury and the Invention of Modern Art

FIONA McKENZIE JOHNSTON

TRIGLYPH
BOOKS

First published in the United Kingdom in 2026 by Triglyph Books.

Triglyph Books
154 Tachbrook Street
London SW1V 2NE
www.triglyphbooks.com

Instagram: @triglyphbooks

Publisher: Clive Aslet and Dylan Thomas
Production Manager: Kate Turner
Design and typesetting: Tetragon, London
Cover design: Steve Turner
Assistant Editor: Devon Harvey
Copyeditor: Henry Howard
Proofreader: Mike Turner

Set in Optima and Adobe Caslon

British Library Cataloguing-in-Publication Data.
A catalogue record for this book is available from the British Library.

ISBN : 978-1-0686914-6-1

Printed and bound sustainably in China.

For Andrew, Sholto and Esmeralda

'If Bloomsbury had produced only Roger, it would be on a par with Athens at its prime.'[1]

VIRGINIA WOOLF

'In so far as taste can be changed by one man, it was changed by Roger Fry.'[2]

KENNETH CLARK

FRONT AND BACK ENDPAPERS: One of the original Omega rug designs put back into production by Christopher Farr, using original artwork held by the Courtauld Gallery.

Contents

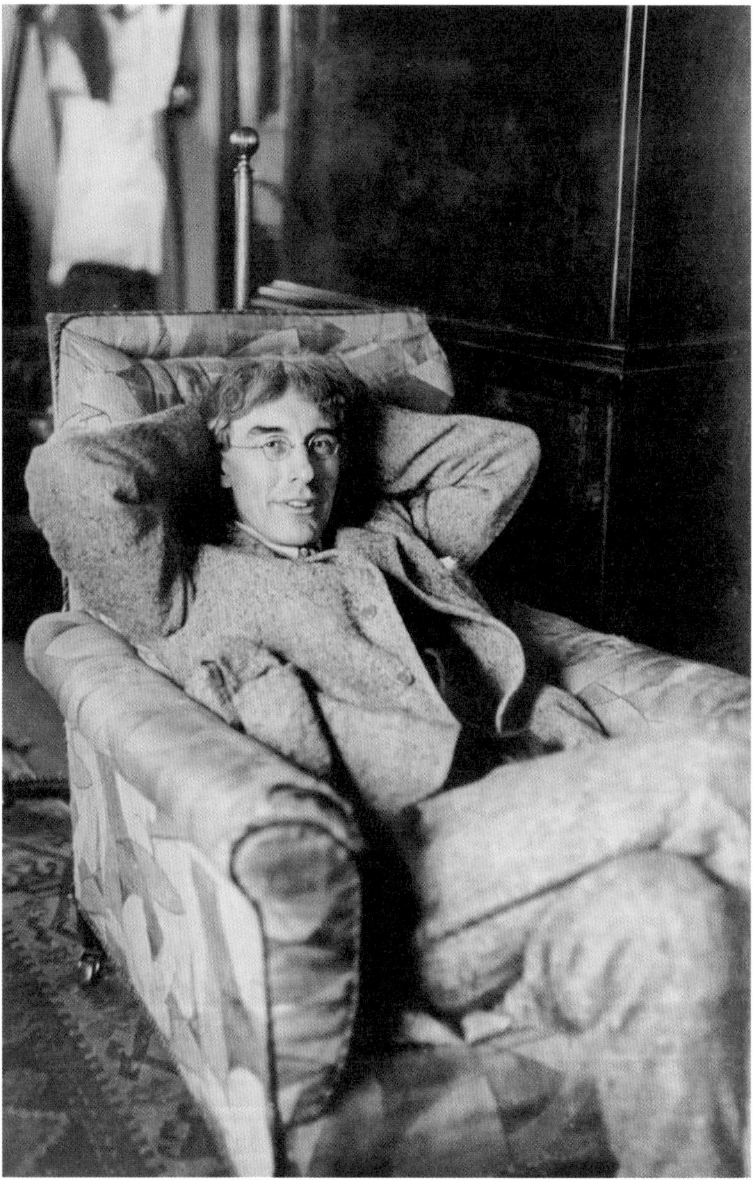

Roger Fry in his study at Durbins, his house in Guildford, in 1918. He is sitting in an armchair covered in an Omega Workshops fabric.

Introduction

THE EXACT DATE OF THE ARRIVAL OF MODERNISM in Britain has long been debated, but one recurring conclusion is that it began with Roger Fry – and what Desmond MacCarthy called the 'Art-Quake' of 1910.[1] *Manet and the Post-Impressionists*, an exhibition organised by Fry in London, introduced the public to the works of Cézanne, Gauguin, Matisse, Van Gogh and Picasso. It horrified an audience accustomed to Classical representation, and the aftershocks continued. Post-Impressionism developed an English following, Fry put on a follow-up show and offered a radical new vision of living via the Omega Workshops, while the generation he'd lectured at the Slade School of Art took art in new directions, including into abstraction.

Fry's preoccupation was with 'form' – a word he used to refer to the visual elements of a picture: the line, the colours, the composition. He believed form gave a work of art its emotional resonance, more than subject matter or narrative content. It was a democratisation of art appreciation, for it required no prior knowledge, only instinct as to whether one liked something. But at the same time, Fry saw Post-Impressionism as a new interpretation of an existing tradition. Linking it, via its emphasis on form, to the mosaics of Byzantium and early Florentine Renaissance frescos, he offered a way out and forward from the established doctrines of portrayal, while simultaneously rearranging the furniture of the British mind.

His infatuation with the Post-Impressionists came as a surprise to many of his contemporaries because Fry was, in 1910, a forty-three-year-old renowned Old Master expert who had only recently left a senior post at the Metropolitan Museum of Art in New York. He was known for his compelling lectures and astute art criticism, as an advisor to wealthy buyers, and as the author of a well-received book on Giovanni Bellini. He was also one of the founders of *The Burlington Magazine*, a picture restorer, and a practising artist in his own right. When it came to jobs in the late nineteenth-century and early twentieth-century art world, Fry worked across them all – although such a portfolio career was less unusual then. No university offered a degree in history of art, and the pool of expertise was consequently shallow (though elbows could be sharp). His polymath approach continued: in the second half of his life his paintings were exhibited in England, France, America and at the Venice Biennale; his books reached a mainstream readership; his lectures were broadcast by the BBC; and leading galleries and museums in New York, Philadelphia and London hold major paintings in whose purchase he played a part.

Fry was also a member of the Bloomsbury Group, the early twentieth-century cluster of British writers, philosophers and artists who numbered among them Clive and Vanessa Bell, Leonard and Virginia Woolf, Duncan Grant, John Maynard Keynes, Desmond MacCarthy and Edward Morgan (more familiar as E.M.) Forster. They came into his life – and he into theirs – the same year as *Manet and the Post-Impressionists*, and the encounter was metamorphic in both directions. Bloomsbury, with Fry, were at the forefront of the modern movement.

Unsurprisingly, given the reach of his influence, there are biographies of Fry in existence. Virginia Woolf's came out in 1940; as one of his closest friends she offers intimate insight into his character and charts his achievements, by way of some delectably Woolfian passages. Frances Spalding published hers in 1980; based on her doctoral thesis, it is triumphantly comprehensive, fascinating, and

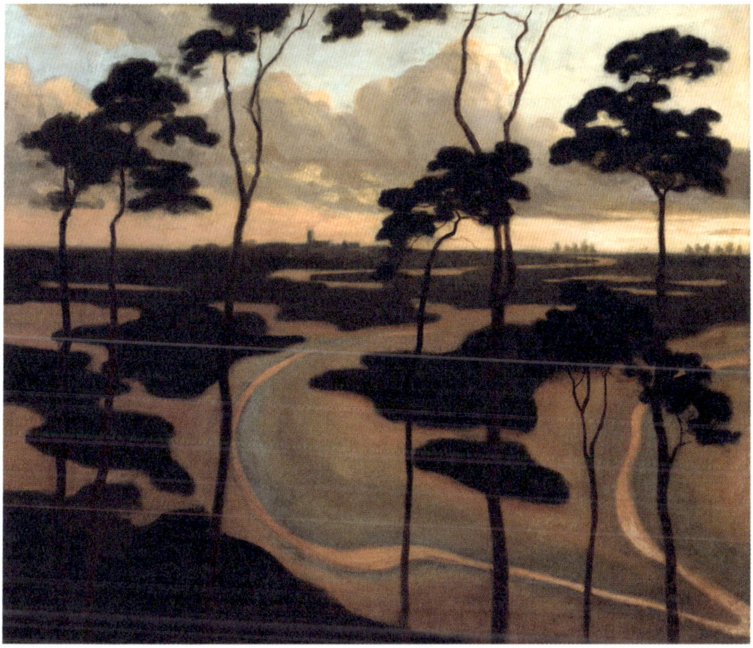

Roger Fry's *Blythburgh, The Estuary*, painted in 1892–3 and showing the influence of the Nabis group.

includes details that Woolf, deferring to Fry's family, left out – including his relationship with Vanessa Bell. Sadly, it is out of print, a fate which has also befallen Denys Sutton's edited volumes of Fry's letters and Richard Shone's captivating *Bloomsbury Portraits*.

My interest in Roger Fry was sparked at the Courtauld Gallery in London, where his impact can ever be felt – he advised Samuel Courtauld and was supportive of the founding of the Institute itself – and where I found his painting of *Blythburgh, The Estuary* of 1892–3 (on long-term loan to the gallery). He had recently returned from studying at the Académie Julian in Paris when he painted it, and the appealing composition shows the influence of the Symbolist Nabis group. Rejected by the New English Art Club, the most progressive exhibiting society of the time, who were then more Impressionist in ethos, it is an early instance of Fry finding beauty in a new perspective.

For Fry, his art was more important than anything else he did. In his lifetime, however, his paintings often didn't receive the approbation he'd hoped for, even among his friends. 'Some of them wondered,' wrote Clive Bell. 'Surely he knew that he was the best critic alive, and, at the bottom of his heart, can he have believed that he was a very good painter?'[2] Time was one of the issues: Vanessa Bell and Duncan Grant, who he is most often shown alongside, committed themselves to their art wholeheartedly. Fry, in comparison, slotted in painting when he could. And while painting undoubtedly made him a better critic, his critical interest in other artists led to some variance in style. When in 1913 Paul Nash visited Fry's friend Robert Trevelyan, who had been collecting Fry's work, Nash couldn't believe that what he was looking at was all by the same hand – or that the hand was Fry's, the 'high priest of art'.[3] But a hundred or so years later, it doesn't take away from the form-informed loveliness of works that are held by the Courtauld, the Tate and the Metropolitan Museum of Art, while the ideas that are imbued in each canvas only increase their charm.

A painter's artistic personality can be quite different from the personality described by their biographer – a point that Fry himself made in his 1927 book on Cézanne, whom he portrayed as a 'disillusioned, suspicious and grumbling misanthrope' in later life, yet a 'heroic figure' in his paintings.[4] But there are parallels between Roger's creative output and his character, and his stylistic transience is mirrored in his professional endeavours. William Rothenstein's observation of Fry as a twenty-something artist who 'sat' at another artist's feet,[5] which chimes with occasional accusations of painterly derivativeness, was answered by Virginia Woolf:

> Roger Fry had a great capacity for laying himself open, trustfully, optimistically, completely to any new Idea, new person, or new experience that came his way. But ... when he had sat long enough at those feet to see where they led, he would get up and go off, sometimes in the opposite direction.[6]

Moreover, it would be done with absolute conviction. Fry once told Vanessa Bell that 'he possessed some tremendous power, some queer force which gave him complete self-confidence and made him able to do all he thought best.'[7]

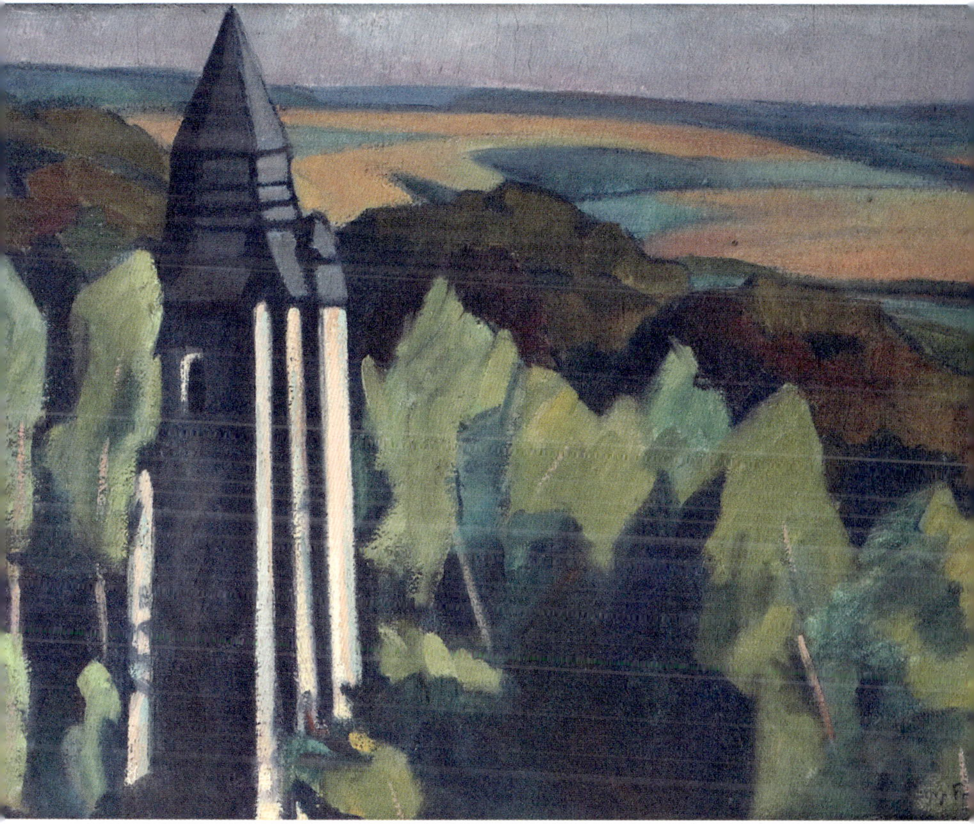

Roger Fry's *Landscape with Bell Tower*, c. 1913.

It could make him infuriatingly obdurate, but equally his conviction is one of the traits that ensured the consistent level of excellence he achieved across so great a variety of pursuits. There were other elements that worked in his favour, including his academic brilliance: before devoting his life to art, he achieved a First in Natural Sciences at Cambridge, where he was elected to the Cambridge Apostles. He spoke several languages, and had trained himself to pick them up quickly, using a method he once explained to Marie Mauron: 'All you need to do is take a book you know quite well, for example the Bible … and to read it with a translation.'[8] He reckoned assigning a few evenings a week would result in fair fluency within a couple of months.

It's a method that is reliant on momentum, and certainly Fry had that, too. The scope of his activity and achievements often sounds utterly exhausting – and it frequently wore out his companions. He thought nothing of bicycling miles to a particular church or valley and painting from first light to last with barely a break for lunch, or catching a pre-dawn train to a city where he'd spend four hours in a gallery before moving onto another city for an afternoon of the same. Articles and lectures were seemingly written on the fly, waiting for trains, on trains, in the time between a church closing its doors and dinner. But his enthusiasm was infectious: 'there was always some new idea afoot, always some new picture standing on a chair to be looked at, some new poet fished out of the obscurity and stood in the light of day,'[9] recalled Woolf. Adding colour to the self-portrait on the cover, she described him as 'brown and animated … he laughed spontaneously, thoroughly, with the whole of him'.[10] She remembered him wearing 'a large ulster coat, every pocket of which was stuffed with a book, a paint box or something intriguing … he had canvases under his arms; his hair flew; his eyes glowed.'[11]

Even in his sixties he was never still, as documented by Clive Bell's precis of twenty-four hours in the life of Fry while a guest at Charleston and, nominally, ill:

> Up and on the motive before breakfast; after breakfast just slips over to Tilton to see Sam Courtauld, arrange about lectures, and telephone to Hindley Smith; painting in Vanessa's studio until lunch; at lunch moans and groans about not being allowed to eat anything, has Lottie put on to cook special invalid dishes but meanwhile makes a hearty meal off roast beef and plum tart; hurries off to Seaford to inspect Hindley Smith's collection; back in time for an early tea so that he can drag Vanessa & Duncan to Wilmington to paint landscape; after dinner just runs through a few of Mallarmé's poems, which he is translating … bed time – 'Oh just time for a game of chess, Julian.' I look out of window at half-past one and see the old object, lying like a tomb, in bed on the terrace, reading by the light of a candle. He had to start early this morning in order to lunch with Lady Colefax. But, while I am dressing, I hear him shouting through the ground floor window – 'I think before I go we've just time to run through *L'après-midi d'un faune*.'[12]

His over-achievement did, occasionally, come with drawbacks. 'Although extraordinarily good and ingenious … he was inclined to be carried away by his enthusiasm for a scheme and brush aside all the details upon which success of failure depended,' recounted Leonard Woolf, who acted as secretary for the *Second Post-Impressionist Exhibition*. 'He conducted business in an extremely unbusinesslike way, and this occasionally led to disastrous results. For instance, he would make agreements with people without recording them in writing.'[13]

That was, in part, due to Fry's scrupulous honesty, and his belief in the inherent goodness of people – which in turn nurtured broad-mindedness and an irrefutable magnanimity. Even when Vanessa Bell fell in love with Duncan Grant, which was devastating for Fry, he never stopped promoting their work and encouraging them. And much of his time was directed towards schemes to improve the income of artists, or, after he founded a charity for the purpose, in the acquiring of paintings for the nation to allow others to benefit from their beauty. It helped here that he came from a respected, upper middle-class Quaker family, and that his unmarried sisters would step in and run his house when necessary, just as Leonard Woolf cleared up business muddles during the *Second Post-Impressionism Exhibition*. In addition, Fry was in receipt of a private income, which enabled him to take risks, to spend weeks abroad looking at pictures (though never in the lap of luxury, and he could make a little go a long way), to devote time to working for free, and to challenge the institutions who employed him.

It was, in many ways, a charmed life, though it came with difficult moments, relatable disappointments, and heartbreak. His marriage to the artist Helen Coombe became a tragedy to which we cannot apply a contemporary verdict. Schizophrenia, which it is now believed she may have suffered from,[14] had not even acquired a name when in 1910 she was committed to the institution that became her home for the rest of her life. Fry's relief, during these times, came from the love of his many friends, and from art.

And it was a desire to spread his appreciation of art that drove Roger Fry. His own writings and his *Last Lectures*, published posthumously with an introduction by Kenneth Clark, are still in print. Their survival is proof of the enduring value of Fry's wide-ranging and significant contribution. In this snapshot commemoration of Fry's brilliance, I've endeavoured to set his extraordinary career against the context of his time, in the hope that it will inspire readers to find out more, to look again at his art and the art which he admired, and to notice anew the beauty of its form.

NOTE

A biography, by its nature, comes with a cast of characters that can prove irritatingly untidy. The huge *dramatis personae* of Roger Fry's life is particularly unwieldy, largely on account of the extraordinary scope of his life, career and its internationalism, but also because of the artistic landscape of the time. The commercial gallery system was less established than it is now, and so artists formed their own exhibiting groups, whose roster of members grew and changed and bled into each other, before re-forming as new groups – all of which can feel impossible to keep track of. I have put together a list of those people whose repeat recurrences merit a brief identifying refresh, as well as a list of pre-war art groups. Neither is exhaustive, and they are not essential to consult. But should you wish to, they can be found on pages 209–215 and pages 216–217.

In quoted excerpts from handwritten sources, very occasional ambiguous spellings – that could be attributed to misinterpretation of handwriting – have been given the benefit of the doubt.

For all historic sums in £, a multiplication by 100 will give an approximate contemporary value.

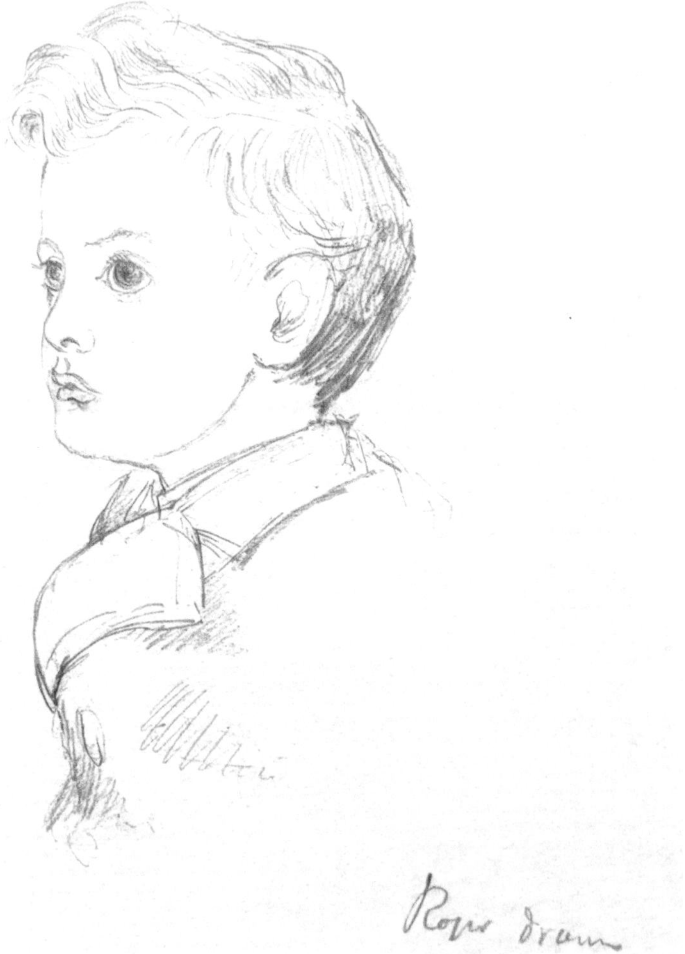

An 1874 drawing of Roger by his mother, Mariabella Fry. Roger would have been seven years old.

ONE

THE EDUCATION OF AN ARTIST

Boating along the Cambridge backs, past ancient Gothic colleges and the fanciful bridges that line that stretch of the River Cam, is to experience the meeting of academic brilliance with wilful dreams. Arguably, the same was mirrored in Roger Fry's throwing over of a First in Natural Sciences for a life devoted to art. He knew it was a risk: 'To fail in art is much more complete a failure and leaves one a more useless encumbrance on the world than to fail in almost anything else – e.g. to be a fourth-rate doctor in the Colonies,' he wrote to his father from Cambridge in February 1888.[1] He also knew the idea would be 'unpleasing'; being an artist was not the career his parents had hoped for him. Nor was it a path they would have predicted.

Roger Elliot Fry was born on December 14, 1866, almost halfway through Queen Victoria's reign over a still-expanding Empire, and five years after the advances of the Industrial Revolution had driven William Morris to found his decorative arts company with the aim of preserving craftsmanship. He was the second son and fifth child of Mariabella, née Hodgkin, and Edward Fry who, at the time of his birth, were living with their family at No. 6, The Grove, Highgate – then still a village outside London – in a terraced Georgian house three doors up from where the poet Samuel Taylor Coleridge had resided thirty-odd years earlier. They were

Quakers, a frivolity-free, pacificist Christian sect whose belief in equality of man regardless of gender, race or class marked them as progressives (famously, Quakers had played a major role in the abolitionist movement). Both Edward and Mariabella had seven or eight recorded generations behind them, reaching back to the seventeenth century when Quakers had been widely persecuted. But by the nineteenth century, the Frys were comfortably upper middle class. The year of Roger's birth coincided with the launch of the first ever mass-produced chocolate bar, Fry's Chocolate Cream. J.S. Fry & Sons, which had been founded in Bristol by Roger's great-grandfather, was being transformed into the largest commercial chocolate producer in Britain by Roger's uncle, Joseph Storrs Fry II.

Edward Fry, a year younger than his brother Joseph, was a distinguished lawyer, who in 1877 was appointed a judge and knighted, in 1883 was made a Lord Justice of Appeal, and from 1902 was also involved in international law at The Hague. Liberal in some regards – he was against some of the traditional Quaker peculiarities such as adherence to 'plain dress' – he upheld absolute respect for the Quaker practices of abstemiousness, hard work and social responsibility. His was a puritan household, and Roger later recounted a moral code 'that was terribly complicated and one didn't always forsee where it would catch you tripping over some apparently indifferent and innocent word or deed'. When it did, 'my father's voice was of such an awful gravity that one shrunk at once to helpless self-condemnation and overpowering shame.' Principles were absolute: aged thirteen, Roger accompanied his father to watch the first telephone being installed at court – and was instructed to return a piece of wire given to him by a workman, it having been likened to a bribe.[2] Tipping was 'truckling to immorality', and moreover, 'we were brought up to the absolute conviction that all men not in regular employment and receipt of a fairly high salary were morally reprehensible, that in fact the world was so arranged that wealth and virtue almost exactly corresponded.'[3]

There were weekly two-hour meetings in the Friends' Meeting House, conducted mostly in silence, and, although there was love, spontaneous physical expressions of affection were in short supply, according to Quaker principles of self-denial and self-control. But there was a Sunday sirloin, teacakes for tea, ice-skating when the ponds at Hampstead Heath froze over – which, for the duration, charged his father with joy – a close-knit extended family, and sisters to play with. Roger's immediately older sister, Alice, died from scarlet fever in 1868, but four more girls were born after him; none, incidentally, were ever to marry. In 1873, Edward and Mariabella moved their family next door, to the larger No. 5, The Grove and in 1874, Edward bought Failand House, set in two hundred acres just outside Bristol, with views over the mouth of the River Severn to the Welsh hills beyond. It became the family's summer house, increasing the children's ready access to the outdoors.

Early schooling took place at home with visiting teachers. Edward Fry would himself have pursued a career in science had he been able to. (Oxford and Cambridge were closed to him; it was only in 1871 that the universities' religious tests were abolished.) He retained his devotion for the subject, and every morning read aloud to his children from scientific textbooks before leaving in a carriage and pair for Lincoln's Inn. There were keen discussions with a neighbour, the renowned scientist Charles Tomlinson, that the children were encouraged to listen to – and Tomlinson would invite the children to tea and show them various scientific objects of wonder. Roger's bedtime toy of choice was a crystal that his grandmother had given him, and he was enthralled by the mosses at Failand, the specimen trees Sir Edward planted there, and, in London, 'a bushy plant of large red oriental poppies'[4] – which he once sat and watched, that he might catch a bud bursting into flower.

Charles Tomlinson also took the Fry children to visit factories that made candles, glass and cut diamonds, which, Roger's sister Agnes recalled, 'raised questions of ... what made good art and bad art, what ornament was justified'.[5] And there was further exposure to art: annual trips to the Royal Academy, where Roger saw works by the Pre-Raphaelites and other prominent Victorians such as George Frederic Watts and Frederic Leighton, and to the National Gallery, where the collection primarily consisted of Italian Renaissance and Dutch and Flemish seventeenth-century paintings. Roger's early experiments in watercolour were encouraged by his mother, who painted landscapes, as did her sister, Elizabeth, a novelist who also produced designs for embroidery and copper and brassware in Arts and Crafts style. Elizabeth's husband was the architect Alfred Waterhouse; between 1873 (when Roger was six years old) and 1881, Waterhouse was engaged in the design and building of the Natural History Museum, the great 'cathedral to nature' that so excited the country, the interiors of which he augmented with decorative animal and plant ornaments, tiles, statues and relief carvings.

Roger's formal education began in 1877 when he was ten. He was sent to board at St George's, Ascot,[6] 'armed with a silver watch my father gave me, and a black leather bible which my mother gave me, with many solemn warnings about sin and the assurance that the bible would always guide me through the difficulties of life'.[7] The school was new and was described by another pupil, Winston Churchill,[8] as 'one of the most fashionable and expensive in the country'.[9] Roger was not, at that time, someone who stood out particularly, and he did not shine in sports, or anything else that small boys put stock in. His letters home mention some bullying, and he was horrified by the (standard for the time) corporal punishment. More pleasant was that his younger cousin Maurice Waterhouse was there too; he had his own garden which he enjoyed planting, he was allowed to keep two snakes, and academically he excelled.

In 1881 he moved to Clifton College in Bristol, where his brother Portsmouth had been before him, and which was exceptional for emphasising science over Classics. Roger's letters from there are full of the experiments he was allowed to carry out on his own, though there's also mention of adorning terracotta plates with pictures of

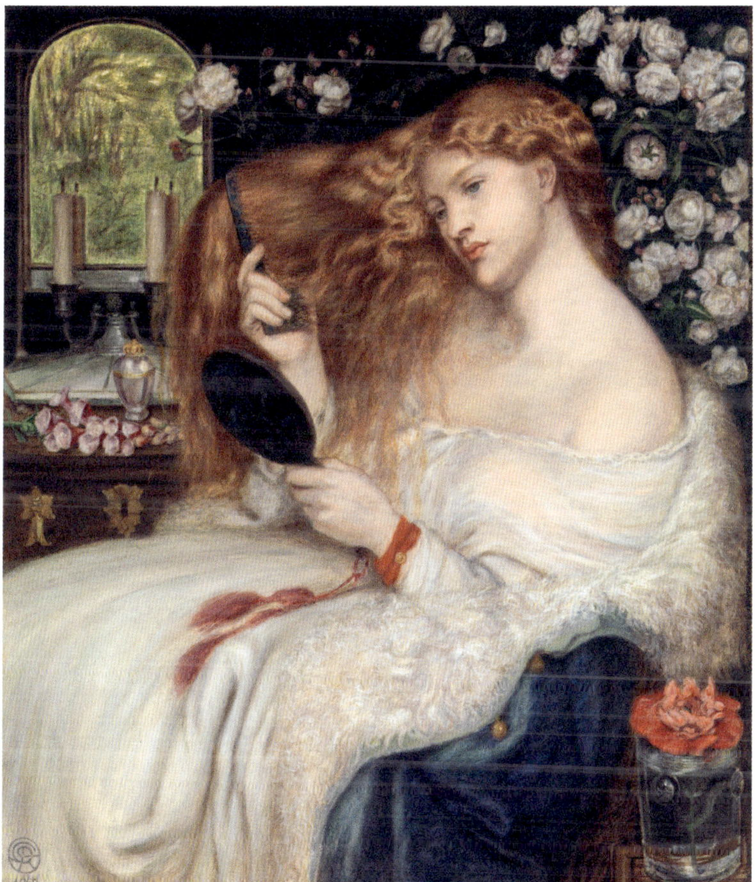

Dante Gabriel Rossetti, *Lady Lilith*, 1867, painted with his assistant Henry Treffry Dunn. Roger acquired it for the Metropolitan Museum of Art in New York in 1908.

flowers. But his time at Clifton was most marked by his friendship with John McTaggart Ellis McTaggart, who was to become one of the leading proponents of philosophical British idealism. The teenage Roger deliberately sought him out after hearing his peers speaking derogatively of his appearance (McTaggart, an awkward-looking boy, was excused from all sports). They undertook weekly Sunday walks, during which the conversation ranged from the day's sermon given by the headmaster, the theologian Canon Wilson, to Dante Gabriel Rossetti's paintings – Roger had read John Ruskin who believed that the duty of an artist was to capture the world accurately, not to idealise it – to grand philosophical debates on the merits, or not, of living under a republic.

In 1885 McTaggart and Roger went up to Cambridge together; McTaggart to Trinity, the still less socially adept Roger, at Canon Wilson's advice, to the smaller King's College. He was awarded a two-year exhibition, the only one given to his intake for science.

If Cambridge changed Roger, the second half of the nineteenth century was also a period of change for Cambridge. Daily services beneath the magnificent fan-vaulted ceiling of King's College Chapel were still compulsory, but the relaxing of religious requirements was leading to a greater diversity. There were female students: Girton College had opened in 1869 and Newnham College in 1871 (though women had to be chaperoned in lectures, had restricted library access, and were not yet granted degrees). Alongside this was an enthusiastic questioning of the established status quo, King's College being particularly remarkable as a place where some elements of homosexuality were less frowned upon than the 1885 Labouchere Amendment, which made all homosexual acts illegal, might suggest. One of the most renowned dons at King's was Oscar Browning, who, having been sacked from Eton for his closeness to some of the boys, had returned to his former college as a Fellow. There, he founded the Dante Society and the

Mozart Society, threw popular Sunday salons, and was a voice for an idealistic type of Greek love.

Roger shared rooms with McTaggart that first year, outside of college. Immediately enlivened by the possibilities, he took up rowing,[10] attended Browning's salons, and, importantly, met Charles Robert Ashbee, who, almost four years older than Roger, was reading history – and who was to become an architect, designer, and one of the prime movers of the Arts and Crafts movement. It was Ashbee who provided direction for Roger's initial move towards art. In the Easter holidays of 1886, he and Roger went to Somerset together, sketching, and spent a whole day marvelling at the Gothic cathedral at Wells, before Roger went home to Failand where he read romantic poetry – Shelley and Walt Whitman – to his sisters. The summer term saw Roger and Ashbee continuing their sketching, cycling through the Fens to find churches and views. Roger was elected to the Cambridge Fine Art Society and added their lectures to his schedule. July saw a visit from Edward Carpenter, a writer and socialist who lived with his male partner on a smallholding outside Sheffield. In his early forties, handsome, and by all accounts engaging (years later, he was the inspiration for E.M. Forster's tale of homosexual love, *Maurice*) the aftermath of his visit saw even greater significance given to both 'romantic' friendships and socialist utopias. Ashbee, when he left Cambridge that summer, went to live at Toynbee Hall, which had been established in East London in 1884 on the premise that the students of Oxford and Cambridge would share their knowledge with the poor, and at the same time develop solutions for endemic poverty.

Despite Ashbee's departure, Roger's interest in art only grew. In October 1886, a new Slade Professor arrived at Cambridge: John Henry Middleton. He had travelled widely through Italy, North America, Mexico, Greece, Egypt and North Africa, and – with William Morris – to Iceland. He'd been apprenticed to the Gothic

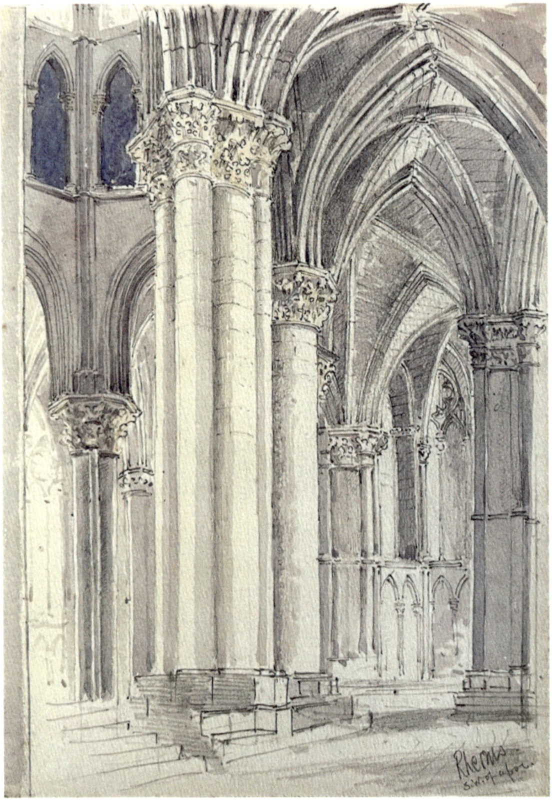

An 1887 sketch by Roger of the interior of Notre Dame de Reims.

Revival architect Sir Gilbert Scott, and had worked as a professional archaeologist. He brought with him paintings by fourteenth- and fifteenth-century Flemish and Italian artists, Rembrandt etchings, Persian tiles, textiles and pottery fragments, as well as a large collection of photographs of other works of art. Roger, who was impressed by him and interested in his ideas, began going to him 'once or twice a week for a sort of informal lecture on art',[11] for which Middleton was typically attired in a dressing gown and a skull cap. Alongside this, Roger spent more time looking at pictures at The Fitzwilliam Museum.

This enthusiasm for art did not preclude an avid appetite for other scholastic disciplines. McTaggart had become a member of the Conversazione Society, an academically elite secret society also known as the 'Cambridge Apostles' (there were twelve members). Another member was one of Ashbee's friends and contemporaries, Goldsworthy Lowes Dickinson, known as Goldie. The son of the portrait painter Lowes Cato Dickinson, he had graduated with a First in Classics and returned to King's to study medicine. In 1887, Roger, too, was elected to this exclusive group, and despite the thesis of secrecy, promptly wrote to tell both Ashbee and his mother. It was a bolster to his self-esteem, and he gladly devoted his Saturday evenings to meetings where the body was nourished by sardines on toast, and the mind by debate on matters of philosophy, politics, ethics and religion. McTaggart, then 'the principal inspiration of the Society'[12] had concluded that the universe was run not by God but consisted of 'souls in ecstatic communion with each other'.[13] Goldie, whom Roger held in worshipful high esteem, similarly put the love of friends first. It was the beginning of Roger's drift away from Quakerism – though, unlike his Waterhouse relations, who had been baptised into the Anglican church in 1877, he never broke with it completely.

It was also the beginning of an increasingly intimate friendship between Roger and Goldie. They breakfasted and lunched together every day, reclined under willow trees watching the moon set and the sun rise, and went night-swimming in Byron's pool before Goldie bade Roger goodnight with 'passionate kisses'. Confessing to 'a tick about boots', Goldie would lie on the floor and get Roger to put his feet on him. There was a walking holiday in Dorset, when they bathed at Weymouth and afterwards lay naked in the sand, holding hands. They were sharing a bed, and Roger allegedly suggested to Goldie, as they embraced, that they should go further – but Goldie, recounting the moment in his posthumously published autobiography, felt such an action would 'lower their love',[14] which was inspiring in him a steady stream of sonnets and other poems. He would send them to Roger: verses that wondered how wild roses could bear to grow 'so far from thee, so lone', accompanied by notes – 'I do hope you ain't missing me as much as I am you – else you must be having a bad time.'[15] Roger copied out some of the poems in his own hand. Liberated from the strictures of his upbringing, intellectually energised, and in receipt of affection, he was happier than he'd ever been.

But standing silently between Roger and his Cambridge friends, including Goldie, was their opinion that 'social service of some kind was the only end worth pursuing in life'. Roger might have discussed the cause with clever enthusiasm, joined Ashbee on a quasi-pilgrimage to Edward Carpenter's house at Millthorpe,[16] and been flattered to have been invited to a post-talk lunch with the famed socialist and writer George Bernard Shaw, but, as he confessed years later in a letter to Shaw, he secretly cherished 'a profound scepticism about all political activity'.[17] Rather, he was increasingly of the belief that art was his only possible métier, his zeal for it exceeding anything else.

In this vein, he sketched and painted whenever he had the chance. Following a holiday on Lake Lucerne with Goldie, McTaggart, and Ferdinand Schiller – another Clifton College friend, whose family owned the house they stayed in – he went to Amiens, and then to Reims. There, sketching outside the cathedral, he met 'the directeur des ecoles nationales de l'art decoratif or something'[18] who showed him where he had made mistakes, gave him motivating advice, and invited him to supper.

Roger applied his developing critical analysis to the fifteenth-century *Madonna and Child* by Verrocchio at Ruskin's St George's Museum in Walkley, and to G.F. Watts's new paintings at Christie and Manson's (now Christie's), of whom he professed himself 'more fully convinced than ever that not only is he the greatest modern painter but one of the greatest men. His portraits are simply grand.'[19] He went to Manchester for the Golden Jubilee exhibition, where, besides works by his uncle Alfred Waterhouse, he delighted in Frederic Leighton's *The Daphnephoria*, a depiction

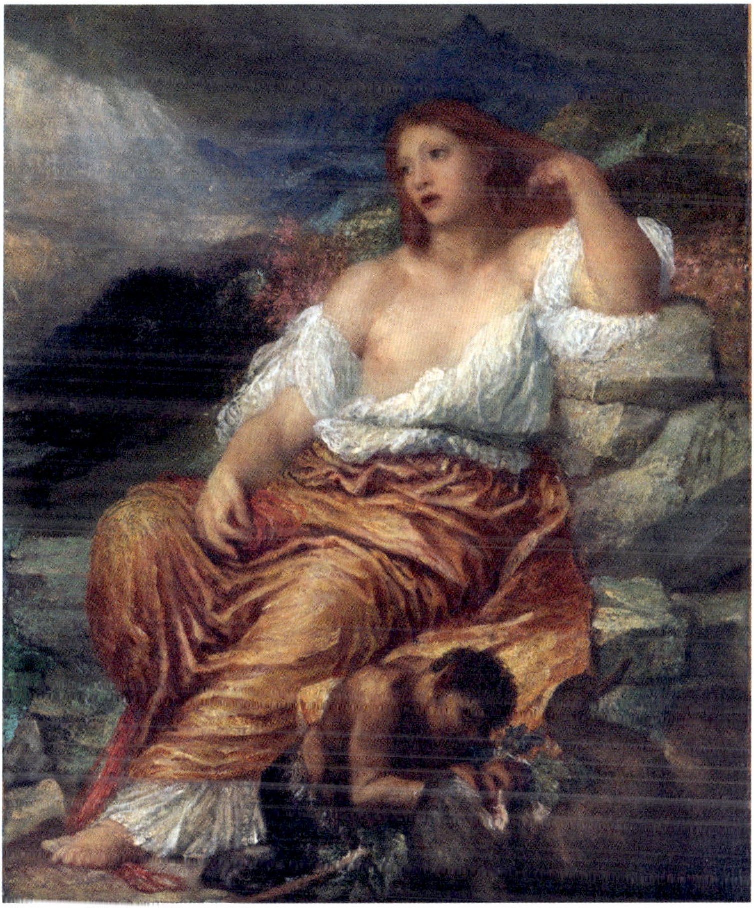

George Frederic Watts, *Ariadne*, 1894; Roger's opinion that Watts was the greatest modern painter was shared by many, and in 1884 he was the first living artist to have a solo exhibition at the Metropolitan Museum of Art in New York.

of a triumphal procession held in Thebes in honour of Apollo with thirty-six figures in Classical dress, as well as paintings by Burne-Jones, Rossetti and other Pre-Raphaelites.

In January 1888, his first published illustration, a 'Sun of Culture' rising behind King's College, appeared on the cover of the *Cambridge Fortnightly*. By February, while planning to take the Tripos in June, he was having regular meetings with the Slade Professor, Middleton, to discuss his future. There was some suggestion of architecture, and that he might apprentice himself to his uncle Alfred Waterhouse – but only if, after he had spent two years as an artist, he discovered that he could progress no further. 'I know what a great thing it is that I ask of you, and what a disappointment it must be,' that letter of February 1888 to his father continued. 'Still I do ask it because I think taking everything into consideration it is what I sincerely think I ought to do.'[20]

Sir Edward did not immediately acquiesce. Roger's First placed the scientific career his father had hoped for within tantalising reach. Upping the ante was that Roger's older brother, Portsmouth, had suffered a climbing accident which had affected both his brain and his mobility. With the help of Middleton, a compromise was reached: Roger would stay at Cambridge another term and study drawing from antique casts and the male figure, while at the same time preparing to sit for a fellowship. In the latter he was unsuccessful, largely because he put too little effort into his dissertation. Eventually, Sir Edward was left with little choice but to accept Roger's determined intention.

The beginning, however, was one of continued compromise, and entailed Roger living at home. The family having moved in 1887, this was now Bayswater, in a house described by Roger as 'huge and palatial', with interiors 'carried out at enormous cost in sham marble stucco ormolu and gilt ... it is an Elysium which I fancy must be haunted by the spirits of all dead builders who are their own architects.'[21] The decor was at odds with the plain style of living, which, combined with necessities such as dressing for dinner and an atmosphere imbued with parental reproach, seemed a stifling step backwards.

Advice as to an appropriate teacher for Roger had been sought from the artists Briton Rivière and Herbert Marshall, a friend of Sir Edward's. They suggested Francis Bate, who ran an art school from Applegarth Studios in Hammersmith, and who had studied on the Continent and encountered the Impressionists. He was also Honorary Secretary of the New English Art Club (NEAC), an exhibiting society which had been founded in 1886 by a group of artists – including John Singer Sargent and Stanhope Forbes – who had returned from Paris with opinions and a style that differed considerably from the established views, literary scenes and moral allegories of the Royal Academy.

Roger began with Bate in January 1889. 'He teaches you more how to analyze your impressions than how to move your pencil and this seems to be the right end to begin,' he wrote to Goldie. A few lines later, he attempted to lure his friend to Bayswater with the promise that afterwards they'd be able to retreat to Roger's private 'room with a fire' where 'I shall work my own wicked will and have Socialists all unbeknown to the rest of my family, and we can plot the destruction of society till any hour of the night.'[22]

There was little else in the way of excitement: Roger read, and went to the theatre and to exhibitions, spent time with his sisters, and missed Goldie. Ashbee was in London, having set up, the year before, a Guild and School of Handicraft in the East End, according to the principles of Ruskin and William Morris, and Roger was invited to give lessons in drawing. But it wasn't, he felt, successful: 'I can't possibly tell them to look for hidden meaning in things.'[23] There was a second failed attempt at the Cambridge fellowship, stymied by Roger's endeavouring to combine art with science. The difficulties of living under 'a veil of ... dishonest compliance'[24] clouded everything, and eventually, predictably, things came to a head. The solution was in Roger's favour, it being decided that he would go to Italy, accompanied by Pip Hughes, the son of a family friend.

'Rome at last,' Roger wrote to Goldie in February 1891, beginning a stream of correspondence that is full of 'splashing fountains and sunburnt domes',[25] but also marble loos that were but a hole in the ground, and unscrupulous managers of pensioni. He and Pip dined out in local trattorias and explored the local countryside, and Roger drew and painted – while voraciously and tirelessly comparing what he'd read about with the reality. He was surprised that 'things I hadn't liked much in casts were so splendid in marble'.[26] And,

> My dear Goldie, I've made a great discovery; Raphael is a great painter – one of the greatest – I never used to believe it & think I was right not to when I had only seen his English works – the fact is he is a fresco painter and not an oil painter.[27]

More of the same followed in Naples, Florence and finally Venice. Palladio's Chiesa del Santissimo Redentore, where Veronese's *Baptism of Christ* hangs in the sacristy, 'toppled over the Ruskin idol'[28] of accurate representation, as Roger deepened his admiration for a more expressive style of painting and the drama of Titian and Tiepolo. Pip had returned home, and Roger took up introductions to Horatio Brown, a historian who specialised in Venice, and John Addington Symonds, poet, literary critic and author of *Renaissance in Italy*, which extended to seven volumes. He also bathed at the Lido – and fell in love, beginning what was to be a not uncomplicated relationship.

The girl was Idonea Widdrington, known as Ida, who was on a tour of Italy with her parents, Cecilia and Shallcross Fitzherbert Widdrington, known as Fitz, and a friend, Ella Pease. Ella came across Roger drawing the Gothic exterior of the church of San Gregorio, and he was invited to join the party for tea, whereupon a Quaker connection was established with Ella. The following day Roger was invited to dine, and then, after Fitz had ascertained that he knew rather a lot about art, to accompany him on his own sketching excursions (Fitz had previously travelled and sketched with Edward Lear). Roger was impressed by how cultured they all were, and how open-minded: Roger and Ida were permitted to explore Venice unchaperoned. The first female he'd ever spent significant time with who wasn't related to him, she'd just had a burgeoning dalliance with a Sicilian army officer quashed by her parents. Ida's mother Cecilia felt Roger was safer, describing him as 'one of those who are not "fire" but can be a real friend'[29] – though she soon found herself as taken by him as her daughter was. Roger wrote to Goldie to tell him that he'd fallen in love, with some trepidation, but received a generous reply: 'I never (in my saner moments) imagined I had, or wanted to have, a monopoly in you. That would be fatal. And it is, I suppose, in the course of nature that men shall fall in love with women.'[30]

And so Roger returned to London in a decidedly positive frame of mind, helped by the fact that the NEAC accepted two of his paintings for exhibition, one of which was a Whistler-ish view of the Basilica of St Mark's at twilight. There was also a deadline on his continuing to live at home, as Sir Edward had decided that, on his coming retirement, he would move permanently to Failand. In the interim, Roger returned to Bate, discussed Euripides with Goldie – with whom his relationship hadn't perceptively changed – and embarked on regular correspondence with both Ida and Cecilia Widdrington. He went up to Newton Hall in Northumberland to stay with them, admired the architectural capriccios that Fitz had painted on the walls, and told Ida that she reminded him of Catherine Earnshaw in Emily Brontë's *Wuthering Heights*.[31]

In January 1892 he embarked on another overseas adventure, for two months' study at the Académie Julian in Paris. A private art school that had been founded in 1867, the rooms were crowded with students from all over the world. A significant proportion were American – though among Roger's fellow English contingent was William Rothenstein, six years Roger's junior but ahead of him in other ways, having started at the Slade aged sixteen. Rothenstein had been in Paris since 1889, had been frequenting the Cirque Fernando with Henri de Toulouse-Lautrec, and found the Académie 'vivid, exhilarating and pregnant with possibilities'[32] – not a sentiment shared by Roger, whom Rothenstein described being 'somewhat shy and uneasy in the free atmosphere of Julian's'.[33] Rothenstein also observed Roger's intelligence, his comparative comfort in 'scientific and philosophical circles'. And notably, Roger had brought part of such a circle with him to Paris. He was sharing an apartment on the rue de Tournon with Goldie, who was working on a play about Mirabeau. They ate together most evenings, went to the theatre, to a performance of Wagner's *Lohengrin*, and in between Roger wrote long letters to both Ida and Cecilia Widdrington, neither of whom knew that he was writing to the other.

Roger also looked at pictures. Whistler's *Arrangement in Grey and Black No. 1*, better known as *Whistler's Mother*, was hanging in the Musée de Luxembourg, having been purchased by the French State the year before, the first work by an American artist to enter a French public collection. He grappled with the concepts behind Neo-Impressionism, and the art of Georges Seurat, Camille Pissarro and Paul Signac. And he saw paintings by the Nabis group – Pierre Bonnard, Édouard Vuillard, Maurice Denis, Félix Vallotton – who had studied at the Académie Julian in the 1880s, were influenced by Paul Gauguin and Japanism, and who, pushing against descriptive naturalism in favour of capturing feeling, employed simplified areas of colour and stylised, decorative forms. But, of the artists who were later to bring Roger lasting fame, 'the name of Cézanne was absolutely unknown to the art students of that day ... throughout my student days in Paris I never once heard of the existence of such a man,'[34] he recounted, years later, in a lecture.

Roger's arrival back in London was initially distinguished by his proposing to Ida, despite having absolutely no income of his own. She – less impetuous when it came to the crunch – turned him

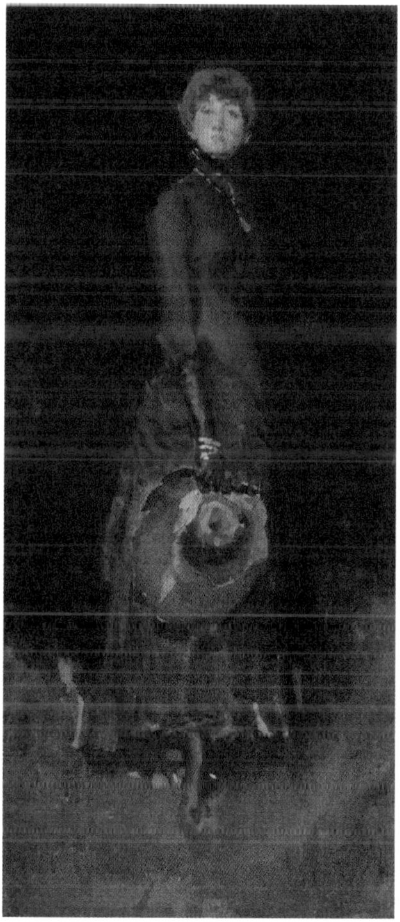

James McNeill Whistler, *Lady in Grey*, c. 1883, acquired by Roger for the Metropolitan Museum of Art in New York in 1906.

down, while professing devastation: she believed Roger to be her 'soul mate' but wasn't prepared to lower her standards of living.[35] Her mother forbade them from corresponding for a year.

While Roger hoped that Ida might change her mind, he found a house with a studio at the river end of Beaufort Street in Chelsea, from where he could work and entertain his friends. One evening Goldie gave a reading of the play he had written in Paris, on another George Bernard Shaw came to dinner, though, a staunch vegetarian, he refused the risotto that Roger had made, believing he could detect traces of chicken. There were trips to concerts and to plays by Ibsen, whose critique of societal norms appealed to their socialist leanings. Roger illustrated a novel by Ashbee set in Arthurian England, *From Whitechapel to Camelot*, and fulfilled some portrait commissions that came via Cecilia Widdrington, whom he saw often, generally chaperoned by her son Gerard.

Progress was marked by Roger's election to the NEAC – though it did not prevent their rejecting his Nabis-influenced painting of Blythburgh Estuary in Suffolk (p. x), depicting dark trees against low-lit marshes. In April, the NEAC had organised the largest show yet in Britian of work by the French Impressionists, with two paintings by Degas, one by Berthe Morisot, one by Jean-François Rafaëlli and three by Monet. Impressionism was controversial in its departure from tradition, and critics and the public declared the works looked 'unfinished', but they were largely reflective of the taste of the other NEAC members.

It was a period of experimentation for Roger, who, despite his stride towards Symbolism, was labelled by William Rothenstein as 'painting in the manner of early English water colour painters'.[36] Different influences were jostling for position, and various NEAC members, including Philip Wilson Steer, were providing advice. Lewis Charles Powles was instructing Roger in traditional methods of oil painting. Charles Ricketts and Charles Shannon (who were a couple, and Roger's neighbours on Beaufort Street where they invited him to their evening gatherings) encouraged other techniques, Shannon being in the process of mastering the Venetian style of oil painting. And then there was Walter Sickert,

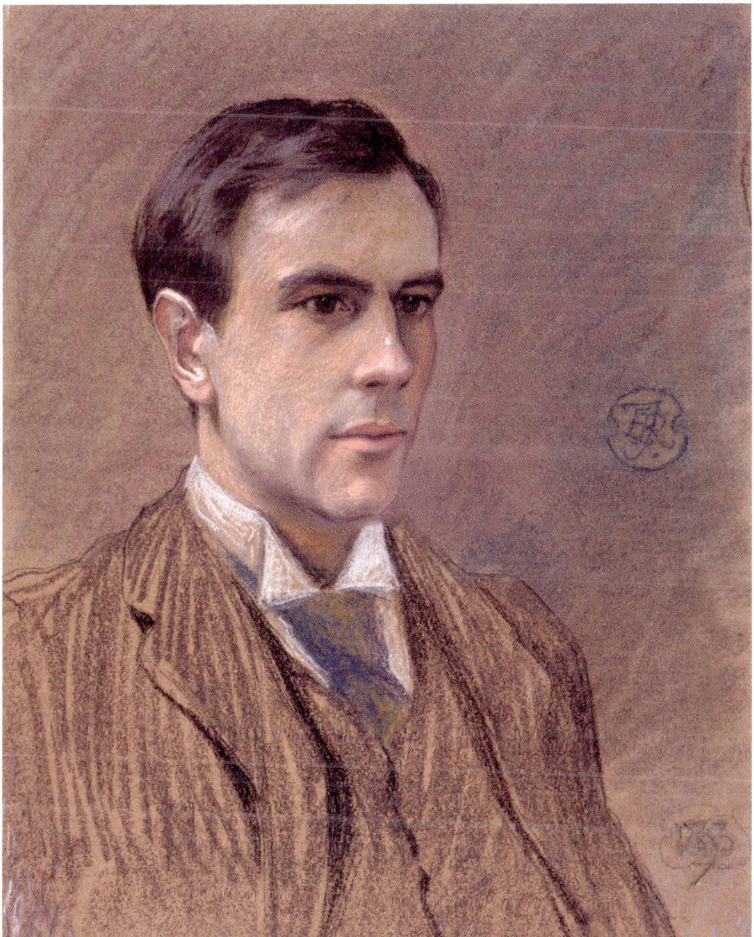

Roger's 1893 drawing, in chalk, of Goldsworthy Lowes Dickinson, now in the collection of the National Portrait Gallery.

whose evening classes, held in William De Morgan's old studio on The Vale, Roger began attending in 1893.

A drawing of Goldie from that year shows Roger's adeptness at capturing likeness and light, and was praised by Sickert. An 1894 painting of Edward Carpenter, which was exhibited by the NEAC and then shown in Liverpool, owes to Whistler, Sickert and perhaps even William Rothenstein who was also taking Sickert's classes, and to whom Roger had recently written, naming one of his portraits as 'exquisite in treatment and … most poetical'.[37]

Throughout, Roger was in regular contact with Cecilia Widdrington, who had even been to stay at Failand with his parents. They had been informed of his love for Ida, though he had given up on wanting to marry her – partly because he felt that she'd never consent to coming second to his art, and his art, he decided, was more important. That spring of 1894, while he was in Wales painting Widdrington family portraits, Roger and Cecilia, who was twenty-three years older than him, became lovers. There was another letter to Goldie: 'I fear I may hurt you,' he wrote. '… [but] I feel that all has happened only draws me nearer to you & you are so generous that I know you feel the same. Yr. Podge.'[38]

Cecilia suggested buying Roger's painting of her son Gerard for £50 – which was a magnanimous offer. It also threw into relief the fact that Roger was nearing thirty, and otherwise still reliant on his parents, who were supporting him to the tune of £300 a year[39] – which would have been £400, but he refused to rule out painting nudes from life. Roger wasn't profligate, but he also wasn't a natural bohemian and had occasional ingrained beliefs, such as that cheap clothes were a poor investment. While he didn't feel he was failing as an artist, he realised that he needed to find a means of increasing his income.

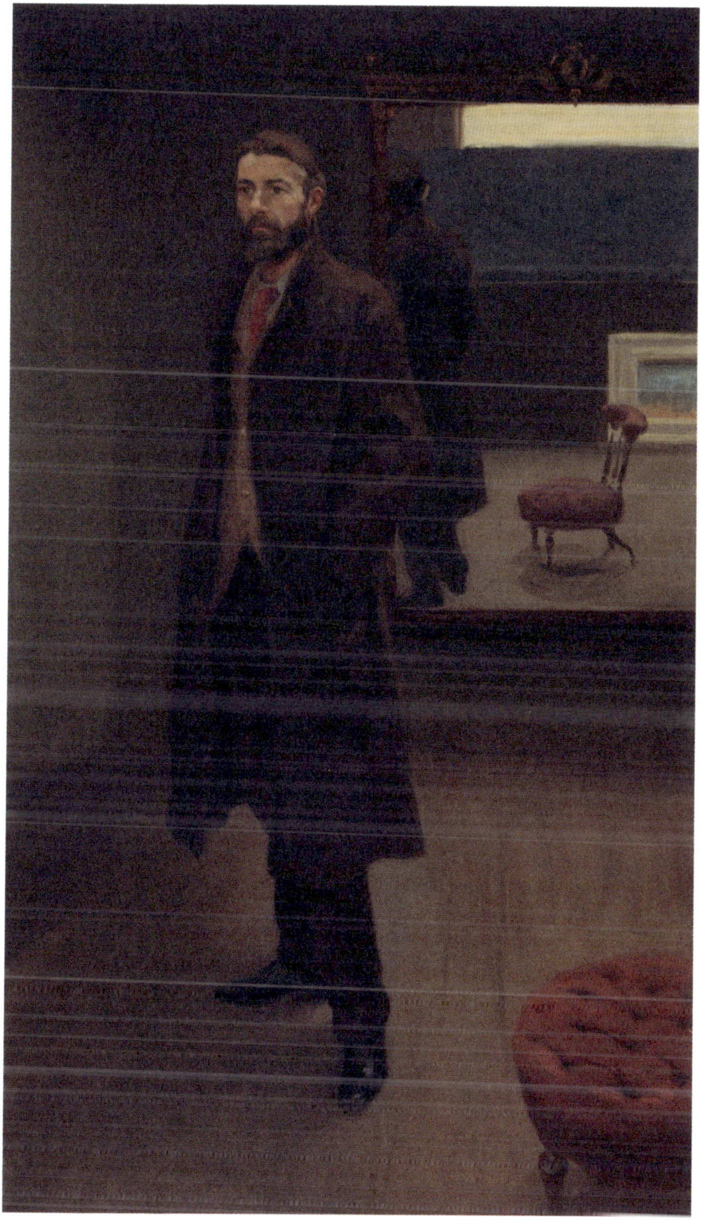

Roger's 1894 painting, in oil, of Edward Carpenter, now in the collection of the National Portrait Gallery having been given to the gallery by Roger in 1930.

TWO

THE MAKING OF AN OLD MASTER EXPERT

THERE WERE, TOWARDS THE END OF THE NINE-teenth century, an increasing number of paintings 'by Giorgione' or 'by Raphael' being offered for sale by cash-strapped members of the English aristocracy. The 1882 Settled Land Act had made it possible for life tenants to part with assets and heirlooms that had previously been part of family settlements – and the Great Agricultural Depression, followed by the 1894 Finance Act which introduced a new death duty levied on the total value of an estate, had made it necessary.

The changes to the law coincided with an escalating interest in art history, which was emerging as an academic discipline in line with the opening of dedicated museums – The Fitzwilliam Museum in 1816, the National Gallery in 1824, the South Kensington Museum (now the V&A) in 1852, the National Portrait Gallery in 1856, the Tate in 1897 – and Felix Slade's posthumous endowing in 1869 of the Slade Professorships at Cambridge, Oxford and University College London, the last of which led to the founding of the Slade School of Art. Curiosity largely came from the new middle classes who were keen to discover a strand of culture that had, until then, been the privilege of the few. But those who had done particularly well from the Industrial Revolution were collecting, too, which made art-historical knowledge helpful when it came to appraising the Old Masters and Grand Tour souvenirs that were up for redistribution, even more so since the situation was being mirrored on the Continent. Sales tended to be arranged privately rather than by auction, and, optimistic attributions aside, straightforward fakes were murkying the waters.

There were thus opportunities for artists with an academic grounding. Roger accepted an invitation to give some talks for the Cambridge University Extension Movement, which was part of an educational programme begun in the 1870s aimed at people who couldn't afford to attend university. Edward Carpenter was involved, speaking on astrology and mathematics, and Goldie had briefly lectured on Classics. Roger's focus was the art of the Italian Renaissance, which he'd studied on his Italian tour.

It was immediately discovered that he had a gift for this form of communication. He was adept at improvising from the black-and-white slide-projected image on the screen in a manner his audience found contagiously exciting; the picture 'became radiant through the mist, and took on the grain and texture of the actual canvas,' Virginia Woolf later described.[1] Even if there were occasional lapses in attendees' concentration, he had a voice, said George Bernard Shaw, that was worth listening to for its own sake.

Further requests followed – and were taken up. A course on Italian art in Eastbourne and Brighton prompted another trip to Italy to prepare, this time with Augustus Moore Daniel, a Cambridge contemporary who was to become, in 1929, Director of the National Gallery. They visited as many galleries and churches as they could in Milan, Bologna, Florence and Bergamo, and in the evenings Roger studied the Italian critic Giovanni Morelli's volumes on art, so as to be better able, with Daniel, to establish authorship of even minor works, and distinguish between the minute individualities of similar painters. Roger described the method as 'scientific',[2] but it also came from getting to know the artists as people: learning their techniques, their moods, their preferred methods and tools. Charles Ashbee joined them for a while, and Roger wrote excitedly of Masaccio to Goldie, 'One of the most tremendous geniuses because he went at one single jump the whole way from the Giottoesque to the complete style of the sixteenth century;' and of Correggio, 'If he isn't the greatest artist Italy or the world ever produced, is almost the most exciting. For a whole day Daniel and I found ourselves absolutely intoxicated with him.'[3]

Painting, too, necessitated travel. In 1894 and 1895 Roger went to La Roche-Guyon in northern France, where the Seine is edged with lime trees and poplars, to apply himself to landscapes. He felt he had been influenced by his recent study of Italian works; he now considered a 'more complete design in a picture'.[4] He experimented with glazes and impastos, and with harvest scenes, working from 6am to dusk, pausing only for twice-daily swims in the river. He cycled from place to place, carrying his apparatus with him, beginning what was to develop into a lasting love for the look of France, as well as its people, food and language. He and Alfred Thornton – another Cambridge contemporary and a fellow artist – visited Giverny, though Monet was not there. The Normandy coast also featured, as did Paris, from where Roger opined that the Louvre's collection was 'finer' than the National Gallery's, and 'they are beginning to arrange the pictures so that they can be seen'.[5] His landscapes were completed in London, and one of them was bought by his friend, the poet Robert (Bob) Trevelyan, a Cambridge Apostle with whom he was now sharing his house on Beaufort Street, for £30 – the price the NEAC asked when they exhibited it.

Roger found another means of making his artistry pay dividends. The Italian Renaissance painters had not contained themselves to canvas but had adorned walls and ceilings in private palazzi, as well as marriage chests, sideboards, beds and boxes. The practice had inspired the Pre-Raphaelites – and now did the same for Roger, who was later to state that 'untold harm has been done to art by the rigid distinction between picture making and applied art,' and point out that '[an artist] will have a subtle sense of proportion and of colour harmony which will enable him to make a definite work of creative art out of an interior'.[6] He advised on some improvements his father was making to Failand: three pairs of wrought-iron gates for the garden, panelling and an archway in the hall. He designed furniture for his friend McTaggart, bookplates for the philosopher Bertrand Russell and curtains for his wife, Alys, and made a wall-painting for a house that Charles Ashbee designed for his mother, which was published in the fine and decorative arts magazine *The Studio*. He decorated the home of the writer Hubert Crackanthorpe, and discovered the frustrations of clients. 'Alas! He has proceeded to furnish it and therewith to destroy all my schemes of colour or at all events to mar them; fancy hanging photographs in a room where I had given him white walls and black wood dados,' Roger wrote to Bob Trevelyan. But it was work he enjoyed, and he wished there was more of it – particularly as, in the spring of 1895, Bob introduced Roger to the artist Helen Coombe, and Roger began thinking, almost at once, about marriage.

Helen, the eighth of twelve children of a Kent-based corn merchant, could not rely on her parents for a living allowance, but was sufficiently successful to have her own studio. Two years older than Roger, she was associated with the Century Guild of Artists, a second-generation Arts and Crafts guild which had been founded in 1882 by Arthur Heygate Mackmurdo. She had a stained-glass window to her name,[7] was working with the musician and instrument-maker Arnold Dolmetsch, and had also exhibited with the NEAC. She was described by Trevelyan as charming and clever – though not intellectual – and as having a beauty in how she moved and spoke: Roger compared her to Spring in Botticelli's *Primavera*. But it wasn't until after they'd been on a bicycling holiday in France in April 1896, along with some other friends, that they started meeting more often and corresponding. Helen asked Roger's advice on the decoration of a harpsichord, advice he gladly gave. By the end of July, she had accepted his marriage proposal.

It was not an engagement that was immediately universally welcomed, as Roger knew it wouldn't be. He wrote to Goldie, promising 'you needn't be afraid that I don't want you,' though acknowledging 'it is momentous and irretrievable and that must make you and Mrs. W[iddrington] apprehensive.'[8] In August, he and Goldie had their own bicycling holiday, in Suffolk.

But Sir Edward and Lady Fry were also reluctant to approve the match. Roger had to reassure them that Helen was of similar class to them, and that there was no history of madness in her family. There are a couple of possible explanations for such a requirement, one being that the Quakers' history of intermarriage had left a worrying legacy of madness (though Helen herself was not a Quaker); the other was that Mackmurdo had suspicions regarding Helen's health and had said something that had reached Roger's parents.[9] Letter-writing ensued. 'She's a distinct personality … awfully and horribly Bohemian and advanced, and she hasn't a sou to her name,'[10] Roger's sister Margery recounted to a friend before she'd even set eyes on Helen. Roger implored his mother: 'If [Sir Edward] chooses to cut off my allowance the whole thing must be broken off which wld. be a much more terrible repetition of the Ida Widdrington affair because then my reason was against my feelings now both go together.'[11] So the family met her: 'she's modern – almost tippling over with modernity,' reckoned Margery,[12] and contained within that code is that Helen smoked. Nevertheless, they came around.

Following more lectures, and an exhibition of contemporary work predominantly by NEAC artists curated by Roger at the

Bijou Theatre in Cambridge, the wedding took place on Thursday December 3, 1896, at the Priory Church of St Bartholomew-the-Great, Smithfield, in the City of London. The service was conducted by the Revd Reginald Alfred Bull, whose wife Agnes was a friend of Helen's. Afterwards, there was a tea party at Helen's mother's house for the modest party of family and friends, and then Roger and Helen, Bob Trevelyan, Selwyn Image – who was also associated with the Century Guild – and a couple of others went out for dinner at Solferino's restaurant, just off Shaftesbury Avenue.

Roger's allowance was not cut, but it was not increased, either. Conceiving that they could live cheaply abroad, they disposed of their London accommodation and set off for France, Algeria, Tunisia and Italy, in that order. There were happy months of painting, and visiting ruins, churches and museums. Roger continued his study of Italian art, bribed his way into the Pitti Palace in Florence to see a recently discovered Botticelli, and enjoyed Helen's instinctive recognition of what she liked, which contrasted with his own need to analyse an artwork before he formed an opinion. They were visited at different points by Bob Trevelyan, Roger's parents and his sister Agnes, and by Goldie, whom at other times Roger wrote to, saying that he wished he were with them. An attempt at returning to London after eight months was foiled when Helen was diagnosed with incipient tuberculosis, and they went back to Ravello where they rented a studio and, besides painting, spent an hour a day reading Dante's *Inferno* in the original. Bob joined them from Christmas, and in February they moved to Rome, as Helen was convinced that there was a doctor following them who aimed to kill her, and they needed to shake him off[13] – a belief that Roger appears to have humoured, while realising that, for practical reasons, he was going to have to prioritise making money. Conveniently, he was almost immediately commissioned to write a 10,000-word monograph on the fifteenth- and sixteenth-century Venetian artist Giovanni Bellini, for a fee of £25.

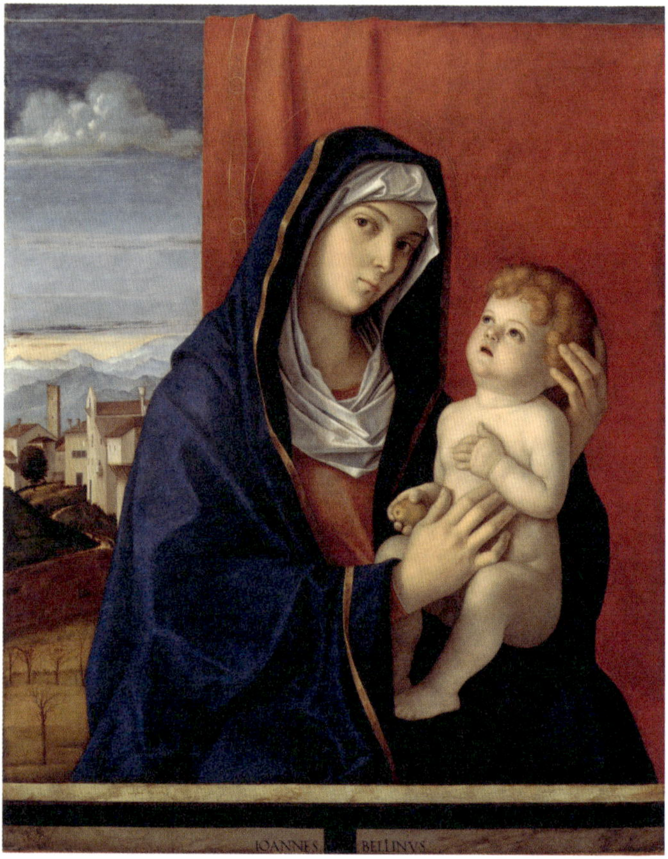

Giovanni Bellini, *Madonna and Child*, late 1480s, acquired by Roger for the Metropolitan Museum of Art in New York in 1908.

The assignment gave Roger the impetus to contact the American Bernard Berenson, who, although only a year older, had already published several important books on the Italian Renaissance including *The Venetian Painters of the Renaissance with an Index to their Works* (1894). Berenson was also advising the American collector, Isabella Stewart Gardner, whose international fame was rising alongside his own. He was living in Florence, as was the art historian Mary Costelloe (whom he married in 1900, after her first husband, who refused to grant her a divorce, died) and Roger and Helen went there to meet him. Friendship was fast, though Berenson initially liked Helen better. He nominated her 'the superior person, exquisitely humorous, and altho' relatively silent … eloquent in her quiet looks'.[14]

It was the calm before the storm. Roger had a series of lectures to give in Cambridge, which necessitated his spending three nights a week there, and he and Helen returned to London in May. By the end of the month Helen's paranoia, glimpses of which had been seen in Ravello, had advanced to such an extent that she had to be committed to an asylum, the Priory in Roehampton. 'I was a fool to be happy yesterday,' Roger wrote to Bob.[15] For weeks he ricocheted between different friends in London, including Walter Sickert's mother, doing his best to work on his book: 'it's difficult to make the jump from Helen, who seems all-important, to the date for Bissolo's death.'[16] He visited her when allowed, and hoped for the best. 'I cannot even now realize what it would mean to me to lose Helen,' he told to his father,[17] who helped with the bills, and never reminded him that there had been concern about her mental health; Sir Edward and Lady Fry had developed a great fondness for their daughter-in-law. Eventually, in mid December, Helen was allowed to return home, to a small, detached house Roger had found in Dorking called Ivy Holt, which he furnished with the help of his sister Margery, who stayed on to assist the transition.

Although Roger could never be entirely relaxed regarding Helen's state of mind, she appeared to have made a full recovery, and there followed a period of contentment which also saw the flourishing of Roger's career and the resumption of Helen's. Once published, Roger's book on Bellini immediately drew attention for its pioneering content – Berenson had given only passing mention to the artist – and its relatability, as Roger had put an emphasis on his own reaction to Bellini's paintings. Henry Newbolt, who had coincided with Roger at Clifton College, asked if he could feature some of Roger's Italian lectures in his *Monthly Review*, and Roger was also appointed art critic of *Pilot*, which included reviewing contemporary art, an area that was gaining in interest among those eager to get to grips with the new movements. Roger quickly gained an eager following, for, like his lecturing, his writing style was accessible, and he had an ability to identify exactly what distinguished one artist from another and to make the differences clear. His analyses weren't always enthusiastic, but Walter Sickert, William Rothenstein and Charles Shannon – respectively his teacher, friend and former neighbour – all benefited from Roger's praise in print. And the job generated more travel: Roger and Helen went to Utrecht, Berlin and Munich, where Roger studied every picture in every gallery, which all 'shut at the absurd hour of 3',[18] before returning to Florence, where they again spent time with Berenson and Mary. Back at home, there was further lecturing, and Roger painted a frieze in the hall of Bob Trevelyan's house, of trees with people mingling beneath them. He was elected to the jury of the NEAC, where his was one of the more conservative voices, and he occasionally clashed with another jury member, Henry Tonks, a surgeon and artist who taught at the Slade.

Peppered through this time were domestic pleasures: in July 1900 Roger and Helen gave a party at Ivy Holt, to present Bob and his new wife, the violinist Elizabeth des Amorie van der Hoeven, known as Bessie, with a clavichord that Helen had decorated for Dolmetsch, and which had been exhibited the year before at the Sixth Exhibition of the Arts and Crafts Exhibition Society at the New Gallery on Regent Street, alongside another by Edward Burne-Jones (Helen's was deemed the more successful).[19] Dolmetsch came to the party and brought a lute, and they sang old English songs by the light of Chinese lanterns. Roger and Helen were happy, and supported each other in their work and creative pursuits, which included dress design, by Roger, for Helen.[20] On the occasions they were apart, they wrote to each other daily, and Roger composed poetry for his wife,[21] as Goldie had once done for him. Weeks after the party for the Trevelyans, Helen announced she was pregnant.

Julian Edward was born in March 1901, less than six weeks after the death of Queen Victoria. Roger only just made it home for the birth, as he'd been spending a few extra days with Goldie in Cambridge after a lecture and had fallen off a horse and couldn't immediately travel. More usefully, Roger's older sister Mariabella, who had trained as a nurse but had never been allowed to work professionally, moved in for a few months. It wasn't long before Helen was expecting a second child. Agnes Pamela, known always as Pamela, was born in May 1902. The Boer war came to an end later that month, and Roger wrote to his sister Margery describing their having again employed the Chinese lanterns 'on little red posts all down our path'. They'd allowed the nurse and all the servants but one to go into town to 'see the jubilations', and when Julian woke up, Roger brought him downstairs 'to console him as he lay on my knees … I never saw anything more lovely than the modelling of his head in that faint warm light. As for Pamela she is no trouble at all.'[22] Roger was, Virginia Woolf noted, 'an enthusiastic father',[23] determined that his children's upbringing should be different from his own.

Meanwhile, he continued lecturing, provided illustrations for a book of Bob's poetry, and was made chief art critic of the literary magazine *The Athenaeum*, a step up from *Pilot*. It devoted a generous space to art which was alternately filled by Roger and an Oxford-educated painter and art historian called Charles Holmes, who was to become Director of the National Portrait Gallery in 1909. Roger also took on some restoration work for Sir Herbert Cook, who had inherited his father's sizeable collection (which had necessitated the adding of a Long Gallery to the house). Among the works were Giorgiones – though Roger thought some of the attributions might be optimistic and was later proved right – and, though it was only authenticated in 2017, a Leonardo da Vinci.[24] Copious letters were exchanged with Berenson on academic points of painterly authorship.

Though there were, on the Continent, dedicated art history journals that carried academic research and good-quality photographs, there was nothing to compare in Britain. It was in 1902 that Roger, Berenson, Charles Holmes and Herbert Horne (who, along with Mackmurdo, had founded the Century Guild of Artists) decided to rectify the situation and found their own publication: *The Burlington Magazine*, named for its address on New Burlington Street. It aimed to appeal to 'students' and collectors alike, and had a consultant committee made up of museum directors past and present, noted experts on such specialities as heraldry and illuminated manuscripts, and academics. While it was to chiefly concern itself with the art of the past, it would not ignore contemporary developments. Roger's next trip abroad, initially accompanied by Helen – they'd left the children at Failand – took in Bruges, where he reviewed an exhibition, France for painting, and, after Helen had gone home, Italy, where he noticed the colour of the walls that paintings were hung against. He also endeavoured, while there, to recruit writers for the new magazine.

Roger's concern for the evolving study of history of art in England extended to the administration of the National Gallery, and what he felt was a related subject, the exodus of valuable paintings abroad, almost entirely to America, aided by such dealers as Joseph Duveen. The National Gallery could acquire nothing without the consent of all the trustees, among whom, Roger pointed out in *The Athenaeum*, were

> gentlemen with very various and in some cases quite empirical tastes – one favours the elegances of eighteenth-century French

> art, another is all for the primitives [early Renaissance artists] … Compromise … will rule all the nation's acquisitions.

Moreover, while trustee discussions were ongoing,

> the private purchaser from across the Atlantic will probably, if the picture is worth having, and no patriotic motives on the owner's part intervene, have written a cheque on the spot and gone off with the object in dispute.[25]

In October, in Venice, he came across two large pictures which he believed to be by Jacobo Bellini, the father of Giovanni, that he felt the National Gallery ought to have. They were for sale at a price he deemed far below their market value, and he wrote to his father asking if he could lend him the money to buy them – he reckoned he'd need between two and three hundred pounds. In contrast to others operating in this field, Roger wasn't intending to make any profit. Rather, 'it would, I think, be a very great distinction for me in the world of picture connoisseurship.'[26] The money was forthcoming, and when Roger brought the paintings home, Sidney Colvin, former Slade Professor of Fine Art at Cambridge, critic and Keeper of Prints and Drawings at the British Museum, supported Roger's attribution. Roger's reputation got the bolstering he hoped for – but the National Gallery did not buy the paintings.

Roger wasn't alone in his opinions regarding public collections. Back in 1857 Ruskin had called for the establishment of a society to save works of art for the nation, and more recently, another art critic, Dugald Sutherland MacColl, who in 1906 became Keeper of the Tate Gallery, had published his concerns, and suggested setting up a public organisation to raise money, since lack of funds was a significant issue. The Chantrey Bequest had been established in the 1870s and was being managed by the Royal Academy of Arts,

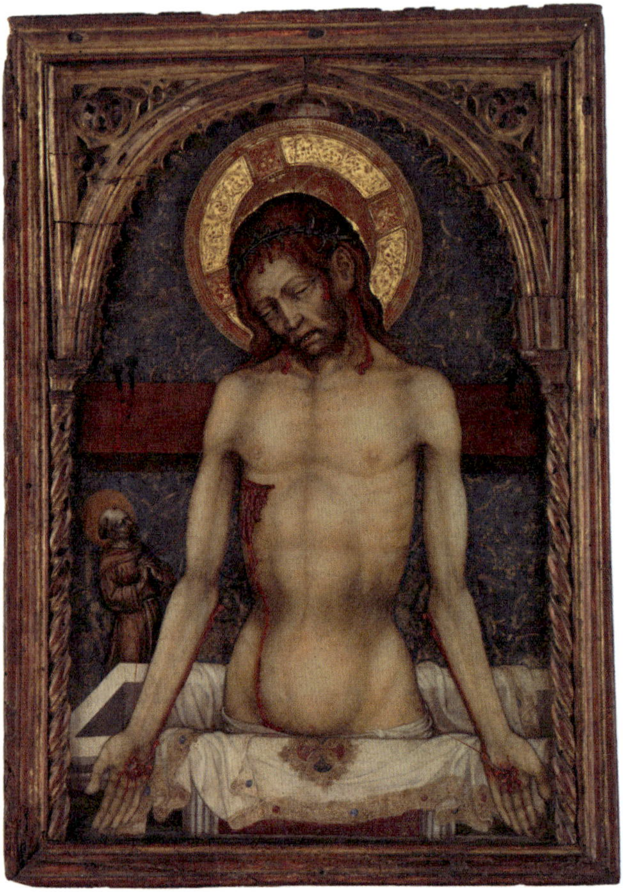

Michele Giambono (Michele Giovanni Bono), *The Man of Sorrows*, c. 1430; acquired by Roger for the Metropolitan Museum of Art in New York in 1906.

but it was specifically to be used for buying paintings and sculpture made in Britain.

The National Art Collections Fund – now called Art Fund – was formed in 1903, by, among others, Roger, MacColl, the artist and patron Christiana Herringham and the banker Robin Benson, a collector of early Italian paintings who owned works by Duccio, Giorgione, Botticelli and Titian. Members of the new society paid a guinea a year and numbered five hundred within the first twelve months.

In April 1903 Roger had a solo show – his first – at the Carfax Gallery, a small commercial enterprise co-founded by John Fothergill and William Rothenstein in 1898, whose early shows had included Auguste Rodin and Augustus John. It was now being run by Robert (Robbie) Ross, who had gone up to King's College just after Roger, and was Oscar Wilde's literary executor and former lover. Roger showed thirty-four watercolours and seven oils. The relative number of watercolours, a medium that dries faster than oils and allows for shorter and more spontaneous painting sessions, is an indication of how little time he was able to devote, in the face of his other pursuits, to painting.

Roger was writing about modern art as well as Old Masters, but his preference lay with the latter. Moreover, the NEAC's rejection of his Blythburgh Estuary painting had thwarted, for now, experiments in that more modern direction. And he was uncertain about Impressionism, particularly the English variety, which was still a dominating force at the NEAC, and which he saw as 'a cul-de-sac'.[27] He'd recently encountered a Chardin still life of some glass vessels and bottles that had been painted as a sign to hang outside a pharmacy – and had had a revelation. The picture had aroused a deep emotional response in him that, at the time, he'd compared to seeing Michelangelo's frescoes in the Sistine Chapel.[28] He'd concluded that this had come from the formal arrangement of the painting, more than what the painting depicted.

Years later MacColl described Roger, at this time, as a 'pastichist of the ancients and opponent of modern French painting'.[29] The show, however, was a success – selling eleven watercolours and two oils at the private view, immediately awarding Roger £79.50.

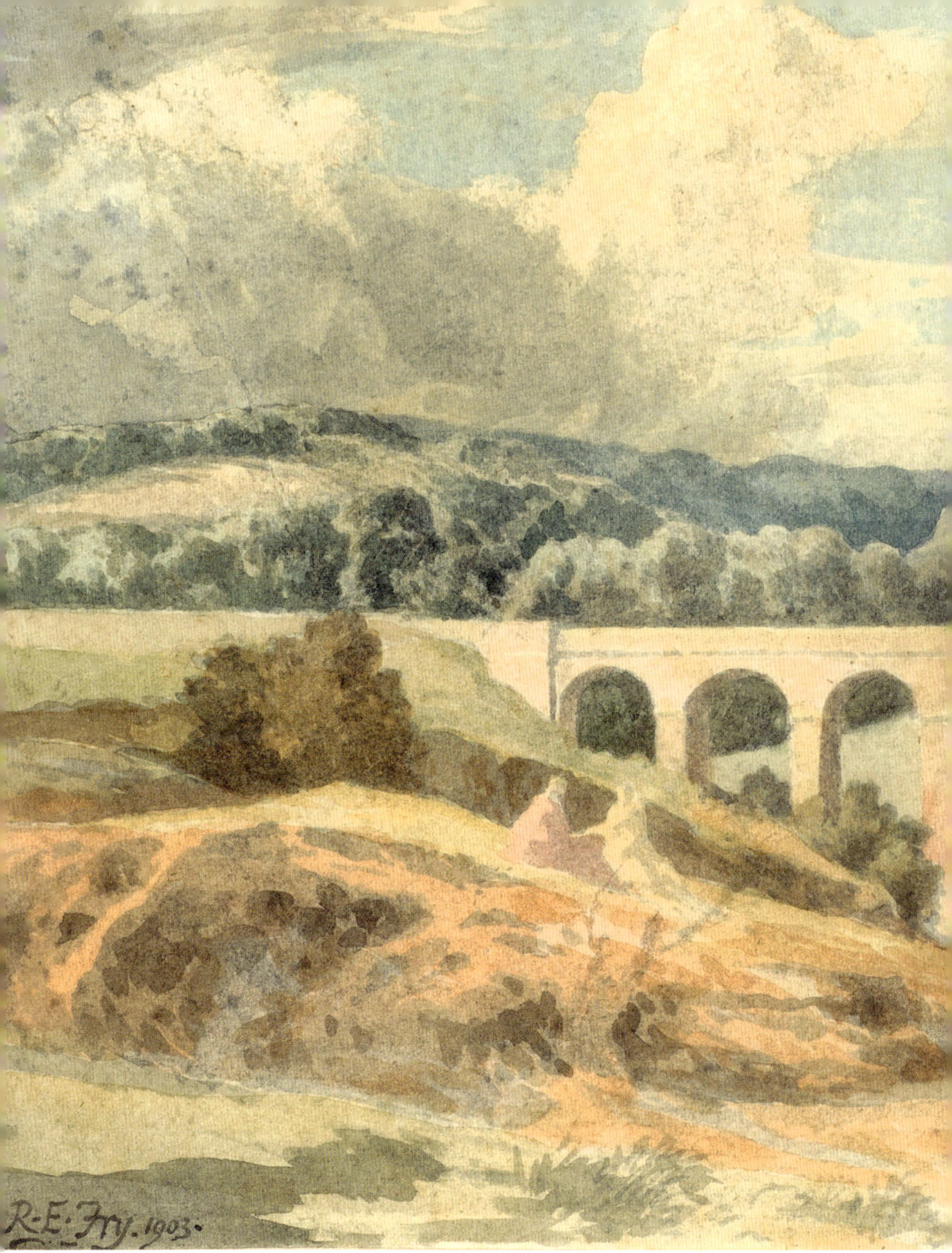
R.E. Fry. 1903.

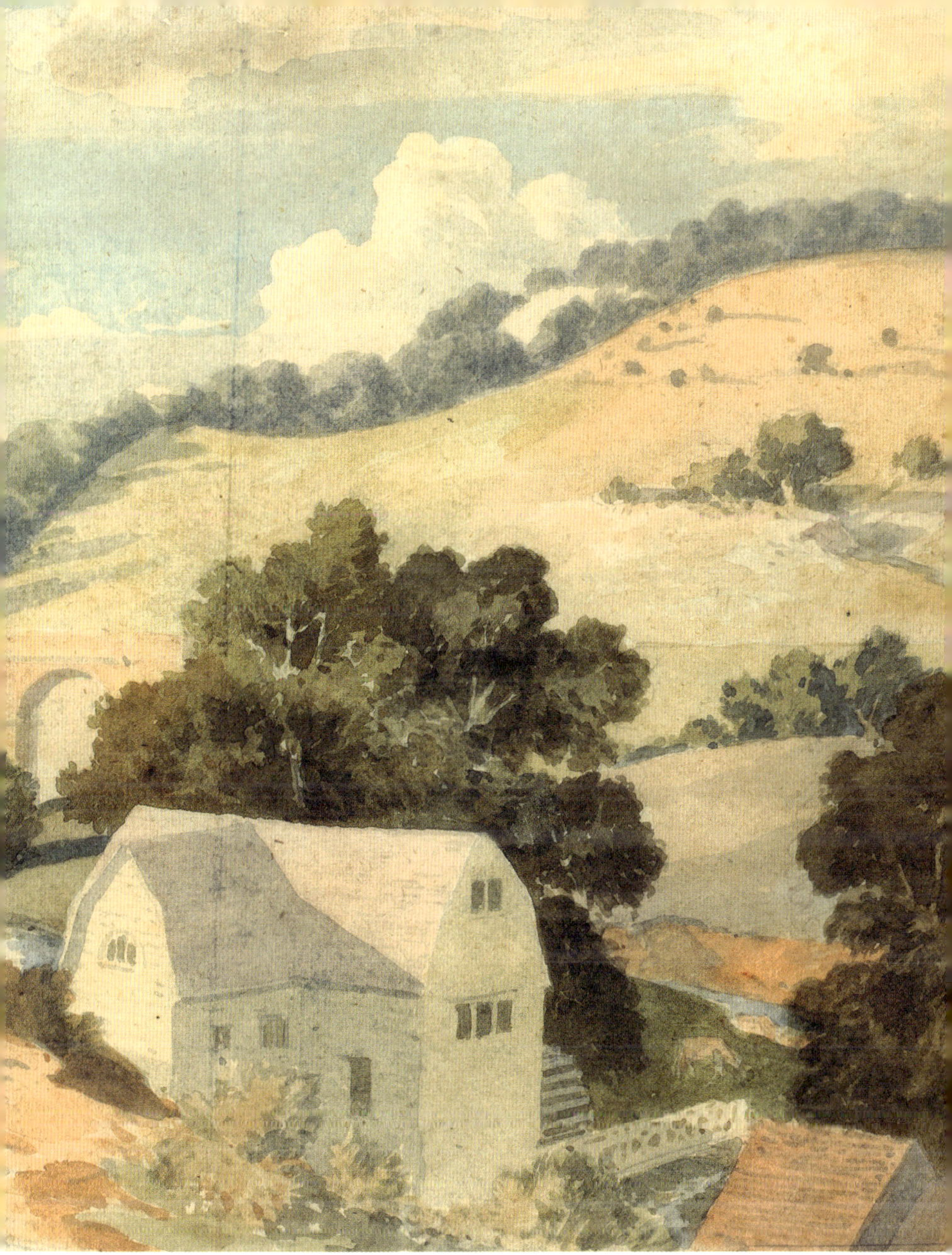

A French Watermill and Aqueduct, 1903, one of the watercolours shown by Roger at the Carfax Gallery in April that year, his first solo show.

Among the buyers was Edward Marsh, a Cambridge Apostle who collected eighteenth- and nineteenth-century work and declared it the best modern show the gallery had ever had. (The watercolour he bought is now in the collection of Queensland Art Gallery, Brisbane.) A painting of Helen's was included, and bought by Mary Berenson, and Robbie Ross told Roger that, excluding Max Beerbohm, it was the most financially successful exhibition that the gallery had put on.

But Helen's health was again on the wane. At the beginning of the year she and Roger had moved back to London, wanting to be able to work but also to attend social engagements more easily. They had found a three-storey terraced house, 22 Willow Road in Hampstead, only a mile from where Roger had grown up and facing directly onto the Heath, and had made it charming. There were blue-and-white silk curtains in the drawing room, and eighteenth-century gilt chairs, an early Italian *Crucifixion* and some late Chinese bronzes[30] – but even so Helen didn't like living there. Roger tried to evade the fact by taking her on a bicycling and painting holiday in France, then renting a house in Sussex for two months, followed by a cottage in Guildford. Making the situation more complicated was that much of her paranoia was directed towards Roger, and the worse she got, the more she railed against him and his family. There was another, albeit shorter, stay in an asylum and when Roger collected her, just before Christmas 1903, he took her to a cottage on the sea front in Lyme Regis, where Margery was helping look after the children. Enough progress was made for them to return to Willow Road in February, and Helen became pregnant once more, but miscarried. In September, she contracted scarlet fever – the disease that had killed Roger's sister Alice – and, although she was rushed to an isolation hospital, and the children to Failand, they caught it too. All came through, but it was a worrying time.

It was also an expensive series of months, with asylum fees, rent for the additional houses, and nurses for Helen while she was at home. Roger, who still owned the two Jacobo Bellinis, enlisted Bernard Berenson's help to sell them – for a profit, since they weren't going to the National Gallery – for which he offered Berenson a commission. And in 1904 he canvassed for the Slade Professorship of Fine Art at Cambridge. However, to his disappointment, his application was opposed by Sir Edward Poynter, Director of the National Gallery and President of the Royal Academy, both institutions that Roger had criticised in print. He'd taken the latter to task over its management of the Chantrey Bequest, for which it was being investigated by a House of Lords committee; it was thought that too much was being spent on works by the Royal Academicians who also administered the money. Although Roger realised he was ruffling the feathers of those who occupied the top branches, he felt no need to rein himself in for future attempts at a Slade Professorship. A couple of months later, writing in *The Athenaeum*, he protested at 'the total incapacity of … the Council of the Royal Academy to buy pictures with intelligence and discretion'.[31]

All the same Roger felt he'd let his parents down. He had, in the last ten years, published a well-reviewed book on Bellini, identified two previously unattributed important Venetian paintings, been involved in the restoration of works in a major private collection, delivered many lectures, written many more articles, and helped found and was closely involved in a new publication – the sum of which had made him one of the most respected Old Master experts in the country. But he didn't have a named position, and that, he felt, was a failure. Besides this, there were worries: not only Helen's health, but also *The Burlington Magazine*, which was struggling financially. It had had to move from its eponymous address to cheaper premises on Berners Street. The magazine's publishers had an agent in New York, where Gilded Age success was defined by the ability to recreate the effects of an English ducal palace by way of portraits and Old Masters. The agent suggested that monetary support could be won there, and that Roger should be the man to go.

THREE

AMERICA AND THE METROPOLITAN MUSEUM

THE GLEAMING EXCESSES OF THE LATE NINETEENTH century in America have been well charted. Rapid industrialisation put approximately twenty per cent of the country's wealth into the hands of an elite few, a cluster of whom – Rockefellers, Astors, Vanderbilts, Carnegies, Fricks, Morgans – lived in New York. Social one-upmanship played out in ostentatious displays of wealth translated into vast new mansions, European travel, competing collections to highlight the owner's cultural sophistication, and philanthropy. When the Metropolitan Museum of Art opened in 1870 the aim was to create a national institution that would inspire and educate the public, but it was simultaneously an ideally conspicuous destination for manifestations of generosity.

Roger, in an English-cut wool suit, arrived in New York in January 1905, after an uncomfortable crossing (he was miserably seasick) and as the Gilded Age was giving way to a focus on social, political and economic reform. A construction boom was underway, and unfinished buildings coupled with streets of unswept snow caused Roger to view the city as being a 'mixture of extreme progress and hopeless barbarism'.[1] He had already suspected that the invitation to raise funds for *The Burlington Magazine* hid an ulterior motive, and his suspicions were confirmed when, having been met off the boat by the art dealer Eugene Glaenzer, he was delivered to William Laffan, owner of the *New York Sun* and trustee of the Metropolitan Museum. The museum's director, Luigi Palma di Cesnola, had died in November. Laffan invited Roger to the museum and suggested that he'd be offered the post, though when the offer was formally made a few days later, it was in fact to be deputy to Sir Caspar Purdon Clarke, the architect and former Director of the South Kensington Museum. But Roger was promised quick promotion if all went well, a salary of £1,600 a year, a travel allowance to spend several months of the year in Europe, and the assurance he'd still be able to write and lecture.

Roger could immediately see challenges. There were undoubtedly treasures in the collection, but other pictures were

> a nightmare ... The blatant forgeries done by any hack Royal Institute man that Agnew could lay hands on are enough to make you stagger, and all these things have been accepted without a murmur.[2]

But they couldn't, it was explained to Roger, be rejected (or even hidden) or else the donations might dry up. In 1901, Jacob S. Rogers of the steam locomotive manufacturing business had left the Metropolitan Museum most of his eight-million-dollar fortune. Indeed, in Roger's estimation, the museum had more funds at its disposal than any other gallery in the world.

The President of the museum was John Pierpont Morgan, the investment banker who dominated Wall Street as head of the firm that became known as J.P. Morgan & Co., and who was a collector on a massive scale. He had started with rare books and manuscripts, progressed to paintings, furniture, jewellery, porcelain, rugs and tapestries, and extended to art from Egypt, Asia and the Islamic world – mostly kept in London to evade import taxes, and verbally promised to the museum on his death. Morgan had appointed fellow millionaire collectors to the board of trustees, which further helped the museum's financial state: if ever more money was needed, Morgan would simply go around the table until he had it. His schedule was so busy that while waiting for an appointment with him, Roger had time to go to Philadelphia to see the collection that John G. Johnson, one of those trustees and Morgan's lawyer, was amassing on his annual trips to Europe. Roger, who instinctively liked the man, admired how Johnson lived with everything he bought. Outstanding paintings, from the Italian Renaissance through to the Impressionists, covered every available inch of wall space including the servants' corridors, and more were propped on chairs and easels. Roger also discovered that Johnson, who urged him to accept the position, had read all his *Athenaeum* articles.

When Roger and Morgan finally met, it was aboard Morgan's private rail car, 'tacked on to the end of a special express', en route to Washington for a dinner with President Roosevelt, whose father, Theodore Roosevelt Sr., had been one of the founders of the Metropolitan Museum. Roger compared the great financier, who was intimidatingly large with massive shoulders and a bulbous purple nose (he suffered from rosacea), to the figure in Domenico Ghirlandaio's *An Old Man and his Grandson* and described him as behaving 'not as a host but exactly as a crowned head and everyone else behaves accordingly'. But Morgan promised Roger money for *The Burlington Magazine* and Roger felt that he would be able to manage a relationship with him, reassuring Helen that Morgan was not somebody who would go back on his word.

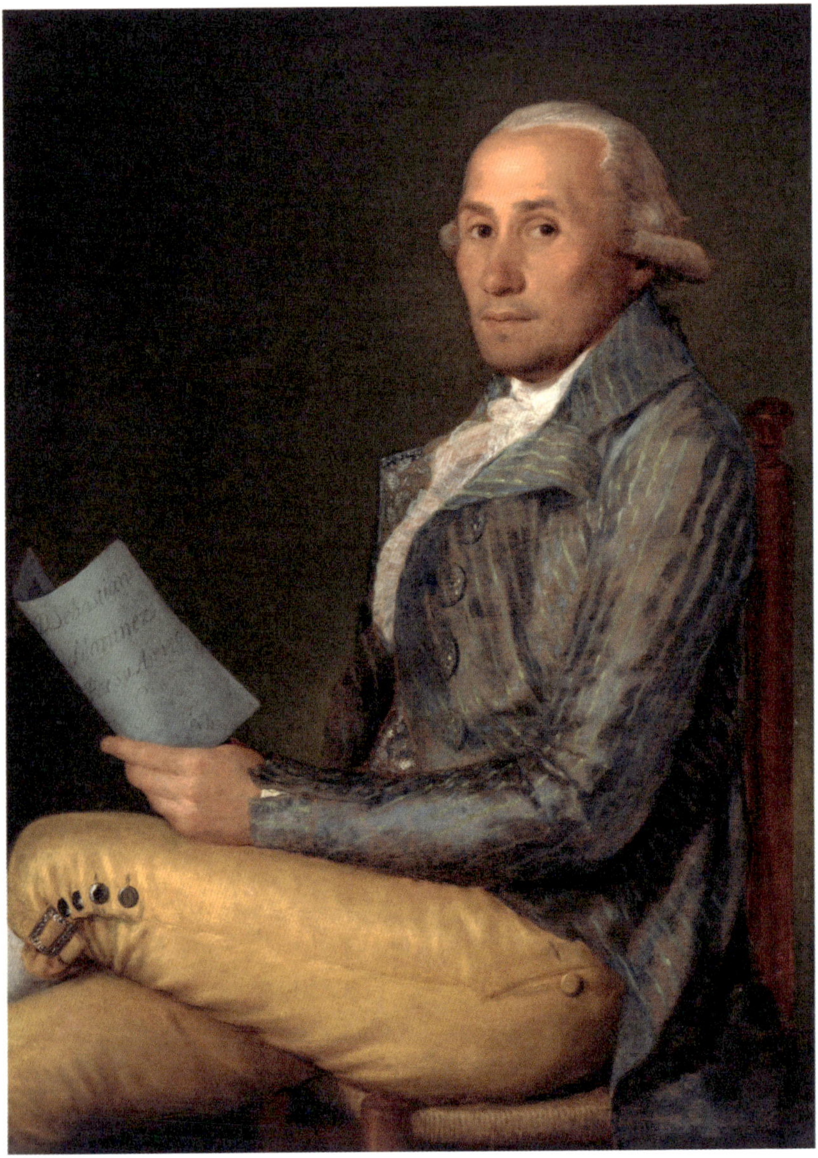

Francisco de Goya y Lucientes, *Sebastián Martínez y Pérez*, 1792; acquired by Roger from Knoedler, one of the New York dealers, for the Metropolitan Museum of Art in New York in 1906.

Roger's interest in the position grew stronger on the way back from Washington, when he met 'the big architects of the country' and

> found them really fine intelligent men all working together with a big idea of the future of art, full of enthusiasm and good sense and with the knowledge that they can carry out their schemes without any difficulty … The feeling that if you have grasped an idea you can realize it, instead of beating your head against the bars of prejudice and prestige, is most invigorating … It's quite a different spirit to that in England.

He was drawn by their wanting to unite with the University in the interests of artistic education, their 'feeling for decorative design', and the idea that, should he accept,

> we should … take a very leading position. Money, I think, would come in plenty, but more than that, real power to shape things … It is extraordinary to find oneself looked up to and one's opinion regarded as it is here. I think that is really the thing that inclines me most. There is going to be an immense boom here in art – everything is shaping and arranging itself for it and I am regarded as the person who can give direction to it in lots of ways.[3]

Even so, Roger was cautious. Helen had written to remind him 'one never has to give one's own answer till one has been alone and then one is in a far better position to give it.'[4] He wanted to be able to talk everything over with her in person, planning that he would settle the business once he'd got home. In the meantime, he reconsidered the offered salary, which he'd begun to fear was insufficient. He explained to Helen that he wanted to be able to give the museum his all and not be in a position where he needed to lecture and write alongside. He also suspected that he'd find himself an unofficial advisor to Morgan for his own collection. He asked Morgan to raise the salary to £2,400. Morgan was furious. Roger now described him as 'a sort of financial steam-engine', who 'likes to be in a position of being surrounded by people he has in his power to make or unmake ... He's much too much a God Almighty".[5] And the Almighty retracted everything, including his offer of funding *The Burlington Magazine*. After a visit to meet Bernard Berenson's client, Isabella Stewart Gardner in Boston, where her collection of works by Botticelli, Vermeer, Rembrandt and Raphael was already housed in her Venetian palazzo-inspired museum, Roger returned to London.

But he had succeeded in his original aims, having secured financial help for *The Burlington Magazine* from John G. Johnson and Henry Clay Frick, as well as Morgan, who had relented on that front. He'd also made helpful connections. He immediately found himself advising Johnson on a Hieronymus Bosch, *The Mocking of Christ* (now in the Philadelphia Museum of Art but reattributed to a follower of Bosch) and then a Bellini *Madonna and Child*, going to look at them on Johnson's behalf to validate the attribution and the quality. Major dealers – Joseph Duveen, Nathan Wildenstein *et al.* – were buying entire collections of masterpieces, but there were overlooked gems to be found elsewhere, and being able to do so in person, in the days when photographs were black and white, and letters crossed the Atlantic by ship, could be lucrative; many advisors were paid on both sides of a transaction. When Berenson procured Titian's *The Rape of Europa* for Isabella Stewart Gardner, working with the dealer Otto Gutekunst of Colnaghi, they added £4,000 to the price, which they agreed to split between them. (Unknown to Gutekunst, Berenson then added a further £2,000.)[6] The seller of the Bosch had thus budgeted a sum for Roger out of the price Johnson had already agreed. But when Roger discovered this, he insisted his 'cut' be deducted from the amount Johnson paid; 'I do not think it a good plan for a critic to take commission from dealers,'[7] he explained.

In March, Roger discovered that he was one of two nominees for the post of director of the National Gallery. Shortly afterwards, he found he was in the running for the same job at the British School at Rome. He was surprised, particularly in light of his recent rejection from the Slade Professorship post, but, frustratingly, nothing immediately came of either. While he was waiting, he took on the writing of a new introduction to Joshua Reynolds's famed *Discourses on Art*, the sermons that the first ever President of the Royal Academy of Arts gave between 1769 and 1790 on subjects including the vital role of the living model, and the nature of genius, originality and taste, thus establishing a framework for understanding art and elevating its status. It was an undertaking that reassured Roger of the worth of his own lecturing and writing.

There was more advisory work; Roger travelled to Vienna, Budapest, Prague, Frankfurt and Berlin, looking at paintings that were on the market – as well as, naturally, at churches and museum collections. His clients included Morgan, who worked with multiple advisors at any one time, and on occasion pitted them against each other. Morgan had been vacillating on Roger's future with the Metropolitan Museum, but in the second half of the year Roger was also asked to look at and secure pictures for its collection. In its report of December 1905, the museum announced that Roger been appointed Curator, though no terms had been agreed.

Right through to January letters went back and forth between Roger and Sir Purdon Clarke, the museum's Director, regarding a contract, as well as a Rubens portrait that King Leopold of Belgium was also considering buying, a Goya, a portrait of Titian by a school-of-Titian artist and a Raphael, sending Roger to Liverpool, Paris and Ghent. Eventually Roger was offered, and accepted, the post of Curator, Paintings. The salary was £1,000 a year, and chief responsibilities were the preservation and presentation of paintings, along with acquisitions to fill gaps in the collection. Crucially, he'd only occasionally need to visit New York, rather than live there, though there was a distinct lack of clarity over exactly how often or for how long he'd be expected to be present.

In February 1906, Roger again crossed the Atlantic. On disembarking the ship, he found journalists awaiting his arrival on the quay: 'I'm quite the rage,' he wrote to Goldie. The museum informed his entire life. He'd start his days with the dealers, and there were high points, particularly the quality of paintings. The spending power of the millionaires and competition between them had sent rates soaring: in 1901, Morgan had paid two million French francs for Raphael's *Colonna Altarpiece*.[8] But so keen were sellers to get their works into the museum, which would increase the worth of everything else they were selling and imbue it with a legitimacy, that, as Roger recorded, 'I've bought heaps of pictures, and have got them at ridiculously low prices.'[9]

The other end of the day could be more taxing. Roger felt permanently on parade with people he'd either never met or had forgotten meeting. Evenings hosted by Mrs Adelaide Douglas, who was well known to be Morgan's mistress (in 1909 he financed the building of her six-storey Louis XVI-inspired house on Park Avenue) came with requests for slide shows. Another society grandee – and museum trustee – wanted to donate a collection of nineteenth-century American art, which Roger didn't rate, and have a room named after him. And then there were the artists, who 'keep asking me to say that theirs is the greatest art the world has ever seen'. But 'the inbetween people are all right. Even when rich, and quite a few are delightful.'[10] Among these were Mark Twain, whose 1873 novel *The Gilded Age* had given the era its name, and whom Roger was seated next to at dinner one night. 'I found him a really fine, generous and liberal-minded gentleman ... He has the courage to speak out for what is honest and humane,'[11] he wrote to his father. Roger devised a test, determining that whether he'd get on with somebody depended on whether they liked the novels of Henry James. If they didn't, well, 'life to them is simple and blankly sentimental,'[12] he explained to Helen.

Helen was helping Roger in his absence, looking at pictures in London on his behalf, and was privy to all Roger's thoughts – which were changeable. He'd received a telegram on his way to New York finally offering him the directorship of the National Gallery, and as his contract with the Metropolitan Museum still wasn't immediately forthcoming, there'd been weeks' worth of deliberation, with the National Gallery 'a huge temptation'.[13] In the end he felt he couldn't go back on his word to the Metropolitan Museum. Added to which, as he explained to Helen, 'I can do ten times as much here as at the National Gallery and I suppose I have big ambitions.'[14]

Part of that ambition was immediately met when Roger was given a gallery in the museum to do with as he wished – along with staff who backed him. The Deputy Director, under Sir Purdon Clarke, was Edward Robinson, formerly Director of the Museum of Fine Arts in Boston, and Roger soon sent all queries his way. Bryson Burroughs, who had trained as a painter in Paris, was appointed Assistant Curator of Paintings, and he and Roger immediately got on. They worked together on cleaning and restoring various works that Roger wanted to exhibit in his gallery, and Roger taught the museum's framers Cennino Cennini's gilding method from the fourteenth century. He had the room replastered (infuriated by the perceived slowness of the builders) and repainted, mixing the colours himself for 'half-tone gold'[15] over pure ultramarine on the walls, and raw umber over a burnt sienna stain on the woodwork.

Roger saw the role of institutions as being to teach the historical sequence of art, but also to spread an aesthetic appreciation, and this exhibition, featuring paintings of 'all periods and of all schools'[16] focused on the latter. Among the pictures – many reframed, and many of them recent acquisitions – were works by Rubens, Van Dyck, Goya, Vermeer, Manet and Turner. There was some controversy on the room's unveiling: *The New York Times* published accusations of 'over cleaning', but elsewhere it was well received, and Roger's star rose. Then, having spent his entire annual budget in a matter of two months (he'd acquired fifty-four paintings including Goya's *Sebastián Martínez y Pérez*, Nicolaes Maes's *Portrait of a Woman*, Peter Wtewael's *Kitchen Scene*, Giambono's *The Man of Sorrows* and Whistler's *Lady in Gray*), Roger sailed for home.

Arriving in London in April, he found Helen recovering from flu and the children ill with colds – and yet was unable to do much to help as, within days, he set off again, to Paris and Brussels, after the museum placed an extra $5,000 in his account for smaller pictures. But in June, Roger and Helen left the children at Failand, and embarked on a trip to France, Switzerland, Luxembourg and Germany that combined work with painting. Back in London, two weeks later, they went to see Oscar Wilde's *Salome*, for which the set was designed by Roger's former Chelsea neighbour Charles Ricketts, 'with ideas of colour that surpassed belief. I've never seen anything so beautiful on the stage,'[17] recounted Roger. There were further European jaunts: he met Morgan in Paris, and the sculptor George Grey Barnard, with whom he discussed purchasing a house and a chapel for the Metropolitan Museum's collection of architectural ensembles (Barnard later bought the Cuxa Cloisters). Then in September, prepped by classes at the Berlitz language school in Hampstead, he and Helen took a holiday in Spain. Roger was struck by the landscape, 'great pyramids of pinky white marble standing up against grey-blue skies, then walls of rock built like architecture stretching for miles, and then vast undulating plains bounded by pale grey hills and everything burnt brown or white except the trees, which look by contrast nearly black.' The cities, too, had beauty, with their 'wonderful coloured tiles used all over buildings'.[18]

October saw Roger back in New York, where he found, to his relief, that the hoo-ha over the overcleaning had blown over, a report conducted by the museum having exonerated him. He began work on the museum's drawings, particularly the Cornelius Vanderbilt bequest – a collection of 670 Italian drawings given to the museum in 1880 by the railroad and shipping tycoon, who had been on the board of trustees. The drawings had been bought in some haste, and Roger realised that many of them were 'school of' or straight copies, so he worked on lowering the attributions to improve the museum's scholarship. At the same time, he made up for this de-weighting by introducing the drawings he had bought over the summer, by Gainsborough, Rembrandt, Leonardo and Ruskin, and donating a portrait of Rodin by William Rothenstein. He also presented the trustees with his ideals. Although some of the collections had been donated with restrictions regarding displaying them together, Roger believed that the museum should aim to divide its galleries by school and period, arranged according to aesthetic principles, and decorated with period furniture and *objets d'art*. He aspired to a gallery for European painting before 1500, another for the Dutch school, and another for the English and French schools of the eighteenth century.[19] Alongside this, he wanted to be able to withdraw and restore pictures, repaint galleries, and redesign the lighting. The suggestions were accepted '*en bloc*'.[20]

Despite these successes, on this trip Roger also requested that his title should be changed to European Advisor, and that he should be allowed to spend less time in New York. He was worried about Helen, and did not feel that his long absences were aiding her health. More, he missed her: 'what happiness to wake in my bed and hear you getting tea ready,'[21] he wrote, adding that he hoped the photographs of Julian and Pamela would arrive soon. He was spending some enjoyable weekends with his assistant Burroughs and his family – which threw into relief the fact that his own family's life was continuing, on the other side of the ocean, without him. His life as an artist, too, was in England. He had five paintings in the NEAC exhibition that winter, four of France and one entitled *Castles in Spain*; to Roger's gratification, they were admired by both William Rothenstein and Charles Holmes. On top of all that, his initial excitement about America had cooled. But although Laffan and Johnson were sympathetic to the appeal, Roger's request for the change in title and role was not granted.

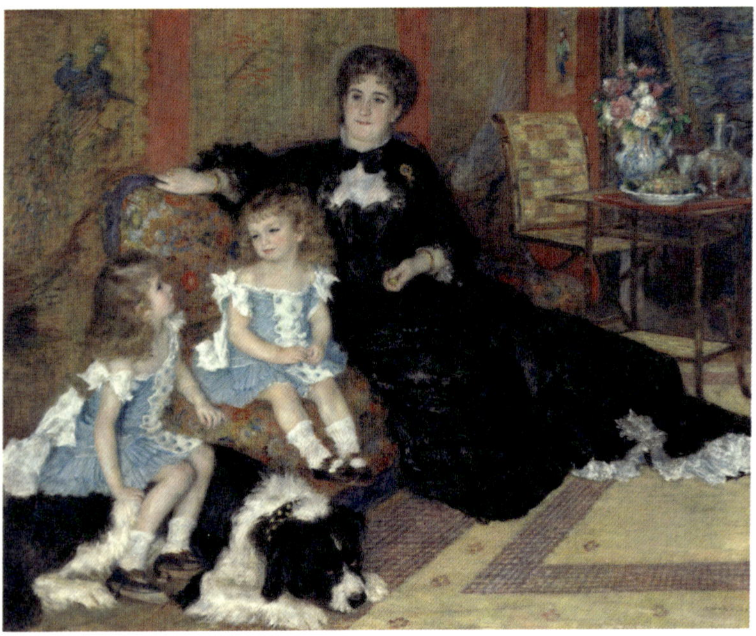

Auguste Renoir's 1878 portrait of the Charpentier family. Roger acquired it for the Metropolitan Museum of Art in New York in 1907.

He eventually sailed for London on December 19. There was a trip to Basel, but he was home again at the end of January and he and Helen took the children to see *Peter Pan* at the Duke of York's Theatre in St Martin's Lane. Two weeks later, Helen had another breakdown. It wasn't so bad as to necessitate another stay in an asylum, but the children were sent to Failand while she was cared for by nurses at home. She again turned against Roger, accusing him of losing the National Gallery job for not having taken her advice,[22] which wasn't quite true. When in March she showed some improvement, Roger took her to a house in Lewes to recuperate.

He was in Lewes when he heard about a change to the Metropolitan Museum's acquisition policy; Roger was asked to focus his spending on fewer but more sensational works. Putting the request into immediate practice, Roger went to Paris where, having negotiated it being kept back from auction, he bought Renoir's *La Famille Charpentier* for $20,000, with the dealer waiving his commission. Painted only thirty years previously, it was the most modern painting to enter the museum's collection during Roger's tenure; in his note to the somewhat hesitant trustees, he compared Renoir to Gainsborough in the way he understood 'the grace of womanhood' and in his treatment of surfaces.[23]

The new directive gave Roger opportunity to suggest certain pictures to Johnson that he might otherwise have secured for the museum. Johnson was in fact already in the habit of buying paintings that Roger had intended for the museum, which Roger found frustrating, and considered wrong; but there was little way around it, as Roger had to notify Johnson of any desired purchase. In May, Roger went to meet Morgan for an exhibition of paintings in Perugia, with the aim of speeding up the process by looking at possible acquisitions together.

Roger found himself part of Morgan's 'triumphal progress' through Italy, along with Morgan's mistress Mrs Adelaide Douglas, and – for the sake of propriety – a chaperone, Morgan's sister Mrs Burns. Years later, writing up the journey, he described the Italians looking at Morgan 'with something like worship. … The mere thought that one man had so much wealth seemed to them ennobling and uplifting and incredibly more romantic than royalty itself.' Everywhere they went, Roger was besieged by optimists hawking heirlooms. In one morning Roger was shown

> Chinese pictures rather recently imported and an immense eighteenth-century carpet … The poor Count had rushed from Rome to Perugia … The family fortunes depended on his success … Before I could get away from him there jumped out from a dark corner of the room a little Levantine or Maltese gibbering in broken English and broken Italian. He had in his hands a large seventeenth-century crucifix which he handed me with feverish gestures. … Once more I tried to get to my petit déjeuner but once more I was stopped, but this time by an elderly lady very refined … She and her sister lived in a Castello ten miles away in the hills and had a wonderful service of Majolica. Wouldn't it be possible for il Morgan to visit them?

By day they spun along, driven by 'a horribly skilful but reckless Italian chauffeur who had his ideas of how an ultra-royal and Morganatic car should be driven, namely to cause as much terror to the inhabitants as possible'. In Assisi, Morgan was 'displeased with the condition' of Giotto's frescos – and he couldn't buy them. In Siena the whole wooden floor of the cathedral was taken up for Morgan to see the mosaics beneath – a privilege that Roger noted had been denied the Queen of Italy, who 'had asked in vain for this'. At San Gimignano the royal book was brought out by the mayor to be signed. And at Ancona, as they drove to the harbour through the square, the military band stopped playing and the whole population followed Morgan's car. A salute was fired as they embarked on Morgan's yacht, and that evening, the town choral society

> serenaded us in boats. They shocked Morgan very much by asking for money and they were rudely refused. It was not so much that he minded parting with money as that the request was a blow to the cherished illusion that everything was done out of pure admiration for his personality.[24]

Florence wasn't mentioned in Roger's write-up, but it was there that he, without Morgan, had a tricky dinner with Berenson and Mary, during which he felt that Berenson was attempting to wrong-foot him into demonstrating ignorance.[25] Also missing from that entertaining account is that in Assisi, Morgan had 'displayed a kind of intelligence'[26] that Roger hadn't expected, and thought Giotto's *Raising of Lazarus* in the lower church the finest picture he had ever seen – though he refused to look at the upper church. Eventually, Morgan returned to New York, while the spoils of his voyage, including the Majolica from the Castello in the hills, were shipped to London. Roger went home to Helen, via Paris, to buy more things both for the museum and Morgan, who was, Roger wrote to Helen, 'mighty pleased with me'.[27] Moreover, he agreed to support Roger's change of title to European Adviser, without reducing the salary.

Helen had sent the children to Failand in Roger's absence, and been on a bicycling holiday with a friend, which Roger hoped would have helped her health. It hadn't. In June, Helen was readmitted to the Priory at Roehampton.

Roger was devastated. Forbidden by the doctors from visiting her, he went bicycling with Goldie and prepared for a pre-arranged exhibition of his work at the Alpine Club Gallery, shared with an artist named Neville Bulwer Lytton, who had trained at the École des Beaux-Arts (he was to win a bronze medal for real tennis at the

Paris Olympics the following year, and much later became 3rd Earl of Lytton). Roger had submitted works for the NEAC's spring show, but they had been rejected – and he'd resigned, telling Rothenstein 'it's no good forcing oneself when one isn't wanted'.[28] At the Alpine Club he showed seven oils and fifty-seven watercolours, and sold twenty-one pictures for a total of £180, while garnering positive reviews. 'I've never had so much recognition of my work,' he wrote to his mother, 'tho' it comes at a time when I have lost my ambitions in that direction, and indeed, in all directions.'[29] He went down to Failand to see the children and made a waterwheel with Julian which they took out into Roger's favourite field, Durbin's Batch, where they made a dam and had a picnic tea. But Helen was constantly on his mind.

He returned to America in October. His visit coincided with the 'Panic' of 1907 – a run on banks that Morgan played a crucial role in ending, lending his own money for the cause. 'All America is ringing with his praises,' Roger reported to his mother, meaning that Morgan was 'in the best of humours'[30] to finalise Roger's resignation as Curator to take up the role of European Advisor on Paintings. Roger's friend and previous deputy, Burroughs, was promoted to Acting Curator.

Arriving back in London in January, Roger was finally able to visit Helen, and by mid February 1908, eight months after she'd been committed, the doctors told Roger that she would, soon, be able to return home. The lease on the house on Willow Road was coming to an end and hoping to replicate the happiness that they had experienced at Ivy Holt in Dorking, Roger began looking for somewhere outside London. Wanting something permanent, and feeling it would help Helen, in the late spring of that year he used £600 his father had recently given him to buy a piece of land on the outskirts of Guildford, close to Chantry Wood and with a southerly view.

Having consulted architects and unimpressed with the beamed, low-ceilinged iterations of Arts and Crafts houses they had come up with, Roger designed Durbins himself. It was named for the field at Failand that he loved, but inspired by the seventeenth-century François Mansart, who introduced Classicism to French architecture, and by the high rooms of Italian Renaissance palazzi. The structure was informed by need; the cheapest method was to build in a block, and Roger conceived the layout from the inside out, fitting the necessary number of rooms around a double-height living room-cum-hall, trimmed by an internal balcony on the back wall. His desire for as much light as possible determined the huge windows, for which he carefully selected panes that were proportional. The whole, before the shutters were added, came in under Roger's initial estimate at £1,000.

While the building work was done, home was a house named Chantry Dene, also in Guildford. The children stayed at Failand

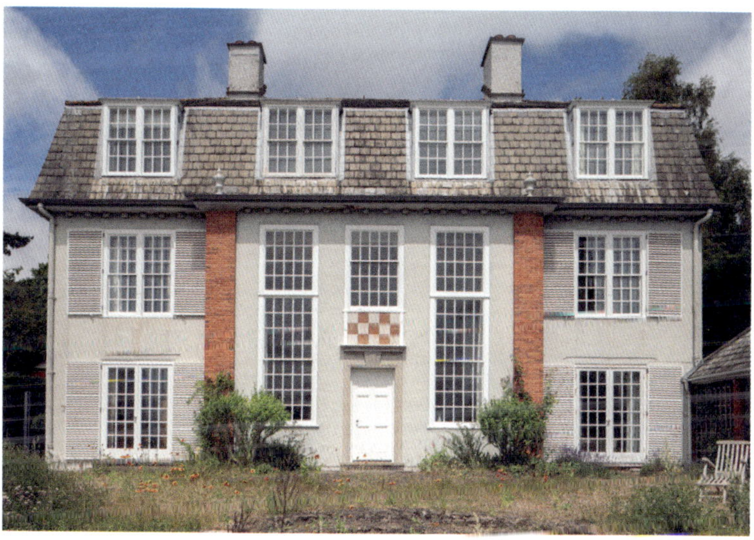

The French-looking garden-facing façade of Durbins, the house designed by Roger in Guildford, as it is today.

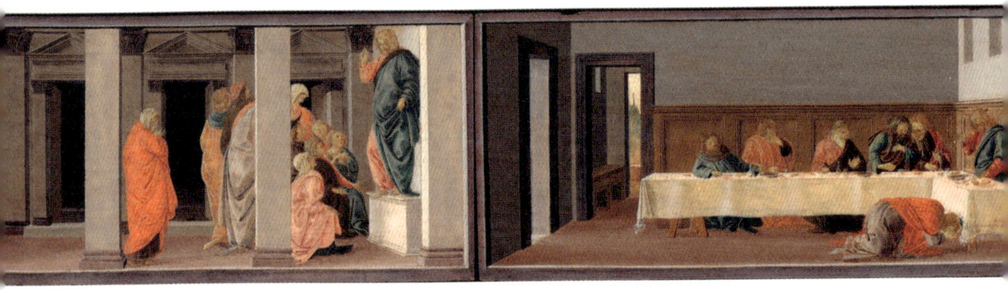

with Roger's sister Joan, as Helen was still unstable. His sister Agnes kept Helen company while Roger went to Paris and Antwerp, his job vital for paying the bills, although his parents were helping with some of them. It was not an easy time; Roger was called back from a trip to Germany, and, although Joan brought the children to visit, even months after she came home Helen still wasn't well enough for them to return full time. She'd be furious with Roger and he'd leave, and then she'd write letters saying how much she wanted him to come back. In November, she declared that she wanted to go with him to Italy – but her doctor advised against it.

It was on that trip to Italy, in November 1908, that Roger proposed that the Metropolitan Museum should acquire four predella panels featuring the life of Mary Magdalene that had been discovered by his fellow founder of *The Burlington Magazine*, Herbert Horne, in Florence. Horne had identified them as having been made for an altarpiece executed for the convent of Sant'Elisabetta delle Convertite which had been established for penitent prostitutes – and as being by Botticelli. Roger agreed with his attribution, but the museum turned them down. Roger, who described Botticelli's sympathy for the Magdalen as being near Rembrandtian, wrote to Johnson about them, who bought them. There was a small squall of argument between Roger, Horne and Berenson, since Berenson initially refuted the attribution, though later he retracted that opinion.

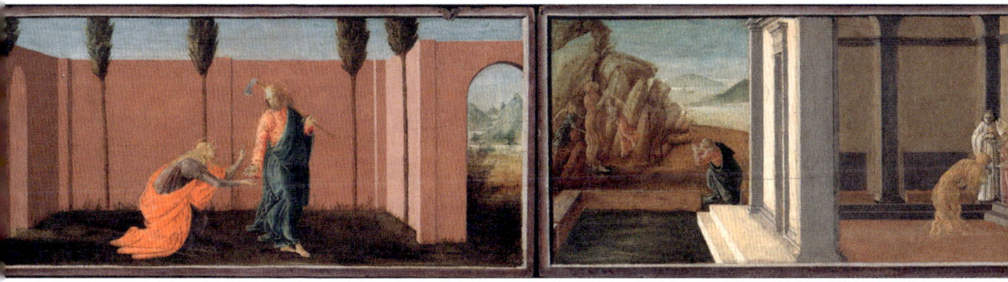

Sandro Botticelli and Filippino Lippi, *Predella Panels from the High Altarpiece of Sant'Elisabetta delle Convertite*, c. 1484, now at the Philadelphia Museum of Art.

Meanwhile, distance was growing between Roger and the Metropolitan Museum. That same month, August Jaccaci, a New York contributor to *The Burlington Magazine*, wrote to warn Roger that he was becoming too remote and his authority at the museum was at risk:

> it is of vital importance that you should come here to regain it and place yourself properly before the Museum people so that they will feel anew your value, your influence and therefore follow your suggestions and lead.[31]

Johnson had said something similar, but, while Roger continued to send letters concerning a Whistler, a Leonardo drawing and more, he did not go to New York. Helen was too ill.

In February 1909, on his way to the ferry to France, he wrote her a jerky letter from the train, using black chalk to profess his continuing love, and implore her to 'make up yr. mind to get well'. He explained that he needed her to agree to what the doctors suggested, and to control 'the impulse to assert yourself in opposition to me'. If not, he couldn't see another option but for to her live 'apart with a nurse & I shall live with the children.' Promising that if that were the case, he'd ensure they'd all see each other 'as often as possible', he concluded: 'It isn't a question of what you or I want

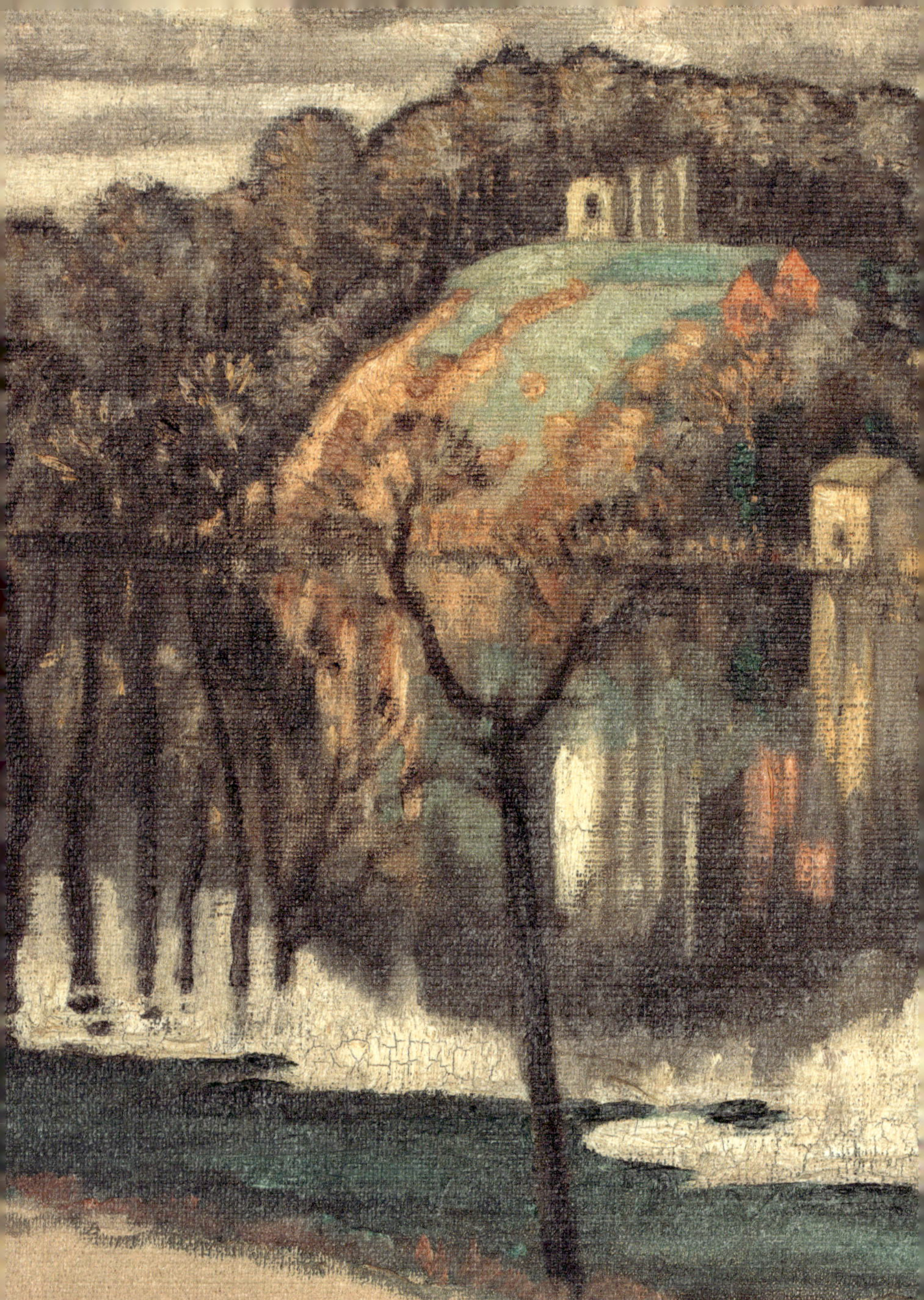

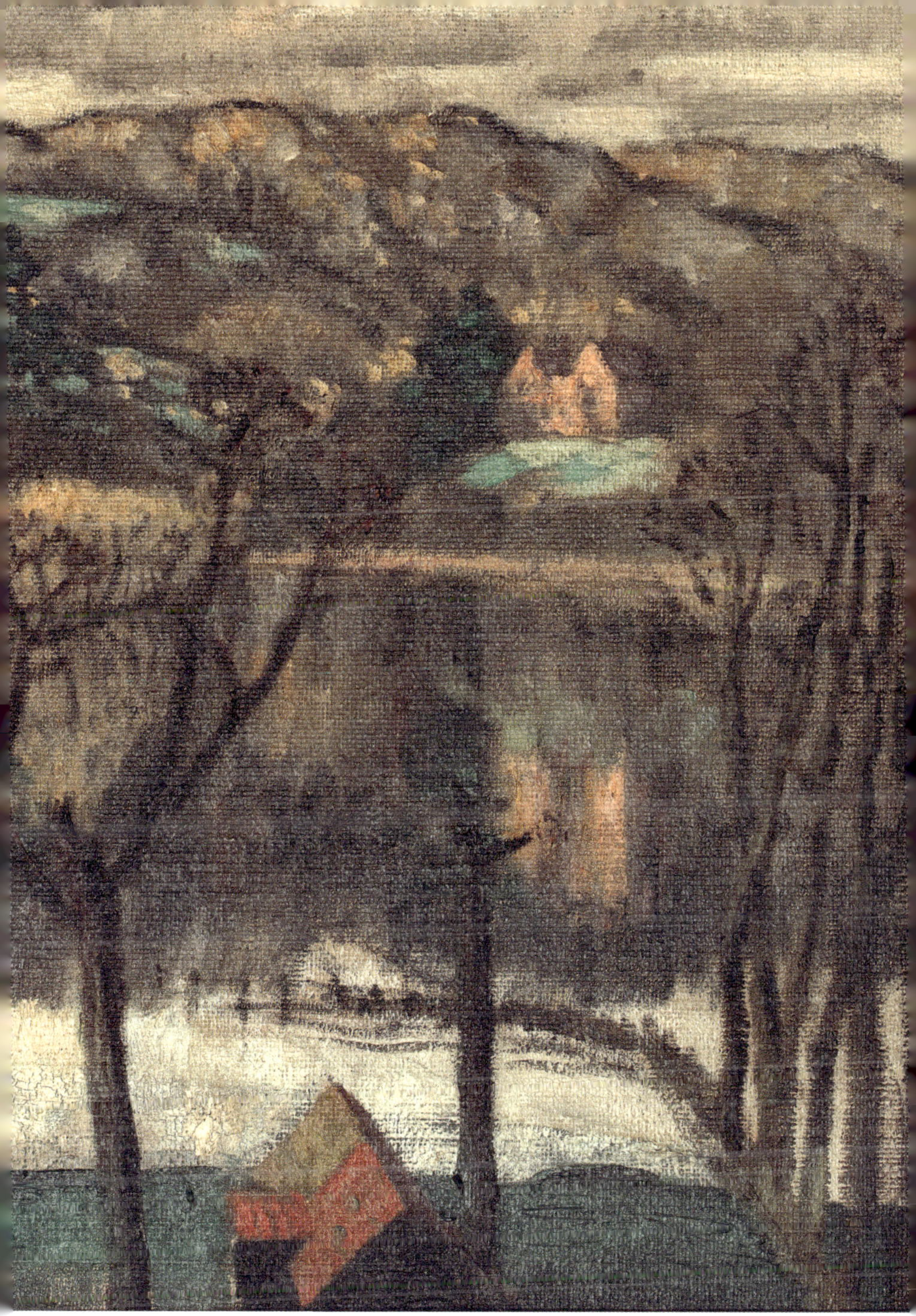

Roger Fry, *Flooded Valley*, 1911.

or wld like best its simply a question what we are *bound* to do for the children's good.'[32]

There were moments of pleasure to be found in art. Roger had taken on co-editing *The Burlington Magazine* with Lionel Cust, Surveyor of the King's Pictures, for which he was paid £150 a year. Taking two days a week, it slotted in alongside his job for the museum. Determined to improve the publication's coverage of modern art, he began paying more attention to contemporary advances. French Impressionism had finally been accepted by the British public, helped by a 1905 exhibition at the Grafton Galleries, organised by the dealer Paul Durand-Ruel. But Roger still wasn't overly enamoured, and in January 1906, he had seen, at the Sixth International Society Exhibition at the New Gallery on Regent Street, two works by Paul Cézanne. In Paris he'd visited the contemporary art dealers, and had met Leo and Gertrude Stein and seen the paintings they'd been buying (to some mockery) by Henri Matisse, who they introduced to Roger, and Pablo Picasso. Both artists were influenced by non-Western art, which was not beholden to academic representation, and Picasso was beginning to explore what would become known as Cubism. Roger's feelings about form that had begun when he'd encountered the Chardin still life in 1903 had developed, and in March 1908, between work, worrying about Helen, and seeing the children, Roger had written to *The Burlington Magazine* condemning its treating modern art 'in a less serious and sympathetic spirit than that which you adopt towards the work of older masters'. He'd defended the 'neo-Impressionists' in general, and Cézanne and Paul Gauguin in particular, whom he defined as 'proto-Byzantines'. He traced, as a comparison, the style of that Eastern Empire that came after the Roman Empire's Classicism, explaining it was not wrought out of a loss in technical ability for realism but was 'a necessary and inevitable reaction from it'. Impressionism,

Roger felt, 'left no power to express the personal attitude and emotional conviction'.[33]

Now he wrote to Simon Bussy, a French artist who'd married the English novelist Dorothy Strachey, to thank him for affording

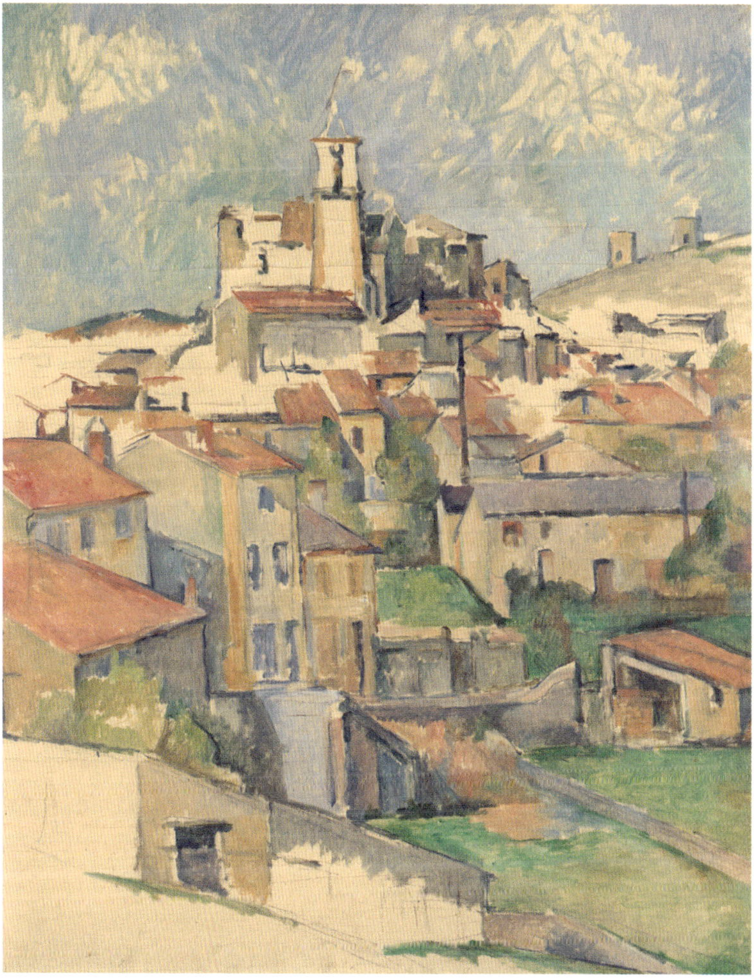

Paul Cézanne, *Gardanne*, 1885–6; Roger may have seen this on a trip to Paris, for it was in the possession of the dealer Ambroise Vollard from 1904/6 until 1924.

him 'the experience of abandoning oneself unreservedly to the enjoyment of beauty in front of a modern picture … when I saw your *Crépuscule d'Été*, I had an extraordinary emotion.'[34] He loved it so much he asked if he could buy it. Then, remembering himself – and his stretched finances – he asked if instead Bussy might be prepared to exchange a pastel for one of his watercolours, which Bussy agreed to. And in April 1909 he wrote an essay for the *New Quarterly* in which he stated that artists

> could dispose once and for all with the idea of likeness to nature, of correctness or incorrectness as a test, and consider only whether the emotional elements inherent in natural form are adequately discovered.[35]

But reality encroached. Roger realised that he was going to have to enact his earlier suggestion, and Helen moved, with a nurse, to a house near Crowborough. And when, that same month, Roger had another solo show at the Carfax Gallery on Ryder Street in St James's, now run by Arthur Clifton, *The Morning Post* wrote that his muted palette pictures – which included a New York skyscraper – 'suggest the work of an old-fashioned dreamer who has wandered in haunted places'.[36]

Helen's illness perhaps affected Roger's tolerance for Morgan's behaviour. In a London gallery he had found a painting attributed to Fra Angelico that had previously belonged to King Leopold of Belgium. Roger reserved it for the museum and wired the trustees for permission to buy it. In the meantime, Morgan stepped in and bought it for himself, the dealer under the impression that Morgan was also acting for the museum, rather than, as was the case, for his own private collection. Roger wrote to Morgan, pointing out that he had seen the painting a few days before Morgan, and adding, 'I think you should know the exact state of the case and therefore trouble you with this.'[37] Morgan was enraged: 'The most remarkable letter I have ever received. I do not propose to answer it until I see you. Bring it back.'[38] Morgan's temper was not improved when the attribution of the painting was queried by Herbert Horne, who said it was too decorative to be by Fra Angelico. (The painting is now attributed to a follower of that artist.) Again, Roger did not to go to New York, despite his presence being expressly commanded.

Roger's fear with Morgan's collection was that, despite Morgan's verbal promises, it would never reach the museum. He wasn't alone in his suspicions: regarding the Fra Angelico, Horne had written to Roger saying 'What Morgan buys will be soon be forgotten: but what the Museum buys will remain.'[39] The premonition held, to an extent: when in 1912, Morgan's collection was shipped to New York following the abolition on import tax on objects over two hundred years old, it was discovered that it was so large that the museum would have to expand to house it. Funds were requested from the City of New York – but the press whipped up opposition, maintaining that the City should not have to pay for Morgan to parade his wealth. Morgan, having refused to finance an extension himself, was so incensed that he left everything, valued at around sixty million dollars, to his son. When he died a proportion of the works did go to the museum, but many of the paintings were sold to pay estate duty. The collection, one of the largest ever to have been amassed by one man, dispersed.

On the other hand, the paintings and drawings that Roger bought for the museum remain there – having given shape and direction, in those early years, to a collection that has become one of the most revered in the world. Eighty miles south-west, John G. Johnson's collection of almost 1,200 paintings, some of which Roger helped him acquire, and others of which Roger restored, are in the Philadelphia Museum of Art.

But in December 1909, Roger's time at the Metropolitan Museum of Art was up. In the same month that Roger and the children moved into Durbins, the trustees held a meeting at which they decided to terminate their arrangement with their European Adviser, with six months' notice. Roger was never to cross the Atlantic again.

FOUR

ART-QUAKE

'In or about December 1910, human character changed.'[1] The year Virginia Woolf spoke of was marked by the death of King Edward VII, the succession of George V and two general elections – but it was the arrival of modernism in England to which she attributed the tectonic shift in temperament. And that came via a highly divisive exhibition, organised by Roger, entitled *Manet and the Post-Impressionists*. It included works by Cézanne, Van Gogh, Gauguin, Matisse and Picasso, drew fury and ridicule from both critics and attendees, and changed the course of British art. It also, Virginia maintained, altered literature, and attitudes to religion, conduct and politics. The exhibition's conception can be traced to a train journey in January 1910, and a fateful meeting between Roger and two key members of what was not yet widely known as the Bloomsbury Group.

The name 'Bloomsbury' derived from where they lived. Vanessa Bell, née Stephen, born in 1879, was the eldest of four siblings. Following her were Thoby, Virginia – who was to marry Leonard Woolf in 1912 – and Adrian. Orphaned by their father's death in 1904, they sold the house they had inherited on Hyde Park Gate and moved to Gordon Square, WC1. It was an area almost unknown to them – and the strike-out was deliberate; in leaving Kensington, they were leaving behind Edwardian upper middle-class societal convention. Once in Bloomsbury, the four jointly hosted 'at homes' on a Thursday evening. Populated mostly by Thoby's Cambridge friends, several of whom were Apostles, the evenings' attendees included John Maynard Keynes, Giles Lytton Strachey (brother of Dorothy), Leonard Woolf, Desmond MacCarthy, Edward Morgan (E.M.) Forster and Clive Bell. Conversation, a continuation of discussions begun at Cambridge, tended towards the philosophical, and specifically the ideas of Bertrand Russell (for whom Roger had designed bookplates in the 1890s) and George Edward Moore, who had both gone up to Cambridge just after Roger left.

But Vanessa and Virginia's interests lay in art and literature. Vanessa had studied at the Royal Academy in 1901, and then briefly at the Slade. In 1905 she'd extended the 'at homes' by way of the Friday Club, which doubled as an exhibiting organisation for artists including Henry Lamb and Mark Gertler. Clive Bell, too, was interested in art – at least the theory of it. He had hung a reproduction Degas in his room at Cambridge and had become further acquainted with the French art scene when he won a scholarship to study in Paris in 1902. Charmingly affable, described by Thoby as 'a sort of mixture between Shelley and a sporting country squire',[2] Clive fell in love with Vanessa, whose beauty came with an appealing sensuousness and wit. He proposed twice before she eventually accepted him in 1906, in the wake of Thoby's premature death from typhoid. They married in 1907, and stayed in Gordon Square, elevating their brand of bohemia with good linen, silver, four servants and an Augustus John painting; the Bell family owned several coal mines.

Virginia and Adrian moved to Fitzroy Square, and the group expanded. Lady Ottoline Morrell, patron of the arts, prominent hostess, famously outré dresser, and her husband, the Liberal MP Philip Morrell (the title was hers, her half-brother was the Duke of Portland) were living in beauty and colour on Bedford Square, where their interiors were based on a Degas painting. And the Stracheys introduced their cousin Duncan Grant, who had been at Westminster School of Art and was encouraged as an artist by Dorothy Strachey's husband, Simon Bussy, whose paintings Roger so admired, and with whom he had organised a swap.

The Bloomsbury Group's refusal to adhere to social mores also applied to romantic relationships. Sex was no longer taboo but openly discussed among them. The homosexuality of many of them had been acknowledged since Cambridge days, and everybody knew of Duncan's affairs with his cousin Lytton Strachey and Maynard Keynes, and, from 1910, his developing relationship with Adrian Stephen. Lytton wrote innuendo-heavy poetry that was passed around, and on one occasion, when he called in on Vanessa and Clive, he was received in their bedroom, where they were in bed.[3] However the evident sexual success of Vanessa and Clive's marriage didn't prevent Clive, following the birth of their son Julian in 1908, embarking first on a serious flirtation with his sister-in-law Virginia and then returning to his pre-marriage mistress. That, too, was part and parcel of Bloomsbury attitudes. 'Perhaps the fidelity of our parents was not the only or … highest form of married life,'[4] wrote Virginia of Vanessa's acceptance of this, though Vanessa was hurt by the Virginia episode (she was more sanguine about the mistress). However, while there may have been sexual freedom within Bloomsbury, appearances were maintained for the outside world, including, often, the servants. And regardless of physical relationships, it was friendship that bound Bloomsbury, along with artistic and intellectual ideals.

Clive and Vanessa were together at Cambridge station when Vanessa recognised Roger, who had taken to wearing a blue shirt and yellow jersey with his tweed suit. Sometime in 1906, she'd encountered him and Helen at a dinner party given by Desmond MacCarthy. Although Vanessa disliked lectures and so had never heard Roger speak, she knew of his reputation, and had expected to be talked at. Instead, Roger had been interested in her opinions, and they had had an intense discussion about John Singer Sargent. Roger, generally, was critical of Sargent's 'glamour and cleverness of brushstroke'[5] and Vanessa spoke in Sargent's defence. Sometime later, Vanessa had been to dinner with Roger and Helen at their house on Willow Road, where she'd thought Helen looked unhappy, and felt for Roger's situation.

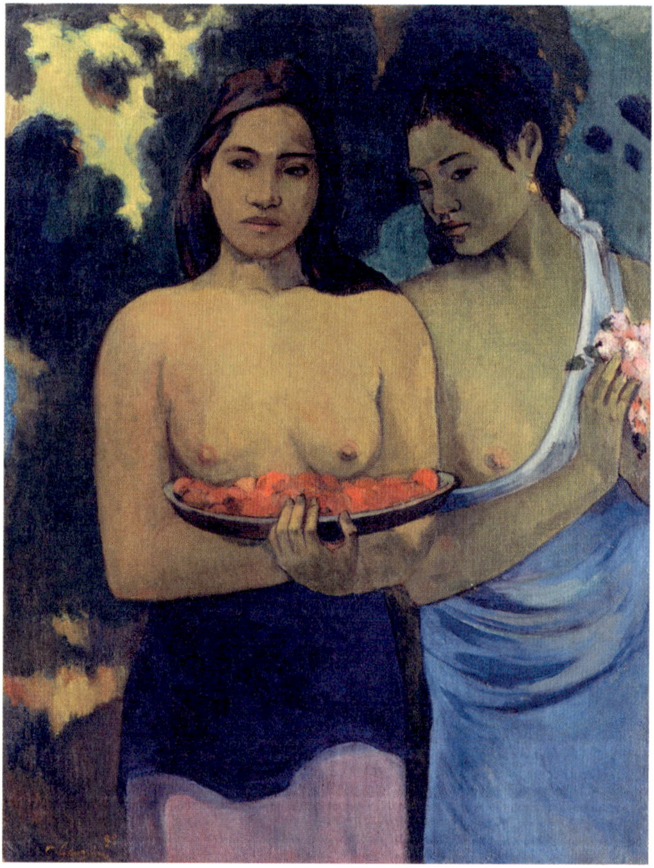

Paul Gauguin, *Two Tahitian Women*, 1899; Roger selected this painting for his Grafton Galleries exhibition *Manet and the Post-Impressionists* in 1910, where it was shown under the title *Deux Torses* – and horrified most of the attendees.

They sat together on the train. Roger, Clive later recalled, had already had the idea for an exhibition that would show the British public the newest French art, by which he was palpably excited. Clive, who decided Roger was the most interesting person he'd met since Cambridge, thought it unlikely to come off but offered to help in any way he could. Roger invited them both to Durbins, and Vanessa asked Roger to speak at one of her Friday Club gatherings at the end of February.

The bonds of friendship were swift to form. The decade and a half or so of age difference 'never seemed of the least importance,'[6] Vanessa wrote. It was helped by their having more friends in common: besides Desmond MacCarthy, there was Ottoline Morrell (who had also been friends with Helen in happier times) and the Berensons. Roger's talk at the Friday Club was a success – 'he had more knowledge and experience than the rest of us put together,' Virginia pointed out[7] – and, within Bloomsbury, he formed a bridge between the philosophers and the artists. Occasionally, when he needed to stay overnight in London, he'd be given a bed at Vanessa and Clive's flat.

By now, he knew of the termination of his contract with the Metropolitan Museum of Art in New York. 'It is useless to make any fuss about it,' he wrote to his father in February.

> If only I could hope that Helen could live at home I would not be so anxious, but that still remains the more expensive of the two establishments. However I am not at the end of my resources ...[8]

The Slade Professorship at Oxford was about to become vacant, for Charles Holmes, Roger's fellow *Burlington Magazine* founder and Director of the National Portrait Gallery, was stepping down. Berenson agreed to give Roger a testimonial, and William

Rothenstein, who had also been going to apply, withdrew when he heard Roger was a candidate. Ultimately, Roger was unsuccessful, again. But there were further irons in the fire.

Roger had been appointed art history lecturer at the Slade School of Art; he spoke on Friday afternoons during termtime to a generation that were later described by Henry Tonks as 'the last crisis of brilliance', and who included Ben Nicholson, Stanley Spencer, Paul Nash, Edward Wadsworth, Mark Gertler, Richard (C.R.W.) Nevinson, Dora Carrington and David Bomberg. Roger was still editor of *The Burlington Magazine*, which he considered increasingly important. And Morgan might have dispensed with his services at the museum, but he was still using Roger as a personal advisor, as were John G. Johnson and Henry Frick, on whose behalf Roger went to Poland in April to buy, for £60,000, Rembrandt's *The Polish Rider*. In May, Roger was commissioned to do a ceiling painting for the saloon at Ardkinglas, a brand new Scottish Baronial-style house on the banks of Loch Fyne, and he rented a barn outside Guildford big enough for the enormous canvas which was to depict Apollo driving his horses across the sky. There were other days when he was working at Hampton Court on the restoration of Andrea Mantegna's *The Picture Bearers*, one of a series on nine huge paintings created in the late fifteenth century that together make up *The Triumphs of Caesar* – an undertaking that was to consume Roger on and off for the next decade.

And, still hoping that Helen would recover sufficiently to be able to come home, he was continuing to improve Durbins. He had commissioned Gertude Jekyll to design and plant the garden, and there were four descending terraced levels, with grand herbaceous borders filled with the oriental poppies of his childhood, blue anchusa and artichokes. A waterlily-filled square pond graced the third level, and there was a semi-nude sculpture by Eric Gill; Gill's first offering, a seven-foot-tall Virgin Mary, was rejected by Roger who felt it was too controversial for the comfort of his sister Joan who, while Helen was ill, was running the house and looking after the children with the help of two servants,[9] a Swiss governess and a full-time gardener. Helen was present on the day that Vanessa and Clive went for lunch but, although Helen noticed that Vanessa was pregnant, she was not well enough to be able to take part in conversation, and Vanessa found herself wanting to hug her. At the same time, Vanessa had some understanding of Roger's plight: Vanessa's sister Virginia had experienced periods of mental illness, during which she, like Helen, pushed away those closest to her. 'I've given up regretting the callus that had to form to let me go through with things. Now and again it gives and I could cry for the utter pity and wastefulness of things,' Roger wrote to Goldie in September.[10]

But, that letter continued, 'life is too urgent.' And most urgent, now, was Roger's changing and developing aesthetic view. His interest in non-Western art was growing. In a review of Helen Tongue's 1909 book *Bushman Paintings* for *The Burlington Magazine*, he praised the South African rock art for its 'peculiar power of visualisation', and in May he went to Munich for the *Masterpieces of Mohammedan Art* exhibition (Matisse also made the journey to see it). He was on the founding committee of the Contemporary Art Society, along with Ottoline and Philip Morrell, Charles Holmes and D.S. MacColl, among others. The line-up crossed over with that of the founding committee of the National Art Collections Fund, and the aims were similar, the only difference being the period of the artworks each group intended to purchase on behalf of Britain's public collections.

But uppermost in Roger's mind were the French artists whose work evoked in him such an emotional response, and was, he felt, a necessary step forward. Part of his delight in being with Clive, Vanessa and the others were that they – unlike his contemporaries – wanted to discuss it. Duncan Grant had also met Matisse, and was similarly familiar with the Parisian avant-garde, having studied in

Paris in 1906–7. The idea for Roger's exhibition languished over the summer months, but in early October he discovered that the Grafton Galleries, an extensive suite of rooms on Grafton Street in Mayfair, had a gap in their programming. He wrote to Charles Holmes, who was now director of the National Portrait Gallery, insisting he join him on another committee: 'It's purely formal, just to give a blessing not to the pictures themselves but to the idea that people may be allowed to look at them. So please be good and do as you're told.'[11] Ottoline Morrell was also appointed, and Desmond MacCarthy was made Secretary, for a fee of £100 plus half the profits, not that any were expected. His position was awarded, Desmond later wrote, not because of his expertise, but because 'I was fond of pictures … [and] we were happy together.'

Days later, Roger and Desmond set off to Paris, Desmond nursing flu, which Roger treated with champagne. There they met Ottoline and Clive (Vanessa regretfully stayed in London as her six-week-old baby was ill, about which Roger, to her gratitude, was not only sympathetic but helpful). Over the following days they saw the Steins, and toured various dealers – Bernheim-Jeune, Ambroise Vollard, Galerie Drouet – where Roger sat in front of paintings with his hands on his knees, groaning repeatedly 'Wonderful, wonderful.'[12]

Happily, they were able to take almost everything Roger wanted, and Paris done, he and Desmond set off for a short bicycling holiday which Roger had promised as lure. Desmond immediately realised that Roger's idea of the distance that could be covered, and pace, were out of sync with his own more conservative ambitions, and so Roger found he had opportunity for sketching, too, as Desmond would subtly draw his attention to the charm of a distant barn, or the contour of approaching hills, and then restfully smoke his pipe while Roger captured the view. After a few days, Desmond continued to Germany and Holland to select more pictures, and Roger returned home; Helen's condition was worsening, and Roger had secured her a place in a Quaker institution, the Retreat in York. His regret for her suffering was immense, and, in a moment's despair, he expressed the unsayable to Goldie: 'If she could only die.'[13]

Manet's name was used in the exhibition title because, a generation older than the other artists included, the public already

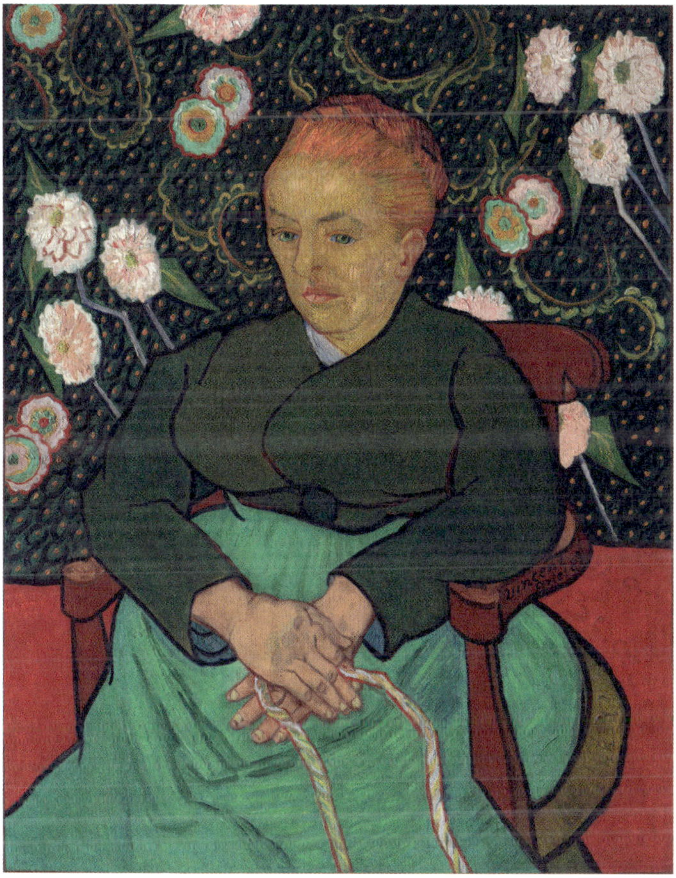

Vincent Van Gogh, *La Berceuse*, 1889; a portrait of Augustine-Alix Pellicot Roulin, included in Roger's Grafton Galleries exhibition *Manet and the Post-Impressionists*. The title translates as 'the lullaby' or 'the woman who rocks the cradle'.

knew his work and liked it. There were eight of his oils, including his last major painting, *Un bar aux Folies Bergère* (now at the Courtauld). Manet was also important because Roger could see a thread between his style and Cézanne's, who was one of the stars of the show with over twenty pictures, including bathers, landscapes, portraits and still lifes. A comparable weight was given to Matisse, Gauguin and Van Gogh, and there were works by Georges Seurat, Paul Signac, André Derain, Maurice de Vlaminck, Picasso (borrowed from the Steins), the Nabis painters Roger had been influenced by in the 1890s – Maurice Denis, Odilon Redon, Félix Vallotton – and more. Post-Impressionism was not yet a phrase, and the term 'Expressionists' was mooted as a possibility, but 'oh, let's just call them Post-Impressionists; at any rate, they came after the Impressionists,' Roger agreed with a journalist who was helping them with publicity.[14] Desmond put the catalogue together, and panicking that Roger would rehang the paintings and mess up the listings, arrived early at the press preview on November 5, 1910, to open the doors to what are now admired as some of the greatest works in the entire lexicon of modern art.

But in 1910, the pictures, and those artists, were decried. Roger knew that it would cause consternation but perhaps hadn't quite conceived the scale. 'A widespread plot to destroy the whole fabric of European painting,' wrote Robbie Ross, late of the Carfax Gallery, for the *Morning Post*.[15] 'The rejection of all that civilisation has done,' determined *The Times*,[16] and 'the output of a lunatic asylum,' said Ebenezer Wake Cook[17] in the *Pall Mall Gazette* – cruelly, for news of Helen's condition had filtered out. Others linked what they saw as painterly insurrection to Ireland's demand for Home Rule, the Welsh coalminers' strike, and the growing, and increasingly violent, Suffrage movement. 'The Post-Impressionists are in the company of the Great Rebels of the World,' declared Christina Walshe in the *Daily Herald*.[18]

The exhibition thus drew a crowd of about four hundred a day, who paid to enter the Grafton Galleries. Almost all came with the intention of agreeing with what they'd read, and the rooms echoed with the sounds of indignation and hysteria – one man laughed so much while looking at Cézanne's portrait of his wife that he had to be taken outside to recover by walking up and down, and Lady Sackville was physically sick.[19] A 'comments' book was provided and filled with complaints, and people sent in pictures that their children had done, asserting their superiority to Cézanne's. The Slade teacher, Henry Tonks, suggested that his students, who were being schooled in accurate drawing from antique casts and life models, stay away from the show their history of art lecturer had organised, to avoid contamination. (They didn't.)

And yet most of the paintings were twenty or even thirty years old. Manet, Van Gogh, Gauguin and Cézanne were all dead. Many of the artists had been shown in England already – earlier in the decade in the International Society Exhibitions at the New Gallery on Regent Street, and earlier that year in Brighton. But on these occasions they had been diluted by the more tempered, muted-coloured work of British artists – and, Roger noted in the case of the Brighton show, sometimes hung too high for proper examination. Now, brought together, the result was an explosion of colour and gesture, unconventional perspective and, noted Paul Nash, then a student at the Slade, 'relentless distortion of the human figure'.[20] It seemed, to most viewers, a complete departure from all that had come before. Gone was polished, academic technique, romantic reminiscences of place, flattering portraiture and identifiable Classical scenes. Of particular irritation for those who saw art in terms of its cultural cachet, and who had perhaps attended Roger's lectures on Italian art, was that one didn't, apparently, need to be acquainted with the traditions of art history to appreciate this new style.

In fact, Roger, who had in 1908 described Cézanne and Gauguin as 'proto-Byzantines', perceived similarities between the Post-Impressionists and early Italian Renaissance painters – Giotto, Duccio, Masaccio, Fra Angelico – who themselves were influenced by Byzantine artistic convention. Both groups, as he saw it, underemphasised descriptive detail to focus on linear design, structure, blocks of pure colour – and used these for the orchestration of emotional impact. In a letter to his mother, he compared the shriek of public resistance with 'the outbreak of militant Philistinism'[21] that had been provoked by the 1878 court case when Whistler sued Ruskin for a review that accused Whistler of 'flinging a pot of paint in the public's face'. Whistler won that case, and similarly, Roger had people on his side: 'Fred Brown, the London Slade Professor … who began by scoffing, wrote me a most generous retraction, saying that he had been completely converted to the ideas embodied by these painters,'[22] he told his father. *The Burlington Magazine*, which, of course, Roger edited, was in favour – and so were several other publications, including *The Art Journal*, *Daily Chronicle* and *English Review*.

Although most of the more established artists of Roger's generation felt themselves 'beyond the reaction and beyond the transition'[23] (and besides, for the most part, were already aware of the Post-Impressionists), there was enthusiasm from young artists and others of their generation who were less well acquainted with what had been happening in France. Roger would gladly go around the pictures with any interested party – he wanted to hear their opinions, too. Vanessa went with him twice, they looked at each in turn and discussed them at length, while she discovered

> a sudden pointing to a possible path, a sudden liberation and encouragement … It was if at last one might say things one had always felt instead of trying to say things that other people told one to feel.[24]

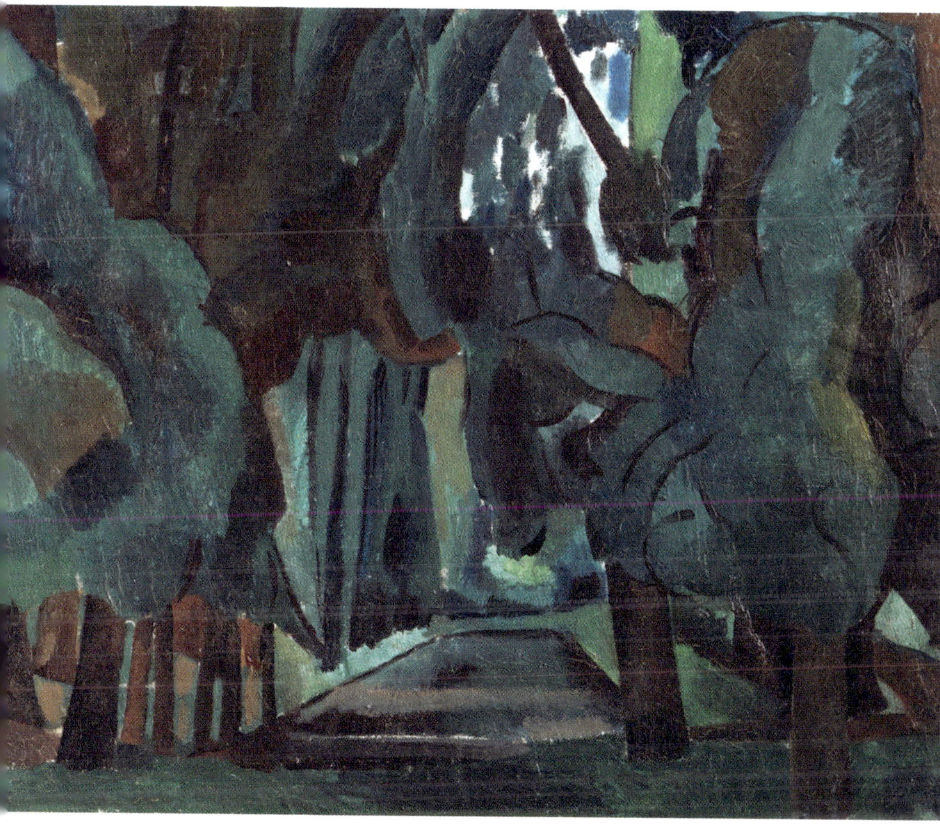

André Derain, *Trees by a Lake, Le Parc de Carrières-St-Denis*, 1909. Roger bought this painting from his exhibition *Manet and the Post-Impressionists*, and lived with it for the rest of his life; it was then given to the Courtauld Gallery.

Ottoline declared herself 'gripped' by Van Gogh, 'with his Vision of Soul in everything',[25] while for Katharine Mansfield, the same artist's paintings had 'taught her something about writing … a kind of freedom, a shaking free'.[26]

And people bought the paintings, including Clive who, not being able to afford a Cézanne – one of which went for £800 – instead acquired a Vlaminck. Roger, who couldn't afford a Cézanne either, bought a landscape by Derain for himself, *Trees by a Lake* (now at the Courtauld) as well as Gauguin's 1891 *Tahitians* which he donated to the Contemporary Art Society who, in turn, gave it to the Tate.

But still there was Helen's illness. Again, Roger had told her – and perhaps himself – that her committal to an asylum was temporary, writing to her 'Surely this illness will pass like a bad dream.'[27] The exhibition proved a distraction – as did his friendships with the Bells and the Morrells; he accompanied Ottoline and Philip to several concerts that winter and entertained them at Durbin's where Ottoline also sat for her portrait. However, in December he went to visit Helen. It was, he described to his sister Margery, 'A very sad Sunday at York.'[28] Having long resisted the specialists' view that her condition was incurable (Helen's doctor described Roger as having 'shown a devotion I have never seen equalled'[29]) he was coming to accept the finality of the circumstance.

Early in 1911, Roger was offered the position of Keeper of the Tate. He turned it down, explaining to his mother that the salary of £350, rising to £500, was insufficient – but at the same time he ascribed his refusal to the indifference he was feeling to 'official life and titles and honours'. Moreover, if he'd accepted, he'd have had to give up his other work, and he was certain he could do more outside the establishment than within it, especially since the exhibition had proved a surprisingly strong commercial success for the Grafton Galleries and they had offered him control of the galleries for the autumn months every year. Additionally, despite the abuse levelled at him from established quarters, Roger had become, as Clive put it, 'the animator and advocate of the younger British painters'[30] (Gertrude Stein described him as having acquired 'disciples'). Roger determined that the next Grafton show must combine the works of the younger British artists with paintings of those from his generation whose names would provide a draw.

Roger also wanted to refocus on his own painting, on which the Post-Impressionists had an immediate effect, not least in terms of the importance of outline: 'the first thing the Neo-Impressionist must do is to recover the long obliterated contour and to fill it with

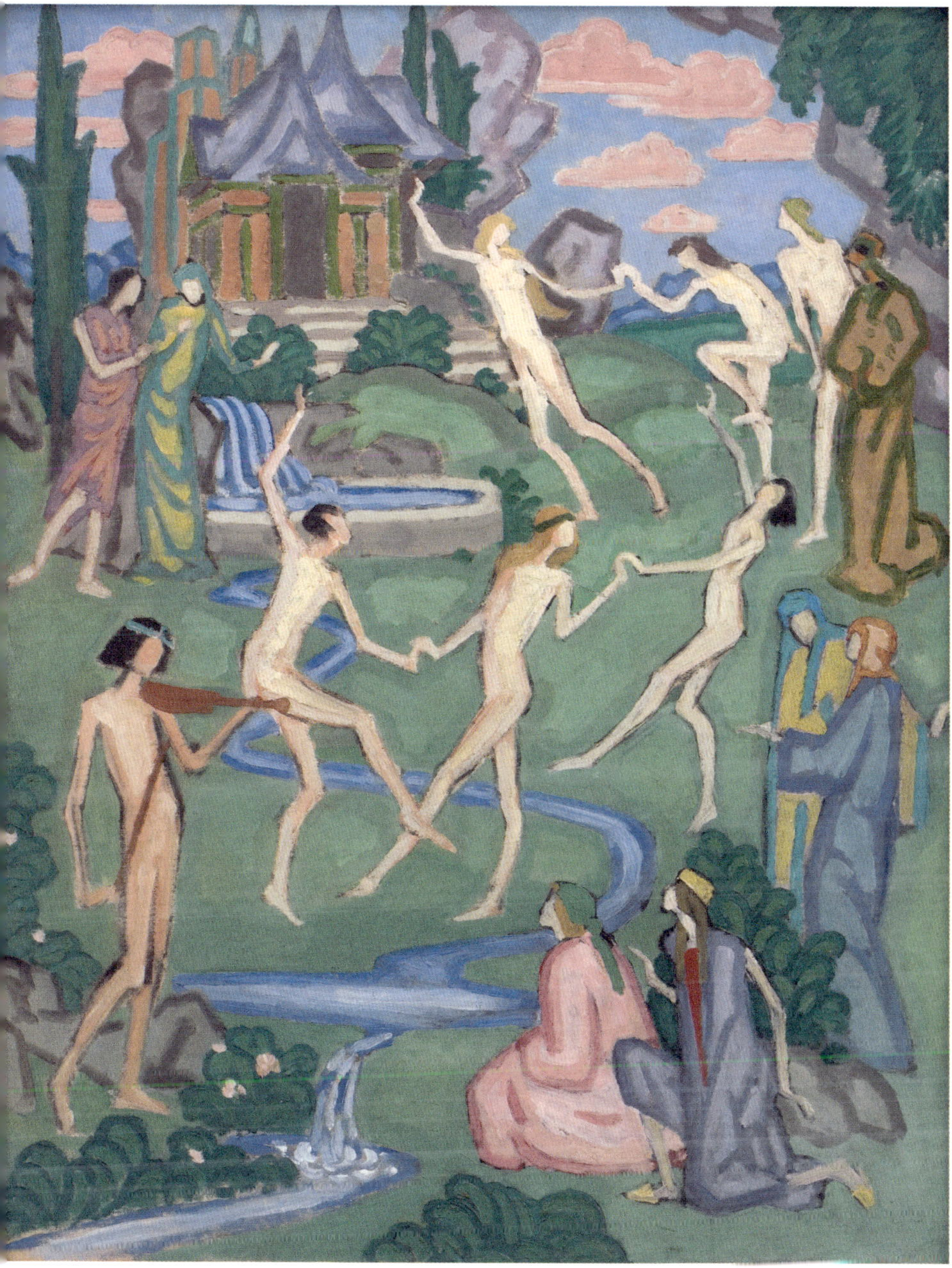

Roger Fry, *Dancers*, 1910; this painting, which showed such immediate Post-Impressionist impact, was bought by Ottoline Morrell.

simple undifferentiated masses,'[31] he'd written in 1908. But there were also repercussions for his subject matter: *Dancers* of late 1910 shows a group of figures cavorting and dancing and playing music, some dressed, some naked, in a fantastical landscape of waterfalls and pink clouds. In the spring of 1911, Roger, writing to Simon Bussy, declared himself 'completely Matissiste'[32] in his painting.

Others, too, were altering their approach. The works of the artists around Walter Sickert – including Lucien Pissarro, Spencer Gore, Augustus John, Harold Gilman – who that year formed themselves into the Camden Town Group, began to show more vivid hues, a freer application of paint and, in the case of Percy Wyndham Lewis, Cubist elements. Duncan, Vanessa and others of the Friday Club embraced bright colour and bold, experimental brushwork.

And Post-Impressionism spilled over into other areas of their lives. For a fancy-dress ball in February at Crosby Hall (now Crosby Moran Hall) in Chelsea, Roger, Clive, Vanessa, Virginia and Co. dressed as Gauguin exotics, by way of some patterned cloth Roger had found that was printed for the African market, and 'Kaffir necklaces'.[33] Their appearance scandalised other attendees, who thought Vanessa and Virginia looked 'practically naked'.[34] Next, Roger, Clive and Vanessa and a Cambridge mathematician named Henry Norton planned a trip to Turkey to look at mosaics and other Byzantine art.

Days before their departure, Roger's friendship with Ottoline, who had bought *Dancers*, tipped into something more. It was not Ottoline's first affair, and she was concurrently beginning another with Bertrand Russell, but it came as a surprise to Roger, who immediately wondered whether he should delay his leaving. In the end he didn't, and at the beginning of April 1911, the party disembarked from the Orient Express in Constantinople.

Roger immediately took control, being equipped with a phrase book from which he had taught himself sufficient Turkish to be able to negotiate travel beyond the traditional tourist route. He bargained for boats that enabled them to see the great mosques and ruined palaces from the water, and even charmed locals into allowing him and Vanessa to sketch them. After a few days, they moved on to Bursa where they planned to stay two days. But Vanessa – who had been pregnant again – miscarried. Clive shrank away from illness. Roger, with his scientific mind and history of caring for Helen, did not.

It was he who watched over Vanessa – although he would slip out for short trips to the bazaar, from which he returned with rugs, silks, glass bottles and more. He used them to decorate her room, affording it an increasingly cluttered vibrancy that communicated some of the essence of where they were. As she improved, he left her for longer, coming back with paintings that he'd prop up for her approval. Vanessa's guilt at having spoiled his holiday was assuaged by their growing intimacy, and the evident pleasure they both found in it. Virginia came out to help bring Vanessa home, but Vanessa and Roger's conversation continued all the way to England. And in mid May, two days after having attended a dinner at the Morrells' house in honour of Winston Churchill, Roger broke with Ottoline.

Vanessa needed to recuperate, and her doctor urged her to do so away from her family. There was a brief stay at Durbins, and in July, she found her own house to rent in Guildford, so that she and Roger could see each other as much as possible. Letters hint at the success of their union: 'You seem to know so exactly what I want, physically and mentally. Being with you is like being on a river and being with most people is like driving a jibbing horse along a bumpy road,'[35] Vanessa told him. He painted her, more than once, lying in a deckchair in the garden. For Vanessa, to have someone so utterly devoted to her was reassuring after Clive's faithlessness, and she admired Roger's ideas. For Roger, it was a relief to be with somebody so alive to life, to have somebody to again discuss his ideas with, and he was in thrall to Vanessa's beauty.

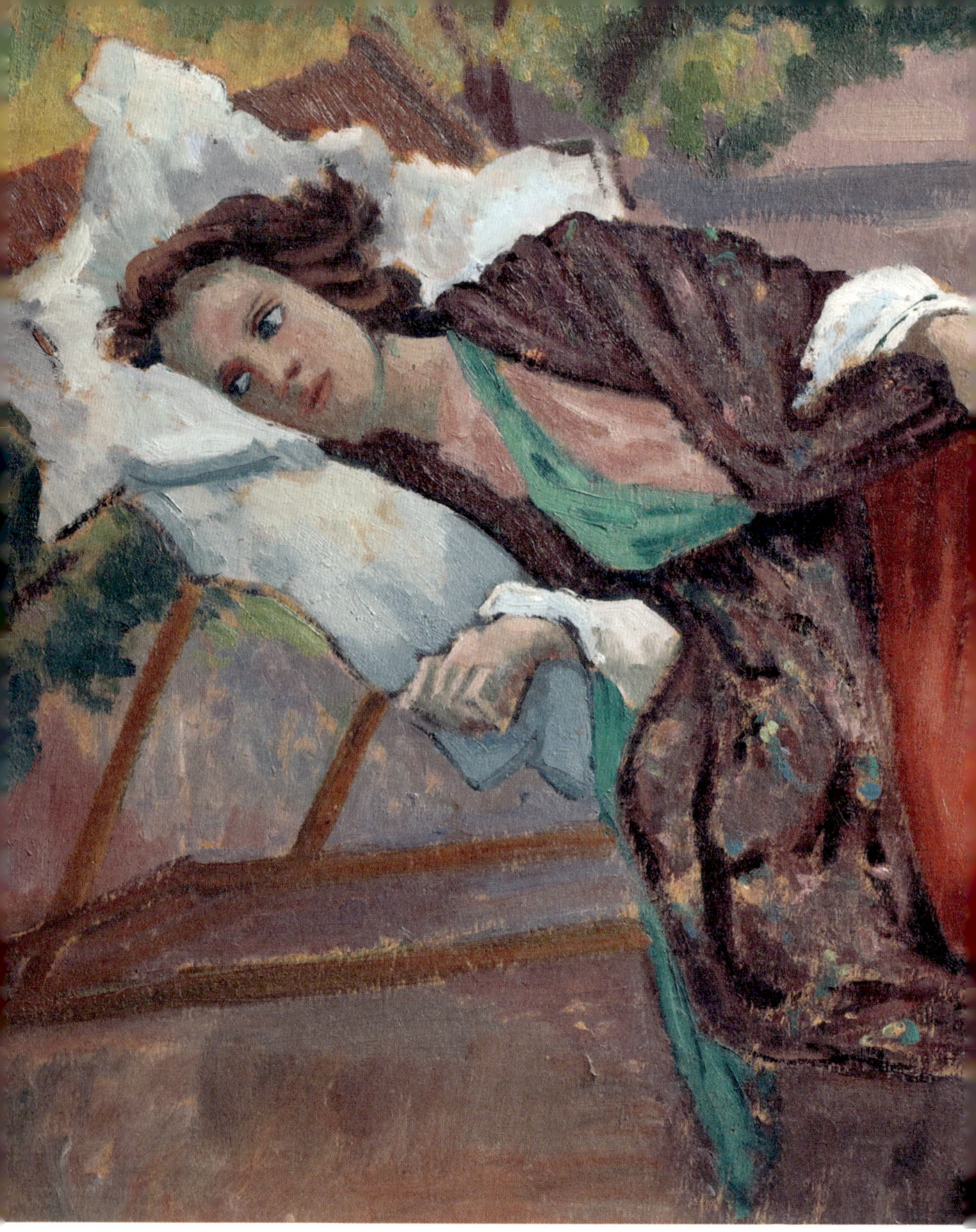

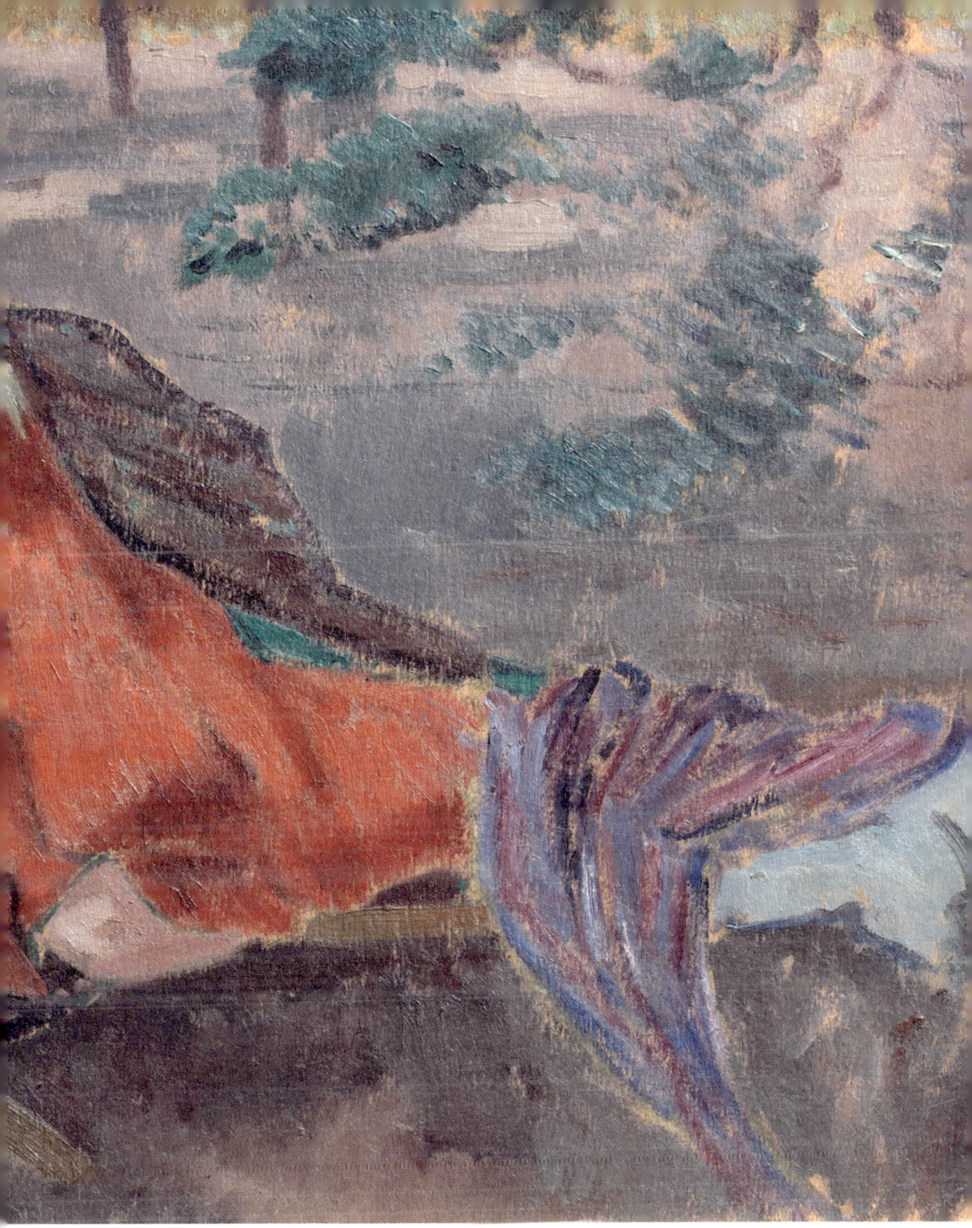

Roger Fry, *Vanessa Bell in a Deckchair*, 1911.

It was a summer of unbroken weeks of balmy weather, and Roger and Vanessa's euphoria was reflected in the public mood. Picadilly was lined with crown-topped poles, between which were strung gold-ribboned laurel swags and garlands for the June coronation of King George V and Queen Mary. The Festival of Empire drew happy crowds to Crystal Palace, and – to the thrill of Roger and others of the Bloomsbury Group – Serge Diaghilev's Ballets Russes were enjoying their first season at the Royal Opera House. The company had launched in Paris two years earlier to instant acclaim, and London audiences, too, were dazzled by the new, emotional approach to choreography that emphasised the body's natural movements, as well as the brightly coloured sets and costumes designed by Russian artists and incorporating elements of Orientalism, Russian folk art, and modern influences that chimed with the Post-Impressionists' preoccupations.

Henri Doucet, a young French artist Roger had met in Paris, came to stay at Durbins and painted Pamela's portrait, and Duncan joined them, to make use of the nine-year-old model. Other days were spent in Southwark. The Borough Polytechnic Murals (now in the Tate) were the idea of Basil Williams, then Chairman of the Polytechnic's House Committee, who wanted to demonstrate that public areas could be made attractive at minimal cost through painted decoration. He had been at Cambridge with Roger and asked him to oversee a scheme for the Polytechnic's dining room, as well as the walls, passageway and staircase leading to it, on the theme of 'London on holiday'. Roger brought in young artists he was now acquainted with: Duncan, Frederick Etchells, Bernard Adeney, and then, when it was realised they needed more hands to meet the completion date, MacDonald Gill (Eric Gill's brother) and Albert Rutherston. Roger painted *The Zoo* and organised for mural-less walls to be decorated in shades of orange, yellow and blue. Other subjects covered were *The Fair, Punch & Judy, Paddling,* and *Toy Sailing Boats*, and Duncan applied himself to two separate canvases (which were glued directly to the walls), *Football* and *Bathers*. His stylised figures are boldly outlined, and the water in the latter is painted as mosaic-like solid bands of blue, turquoise, green and white. All the paintings were given decorative borders, in the Byzantine tradition. Roger was delighted when a young mechanic declared that although he knew nothing about art, the new murals

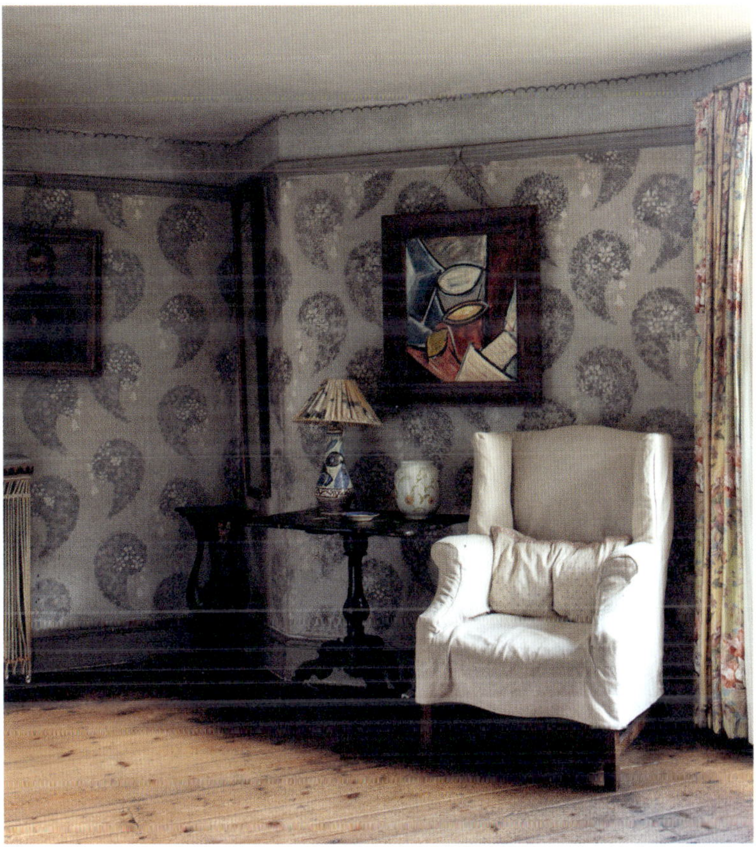

The garden room at Charleston.

made him 'want to whistle',[36] and the *Evening Standard* declared them the most important art event of the year.

Clive had not yet been informed of Roger and Vanessa's affair by the time of the Bell family holiday to Studland Bay in September. Vanessa was still sleeping with Clive and wasn't entirely sure how he would react, and she was wary that he might be less accepting of infidelity than she was. 'If he gets jealous now it will put an end to everything,'[37] she warned Roger, explaining why she was going to have to try hard not to sketch him more than she might if she weren't in love with him. Roger joined them for the first three days, and then took a house nearby for himself, his children and their governess. One morning, for reasons that remain undetermined,

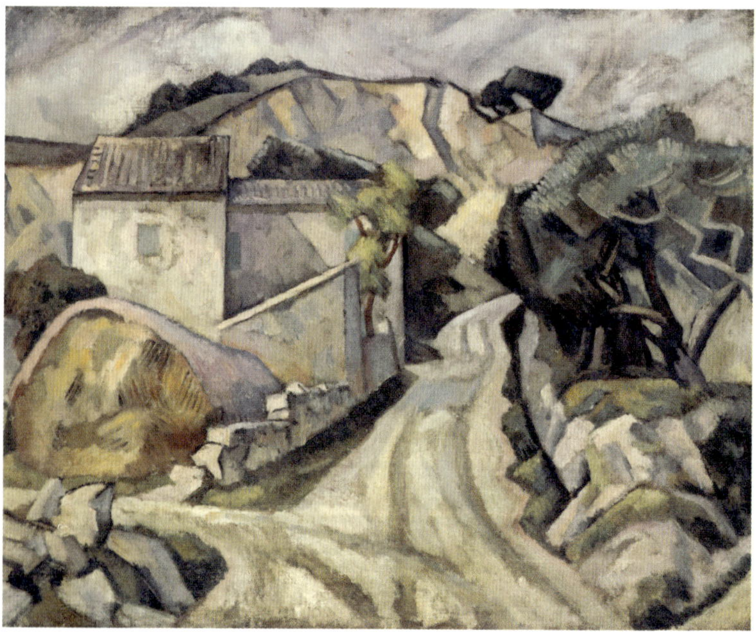

Roger Fry, *White Road with Farm*, c. 1912.

Vanessa, Clive and Roger got up very early and photographed each other naked on the beach.

October saw Roger and Duncan in Paris meeting Vanessa and Clive, who had just bought a Picasso – the first to enter a British private collection. *Pots et Citron* was a small Cubist still life and cost £4. In a buoyant mood, they all went to the Salon d'Automne where a whole room was devoted to Cubism, which Roger reviewed. Then, while Vanessa returned home, Roger, Duncan and Clive set off for rural France, Roger and Duncan travelling by bicycle, Clive by train.

'Dear Vanessa I love you et voila tout. Il n'y a plus rien à dire except that I think you deserve more than I can ever give you. Only it's so perfect that I'm not a bit anxious,'[38] Roger wrote, missing her, though he enjoyed Duncan's company. 'He loves these churches as I do & my dear as you would … He is sensitive in just the way I like.'[39] The whole trip had a galvanising effect on Roger, and the landscapes Roger developed from the trip incorporate fragmented, geometric shapes.

Roger's idea for the Grafton Galleries exhibition of the works of the young English artists combined with more established names did not come off: several of those more established artists, including William Rothenstein, were less taken up with the cause of Post-Impressionism and treated Roger's fixation with some incomprehension. Rothenstein was unwilling to commit his work unless there was a selection committee, an idea that Roger baulked at. Relations between Roger and Rothenstein, as well as others of his contemporaries, cooled.

Nevertheless, in what was a decidedly avant-garde exhibition for a British artist, Roger showed fifty-two of his own new paintings at a solo show at the Alpine Club in January 1912. The reviews were mostly positive, though some required wading through a slew of backhanded compliments. 'Mr Fry makes quite English what

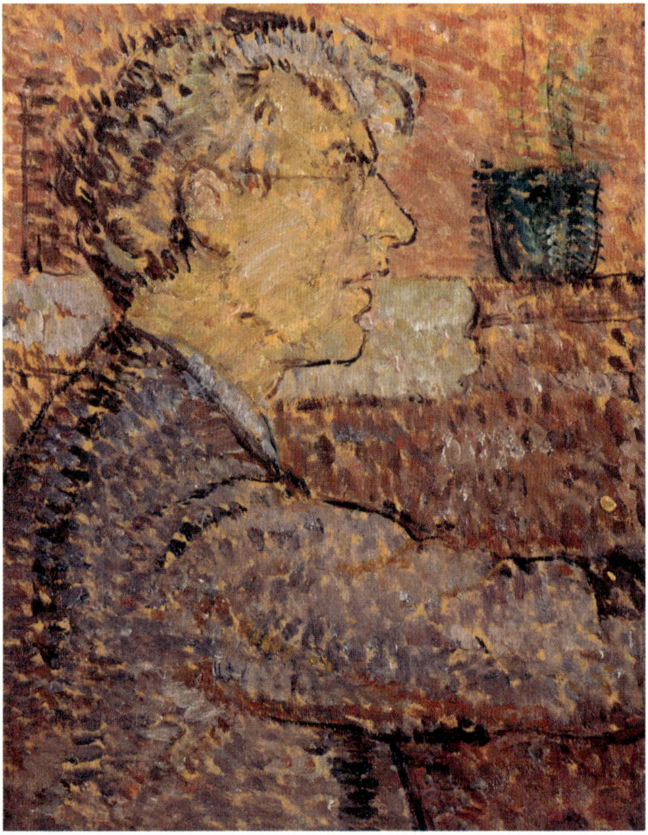

Vanessa Bell's portrait of Roger, painted in 1912 when they were on holiday on the Isle of Wight and experimenting with Duncan Grant's 'leopard' technique, a pseudo-pointillism that was also inspired by mosaics.

proceeds from France. There is none of the unpleasant atmosphere emanating from the canvases of Van Gogh or Matisse, or the appalling sense of evil which no aesthetic formula can obviate when contemplating the undoubtedly interesting work of Gauguin, or the atrophied and perverted work of Picasso,'[40] wrote Robbie Ross in the *Morning Post*.

The painterly probing continued. When Roger joined Vanessa on holiday on the Isle of Wight, they painted each other using Duncan's 'leopard' technique which, inspired by both pointillism and mosaics, used dabs of paint to create an overall image. Roger wasn't thrilled with his attempts at spotting, though he applied himself as industriously as ever; Vanessa's portrait of him was more successful (it is now in the National Portrait Gallery). And, later that spring,[41] Roger, Vanessa and Duncan adorned the hall at Durbins with Matisse-inspired, life-sized nudes, while Roger and Duncan began a mosaic in the summerhouse.

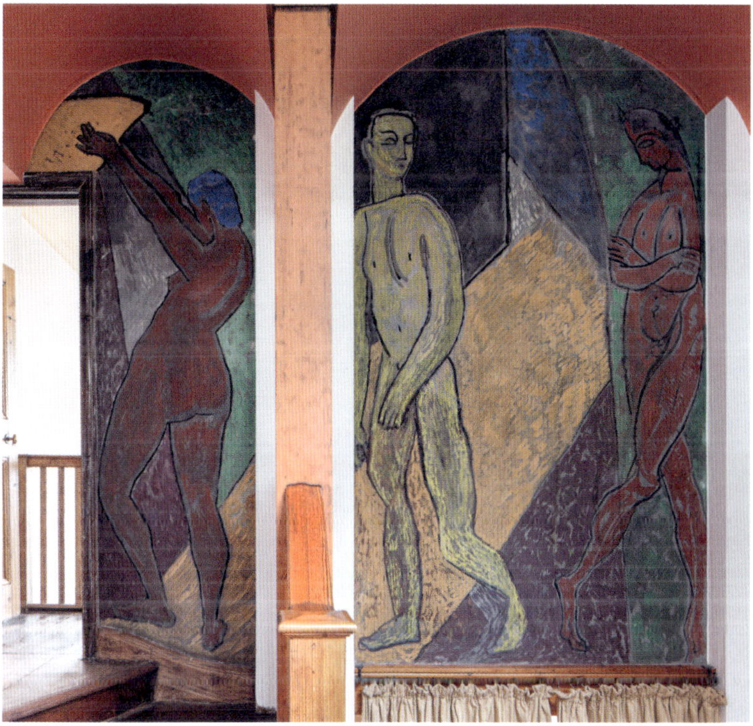

The entrance hall at Durbins, adorned with Matisse-inspired life-sized nudes by Roger Fry, Vanessa Bell and Duncan Grant.

In May 1912, a few of Roger's, Vanessa's and Duncan's paintings were exhibited at the Galerie Barbazanges in Paris. The gallery was run by Charles Vildrac, a poet and art dealer with whom Roger had become friends on his numerous trips to the city. Vanessa and Clive went with Roger to oversee the hanging of the show. It also featured works by the Camden Town Group – Walter Sickert, Lucien Pissarro, Augustus John, Henry Lamb, Spencer Gore – who had invited Duncan to join them after their first exhibition. Roger, Vanessa and Clive progressed to Italy, where Vanessa, to her irritation, came down with measles; Roger, again, looked after her. They saw the Berensons in Florence, and Clive observed that Roger was as famous there as he was in London, continually being stopped

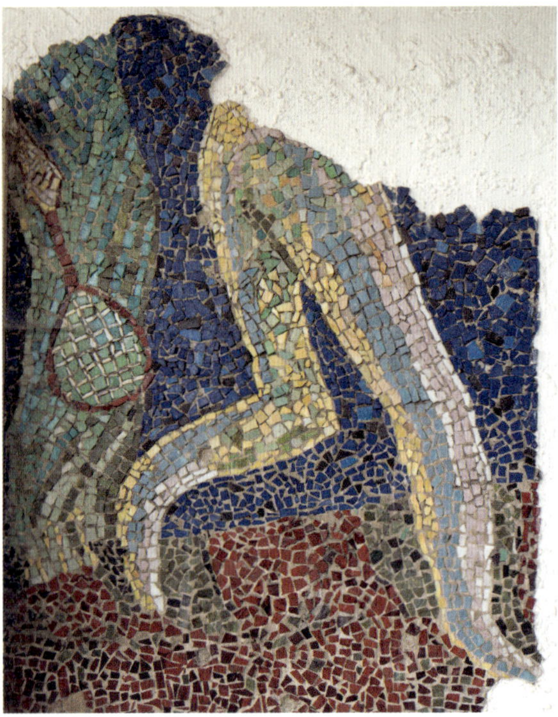

The mosaic that Roger and Duncan Grant began in the summerhouse at Durbins. Conceivably, they lost the impetus to finish it because the scale is wrong; the heads would have been cut off by the roof.

in the street. In August, immediately after Virginia and Leonard Woolf's wedding, which they all attended, Roger, Vanessa and Clive set off to Cologne for the last, most ambitious and most controversial of the exhibitions organised by the Sonderbund westdeutscher Kunstfreunde und Künstler. More commonly known simply as the Sonderbund, it had been formed in 1909 and introduced Post-Impressionism to Germany, as Roger's Grafton Galleries shows did to Britain. In 1912 there was a special focus on Edvard Munch, alongside 125 Van Goghs, works by Braque, Picasso, Cézanne, Gauguin, Seurat, Signac (among them several paintings that Roger had shown in *Manet and the Post-Impressionists*), and the German Expressionists Wassily Kandinsky and August Macke.

Vanessa was increasingly interested in and affected by what Duncan was doing. A letter to Roger in July 1912 had concerned Duncan's painting *The Queen of Sheba*, which had just arrived back from being shown in Wales. Vanessa explained to Roger that she felt

> the whole conception was really sweet and too pretty and small ... I thought that the usual English sweetness was coming in and spoiling it all. I am saying horrid things ... But I also thought perhaps I think all this now because I have been seeing all those French pictures ... Perhaps these look so bad by comparison to Derain, Picaso, Matisse, etc. I want you to come and put them in their right place again.[42]

Vanessa and Virginia had together taken the lease on Asheham House, outside Lewes in East Sussex. Now, while Virginia was still on her honeymoon, Vanessa invited a flow of fellow artists to stay and paint, including Roger (who helped her get the house ready), Frederick Etchells and his sister Jessie, Roger's friend Henri Doucet, and Duncan.

Roger, however, had less time for painting that August, as he was occupied with the organisation of his next Grafton Galleries exhibition. 'The British public has dozed off again since the last show and needs another electric shock,'[43] he wrote to his mother. At the same time, London's contemporary art scene had moved forward. In 1911, the Stafford Gallery had shown Cézanne and Gauguin. In March 1912 the Sackville Gallery, who usually specialised in Old Masters, had welcomed the Italian Futurists. Filippo Tommaso Marinetti, author of the *Manifesto of Futurism*, gave Roger a copy of that proclamation, which was also printed in the catalogue. Roger saw the paintings but felt that the artists failed to deliver the visual equivalent of their creed, which rejected the past in favour of speed, machinery, violence, youth and industry. But it fuelled his ambitions for the *Second Post-Impressionist Exhibition*.

On this occasion, Roger aimed to present a narrative within the Post-Impressionist movement – and to demonstrate that the British artists were part of a global aesthetic progression. Roger wrote to Leonard while he was on his honeymoon asking him to take on the role of secretary, which Leonard agreed to do. The Ballets Russes had returned to London that summer, Anton Chekhov's *The Seagull* had had its London premiere in the spring, Fyodor Dostoevsky's *The Brothers Karamazov* had just been published in English, and with all this in mind Roger also directed the Russian artist, mosaicist and poet Boris Anrep to go to Moscow to select works for a Russian section. Clive, who by now knew of Roger and Vanessa's affair and was accepting of it, was given responsibility of the British section, and Roger went back to Paris to again do the rounds of the leading dealers and collectors. Duncan designed the catalogue cover, to an idea of Vanessa's: a deliberately provocative, Cubist-inspired illustration of a woman looking horrified by what she was seeing.

Cézanne was taken as the 'Old Master' starting point, from which the show segued to thirty-four drawings and paintings by

Matisse, including two that were bigger than life-size, and seven bronzes. There were works by Matisse's fellow Fauvists, André Derain, Kees van Dongen and Maurice de Vlaminck, whose interest in African and Oceanic art influenced their use of bold colours and simplified forms. Also featured were Picasso (including Clive and Vanessa's picture), Braque, Jean Marchand, Auguste Chabaud and five pictures by Henri Doucet.

The Russian selection was initially disappointing: Anrep returned with works by, among others, Nicholas Roerich, Konstantin Bogaevsky, Vladimir Komarovsky – all of whom were essentially Symbolist in their approach. 'They're rather pretty and romantic – well, I daresay it's as well the British Public should have something it'll like,' Roger wrote to Duncan.[44] The problem was to do with shipping, and the assortment improved for the unofficial, second *Second Post-Impressionist Exhibition*, a rehang made possible when the Grafton Galleries' January show fell through, and certain of the works in the exhibition that were on consignment had to go back to Paris. Among the late arrivals were paintings by Mikhail Larionov (who had helped Anrep with his selection) and Natalia Goncharova. Two of the most advanced of the contemporary Russian artists, their Neo-Primitivism drew on folk art and Byzantine icons, as well as on Cubism and Futurism. Other January additions included Matisse's plaster relief *Le Dos* (a bronze is now in the Tate), and a solo show of thirty-three Cézannes that were given their own room.

Clive, meanwhile, selected pieces by Roger, Vanessa, Duncan, Frederick and Jessie Etchells, Eric Gill, Wyndham Lewis, Spencer Gore and Stanley Spencer, who had only just graduated from the Slade. Roger contributed, from his own collection, Vanessa's *Nosegay*, Duncan's *The Queen of Sheba*, Boris Anrep's *The Man Building a Well to Water the Cattle*, and an Eric Gill garden sculpture – possibly the statue of the Virgin that he'd deemed unsuitable for Durbins.

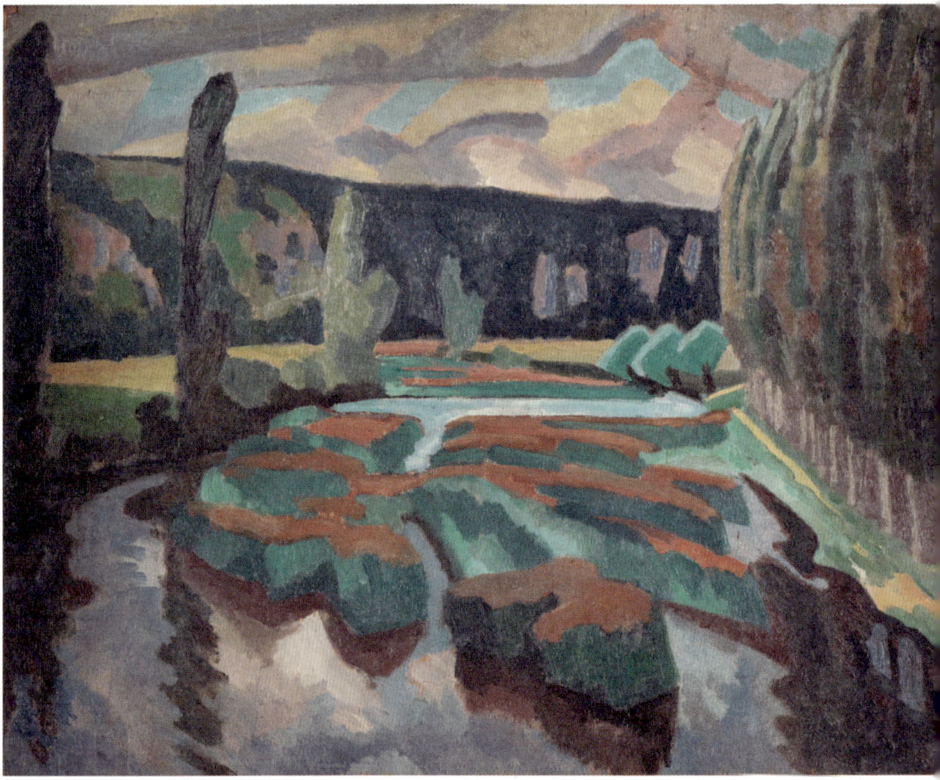

Roger Fry, *River with Poplars,* c. 1912. The view is from the bridge at Angles-sur-L'Anglin, near Poitiers. A painting by Roger called *Angles sur l'Anglin* was shown in the *Second Post-Impressionist Exhibition,* and it could have been this one. It is now in the Tate's collection.

When the exhibition opened again, nine out of ten of the visitors 'either roared with laughter at the pictures or were enraged by them,'[45] Leonard Woolf observed. There was some pointed unkindness: 'There is no eccentricity, no affectation, no mannerism in French that does not find a ready echo in English Post-Impressionism. And let it be said at once, like every echo, it is feebler than the original sound,'[46] reported *The Observer*.

Roger answered the more general criticism in *The Nation*, pointing out that

> every new work of creative design is ugly until it becomes beautiful … we usually apply the word beautiful to those works of art in which familiarity has enabled us to grasp the unity easily, and … we find ugly those works in which we still perceive the unity only by an effort.

Again, he endeavoured to explain that the art in which others saw 'a complete repudiation of all past tradition' was in fact

> in line with the older and longer and more universal tradition, with the art of all countries that has used form for its expressive, not for its descriptive, qualities.[47]

As for the first exhibition, Roger was present in the galleries and available for on-the-spot exchanges of ideas and explanations, given patiently and, Leonard recalled, 'via an extraordinarily interesting lecture'.[48] Henry James appeared one day and confessed to his hesitation over Matisse and Picasso; Roger took him down into the basement for tea and did his best 'to convey to the great novelist … that Cézanne and Flaubert were, in a manner of speaking, after the same thing'.[49] Indeed, to emphasise that Post-Impressionism didn't only apply to art, Roger had arranged a programme of accompanying lectures in the gallery, concerning poetry, music and more.

And it was again a commercial success: the mass of attendees ensured good takings on the door and works, Clive recorded, sold 'like hot cakes'.[50] It was, however, less beneficial to the artists than they'd originally thought it might be; Roger had agreed overly generous contracts which, when it came to payment, he was forced by necessity to ignore, although nobody complained except Wyndham Lewis, whose work, which showed the influence of Futurism, had also drawn the heaviest criticism. Among the buyers was the French poet and gallerist Charles Vildrac, who had been invited to present a lecture on modern French literature and bought Duncan's portrait of Henri Doucet. Edward Marsh, who had previously acquired one of Roger's works, now bought Duncan's *The Queen of Sheba*, which had been owned by Roger. Marsh donated it to the Contemporary Art Society, who in turn gave it to the Tate in 1917, making it Duncan's first work in a national collection.

Later, Clive proposed that 'between the first Post-Impressionism exhibition and the first war … Roger Fry changed more than he had changed in all the years between Cambridge and that exhibition.'[51] Roger hadn't entirely abandoned the Old Masters – there was *The Burlington Magazine*, his lecturing, continuing restoration work, and his position on the National Art Collections Fund which, since its inception in 1903, had acquired for the nation Velázquez's *The Toilet of Venus* (known as the Rokeby Venus, now in the National Gallery), Hans Holbein's *Christina of Denmark, Duchess of Milan* (also in the National Gallery) and Whistler's *Nocturne: Blue and Gold – Old Battersea Bridge* (now in the Tate). But, in the minds of the public, he had become part of Modern Art and Bloomsbury, and those associations liberated him from the expectations of convention. They also, as he observed in a letter to his mother listing his perceived failings, rendered him unemployable when it came to the significant institutional posts, on account of having infuriated so many of his contemporaries and incited such mockery and scorn.

At the same time, Roger had become the most influential man in the entire British art world. He 'could place his words where he would. *The Times* felt bound to print letters from him in large type on the leader page,' noted Clive.[52] 'Form' – the word Roger used to describe the non-representational elements of a work, such as the lines, the colours, and the overall design – entered the art wordbook.

Most importantly, Roger had altered an aesthetic, providing what he described as the 'kind of spiritual high-tension' in which art can flourish, and bringing people with him.[53] And, in exposing Vanessa and Duncan's works to a wider audience, he had established them, and by extension Bloomsbury, as his co-leaders of the new movement. It necessitated the formation of a new exhibiting society specifically for artists who were developing Roger's idea of a Post-Impressionist style. They called themselves the Grafton Group – and they had another project up their sleeves, too.

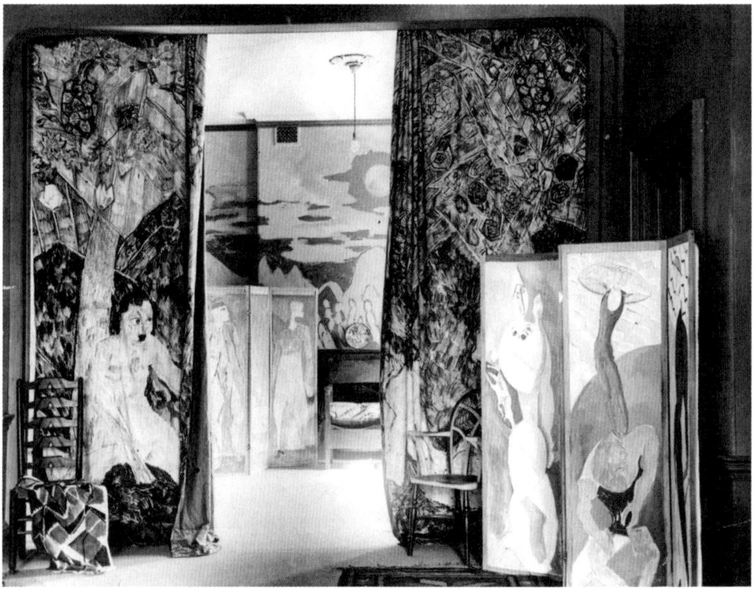

The Omega Workshops in 1913, with Henri Doucet's curtains featuring Adam and Eve, and what were – if you can imagine it in colour – vibrant murals on the walls.

FIVE

INTERIOR INNOVATIONS AND THE OMEGA WORKSHOPS

When the doors to the Omega Workshops opened on July 8, 1913, the press and invited guests were greeted by a radically exuberant vision. Typically, middle- and upper-class interiors were either still steeped in ponderous Victoriana, or were afforded a comparative Edwardian lightness in tasteful pastels. Ethel Sands, a London Group artist and society hostess, decorated her seventeenth-century Oxfordshire manor house with pale grey walls, white lawn curtains, Japanese panels, Augustus John drawings and chintz; Vanessa described it as having a 'fatal prettiness'.[1]

At Omega, under Roger's direction, the walls were covered in vivid murals, while a pair of Henri Doucet-designed curtains featured life-size representations of Adam and Eve in a fauvist-hued Garden of Eden. Screens by Duncan Grant and Wyndham Lewis were adorned with boldly cavorting figures, and a 'conversational' chair had bright blue and yellow legs and a back that sported bands of blue and green. Abstract patterned textiles – conceived by Vanessa, Roger and Frederick Etchells – were made into cushions and bedspreads. There were other things, too: embroidery from

Natalia Goncharova's production studio in Ukraine that combined influences from folklore with futurism and suprematism;[2] reproduction Byzantine mosaics, beads, silks and pots from Turkey; the cloth Roger had found that was woven in Manchester for African export. It was a new look for homes, and a new approach to communal artistic practice.

It was during the *Second Post-Impressionist Exhibition* at the end of 1912 that Roger's idea for the Omega Workshops, to be run with Vanessa and Duncan, had crystallised sufficiently for him to write to George Bernard Shaw about it. The letter outlines his plan to begin 'a workshop for decorative and applied art' to be staffed by 'young artists' (he specified those who had worked on the murals at Borough Polytechnic)

> whose painting shows strong decorative feeling, who will be glad to use their talents on applied art both as a means of livelihood and as an advantage to their work as painters and sculptors.

He pointed out that the Post-Impressionist movement was 'quite as definitely decorative' as the Pre-Raphaelites had been, and that 'its influence on general design is destined to be as marked'.[3]

In referring to the Pre-Raphaelites, Roger cited the enduring legacy of William Morris. Roger had had peripheral involvement with the second-generation, socialist-leaning Arts and Crafts guilds, namely, the Guild and School of Handicraft that his Cambridge friend Charles Ashbee had established while a resident at Toynbee Hall, and the Century Guild of Artists with which his wife, Helen, had been associated. He shared their distaste for mass production and their belief in the value of craft. However, they were less his inspiration for Omega than were the Wiener Werkstätte – which evolved out of the Vienna Secession and was considered a pioneer in modern design – and, more importantly, the Atelier Martine, the interior design business owned and operated by the Parisian couturier Paul Poiret. His workshop was above Charles Vildrac's Galerie Barbazanges, where Roger had organised an exhibition in 1912, and Poiret, like Roger, had been entranced by the Ballets Russes. He had commissioned the Fauvist artist Raoul Dufy to design stationery and fabrics, and ran an experimental partnership school for working-class girls called the École Martine where impressions from visits to the zoo, the market and the aquarium were rendered upon textiles, pottery and furniture. The products, as Roger pointed out to Shaw, 'added gaiety and charm … to an interior'. It is notable that Roger had included nine 'vases en faïence' in the 1910 *Manet and the Post-Impressionists* exhibition, decorated by Derain, Matisse and others.

Essentially, Roger's motivation was aesthetic, rather than pertaining to craftsmanship and high standards of making, although he did tell Shaw that he hoped to develop into furniture construction. He wanted to remove the division between the decorative and fine arts, so that others might discover they were as happy painting a plate as a canvas, and to see Post-Impressionist form used in design, albeit in 'a definitely English tradition'.[4] He also aspired to create a means for artists, who for the most part knew nothing about such aspects of craft as waxing, lacquering or varnishing, to earn a sufficient living in three mornings a week that the rest of the time 'they would be free to paint pictures, as poets wrote poetry, for pleasure not money'.[5] The salary, thirty shillings a week, was more than Roger paid his gardener. That, and the fact that he initially thought the scheme might become a co-operative or profit-share, was as near as the Omega Workshops came to the Ruskin-based philosophy and social reforming zeal of Morris and Co.

Shaw sent Roger £250, and by February 1913 Roger had raised another £1,250. A lease was taken on 33 Fitzroy Square, a corner house on an irrefutably elegant Adam-designed square that had

Pre-Raphaelite history (they had lived and exhibited in various of the houses), Guild connotations (Mackmurdo had an office on Fitzroy Street) and Bloomsbury credentials (Virginia and Adrian Stephen, Duncan and Maynard Keynes had all lived on the square). It was close to Heal's furniture shop on Tottenham Court Road, and convenient for the artists who were beginning to move into the area. Finally, it was a good size: the top floors were let, but there was a cellar that could be used for storage, the ground floor was to be the show room, and the first floor the workshop.

That March, when the newly formed Grafton Group held their first exhibition at the Alpine Club, some Omega furniture – pre-made, rubbed of its varnish, and refinished – was included: a painted table by Frederick Etchells, a screen by Duncan sporting bright blue sheep. However, the artists' names were not attached; the founding ethos of the workshops was anonymity, which Roger felt would encourage experimentation. Everything was to be signed only with the Greek omega symbol: Ω. Roger decided to carry this spirit through to the paintings in the exhibition. Works by him, Vanessa, Duncan, Wyndham Lewis and Frederick Etchells, as well as some invited artists, were presented without any accompanying information. Neither critics nor the public were overly receptive to Roger's new incognito approach, but there were some sales, including of the furniture. And in May, when Roger, Vanessa, Duncan and Clive went to Italy for a holiday of painting and looking at churches - 'I've no doubt now that Piero della Francesca is the greatest artist of Italy after Giotto,'[6] Roger wrote to Goldie following an excursion to Arezzo – they returned with 'large quantities of crockery' to be painted and overglazed and 'boxes for the shop'.[7]

The 'shop', in the immediate run up to opening, became a frenzied maelstrom of activity, the rooms filled with the scent of varnish solvent, glue and paint. A clutch of female Slade students, brought in as assistants and christened 'cropheads' by Virginia Woolf, discovered that powdered alizarin crimson, when breathed in, worked its way out again through their skin, turning their undergarments pale pink.[8] In June there was an 'Alpha to Omega' themed dinner at a nearby Italian restaurant that was envisaged, by Vanessa, as a faintly dissolute bacchanalia of dancing, kissing and shopping that would lure the aristocrats into thinking they were 'really in the thick of things'.[9] Whether or not Roger wore an Omega waistcoat, made up in 'Cracow' upholstery fabric, has not been recorded, but the event was evidently successful. The first Omega patrons included the Countess of Drogheda, Lady Desborough, and Princess Lichnowsky, the wife of the German Ambassador, who was so enamoured of Omega that she named several of the fabrics.

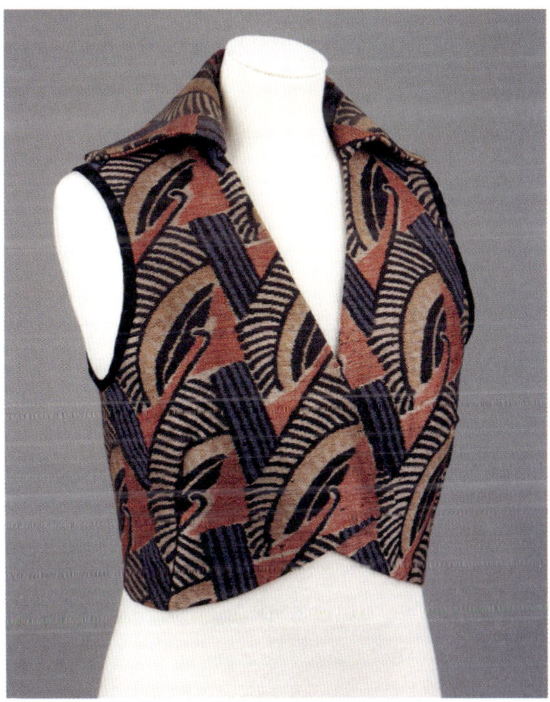

An Omega Workshops Waistcoat in 'Cracow' fabric, designed by Roger in 1913. The garment was made by Joy Brown, the Omega's seamstress, and the fabric – a jacquard weave – was produced by A.H. Lee and Sons.

Ottoline Morrell brought her society friends, among them the rebellious trio of *jeunesse dorée*, Diana Manners, Iris Tree and Nancy Cunard. The poet Rupert Brooke (a schoolfriend of Duncan's) came as did Morgan Forster, Virginia Woolf, Maynard Keynes, Bertrand Russell, Augustus John, Goldie, and, in an apparent move away from the 'pretty', Ethel Sands.

Although to the outward observer there was an Omega 'look', there was no ordained style. Roger advocated for gaiety and joy, for 'free play' being an aid to 'the delight in creation',[10] and the artists didn't only come from the Grafton Group, but from the London Group (newly formed from an amalgamation between the Camden Town Group and the English Cubists) and, indeed, from no group at all. Nina Hamnett, 'feeling brave one morning,' presented herself; Roger, 'a charming man with grey hair',[11] assessed her and then said she could come back the next day and start work, whereupon she was taught batik, a dying technique using wax resist. A couple of months later, Nina, in turn, introduced Henri Gaudier-Brzeska.

Roger designed simple chairs and other pieces of furniture, sometimes based on existing examples, and made by professionals outside the workshops, that could be embellished in different ways. There were Ballets Russes-influenced dancers and acrobats, there was increasing abstraction, and there were some distinctly Cubist leanings. Marquetry (commissioned out to John Joseph Kallenborn & Sons) lent itself to angular forms, and designs by Gaudier-Brzeska, Vanessa and Duncan were turned into trays; Duncan's design of a woman on an elephant was particularly popular. Events from life had an impact; in August 1913, some of Bloomsbury and their Neo-Pagan friends (a group of Cambridge-educated outdoorsy individuals including Rupert Brooke) went on a camping holiday in Norfolk, during which Roger, true to competent form, kept everybody fed with omelettes and stews made over a fire. Vanessa turned

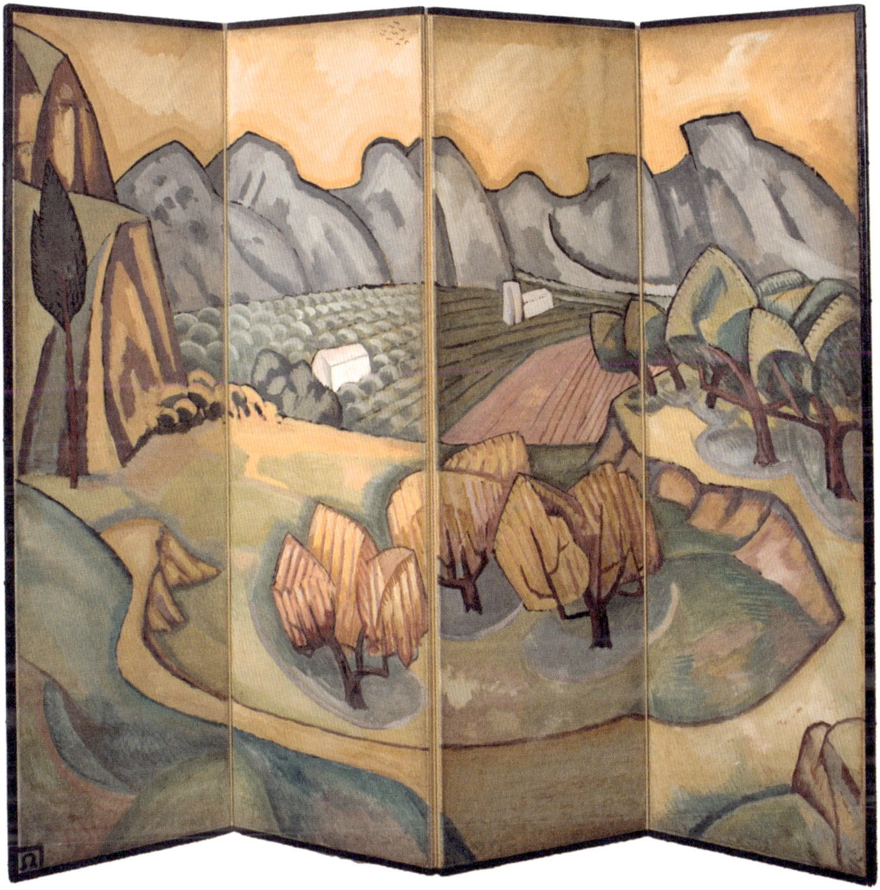

Roger's *Provençal Valley* Screen of 1913, featuring a landscape he discovered while on his autumn painting holiday, in and around Avignon, with Henri Doucet that same year

the experience into a screen featuring stylised tents – although in truth she eschewed those for a bed in a nearby farmhouse – and Post-Impressionist figures. Roger adorned another screen with a remembered view of a Provençal valley and painted bold flowers on a wardrobe.

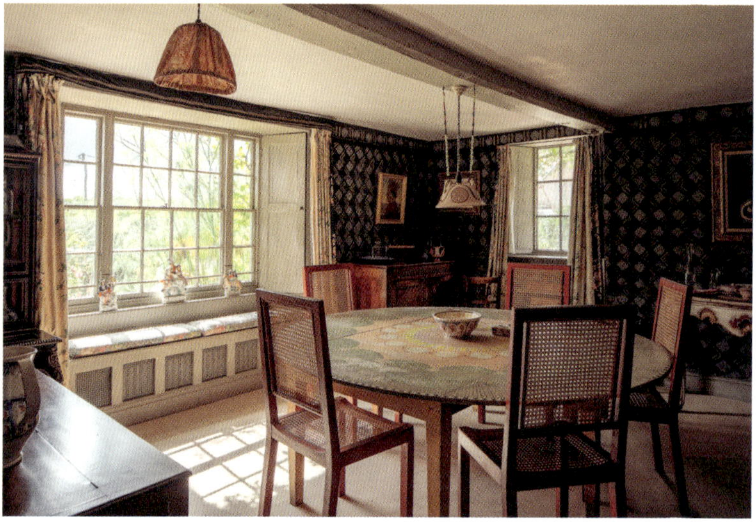

The dining room at Charleston, with Omega chairs, designed by Roger and made by the Dryad Company, Leicester.

Nothing was too small: lampshades, fans, pencil boxes and umbrellas were all considered ripe for renovation. Equally, the Omega artists could work to commission: there was a 'bank' of designs waiting to be made up, or customers could order items bespoke, whether a mural, a fabric (produced by external companies including Besselièvre and Allan Walton Textiles), a rug design (loom woven by Wilton), a set of china or even an entire decorative scheme.

It was such a scheme that, in October, caused a major schism within the Omega. The Ideal Home Show had been conceived by the *Daily Mail* in 1908 to bring together everything interior-associated and showcase the latest inventions and designs. The story goes that the newspaper's art critic, Paul George Konody, had recommended the London Group artists Spencer Gore and Wyndham Lewis, who, in 1912, had decorated a decadent new subterranean nightclub on Heddon Street, The Cave of the Golden Calf, with Futurist–Ballets Russes-inspired murals. Konody had also suggested the Omega Workshops, which Gore and Lewis were part of – the half-formed concept being that all of them could design a room together. In July, within days of the workshops' opening, Gore was invited to see an agent connected to the show and left the meeting with the understanding that he had been officially commissioned, with Lewis, for the decoration of that room, and that the Omega would provide furniture. Not having time for the commission, he wanted to hand it all to Lewis, and went straight over to Fitzroy Square. He didn't find either Lewis or Roger, so left a message with Duncan. At about the same time, Roger received a letter commissioning the Omega Workshops, which didn't name either Lewis or Gore; nor did the message left by Gore ever reach him. Artists were free to come and go from the Omega as the mood took them or their finances dictated, and Gore didn't reappear at Fitzroy Square until September. Meanwhile, Lewis heard about the commission and that it had been given to the Omega, and asked Roger what his contribution should be. Allegedly, Roger suggested that Lewis should carve a mantelpiece and said that he thought that the walls would not be muralled. Later, Roger said that Lewis had asked to do the carvings.[12]

August and September saw Roger, Vanessa and Duncan up and down from Durbins and Asheham, where Roger camped in a nearby field with his children. Once they all returned to Fitzroy Square, shortly before the exhibition opened in October, the situation came to a head. Lewis had not done the carvings, he discovered that there were to be murals after all (the idea for the scheme had perhaps changed in the intervening months), and, more, he found out from Gore that – according to Gore's understanding – he, Lewis, should have done them. Lewis and Roger's relationship was already on shaky ground after the bookkeeping difficulties of the *Second*

Post-Impressionism Exhibition, and Lewis decided that Roger had deliberately lied to him. Compounding Lewis's sense of injury was that Roger had forgotten to ask him if he had any paintings for a Grafton Group exhibition in Liverpool.

While Roger was on a pre-arranged painting holiday in Avignon with Henri Doucet, Lewis – who suffered what has been called a persecution-mania[13] – circulated a round-robin to all the workshops' friends and patrons, also signed by Edward Wadsworth, Frederick Etchells and Cuthbert Hamilton. Announcing their departure from the venture, it accused Roger of being disorganised and the Omega Workshops of being badly managed. It also criticised the aesthetic: 'The Idol is still Prettiness.'"[14]

Before Lewis's letter was sent out, Roger had attempted to clear things up with Gore, while in its wake Vanessa received a letter from the *Daily Mail* stating in unequivocal terms that the Ideal Home Show commission had been given to Roger without any conditions regarding which of the Omega artists should be involved. At this point Roger could have sued – which, it is thought, is what Lewis wanted. However, Roger didn't; which was partly down to his inherent pacifism, and he doubtless also recalled the Whistler–Ruskin case (although Whistler won, he was only awarded a farthing, making the trial a costly point of principle). Clive encouraged this stance:

> I wonder whether it wouldn't be best to let the whole thing slide … After all, why should you wrangle with four grubby little ill-bred painters? The whole thing's a matter of character, and surely yours is good enough to stand a little scurrilous rhetoric.[15]

But it was a loss of talent for the workshops, there was hurt over Etchells' defection – he had been part of the Borough Polytechnic murals and a guest at Asheham – and the argument dominated

London's artistic circle for weeks. Lewis, who never let go of his vitriol against Roger and Bloomsbury, located another premises on Great Ormond Street and founded the Rebel Art Centre, which lasted four months before a furious argument with his financial backer terminated that experiment, though not before he had published the Vorticist manifesto in *Blast* magazine.

Arguably, there had been some truth in Lewis's letter, including the accusation of 'pretty', which could apply to the fans, the parasols,

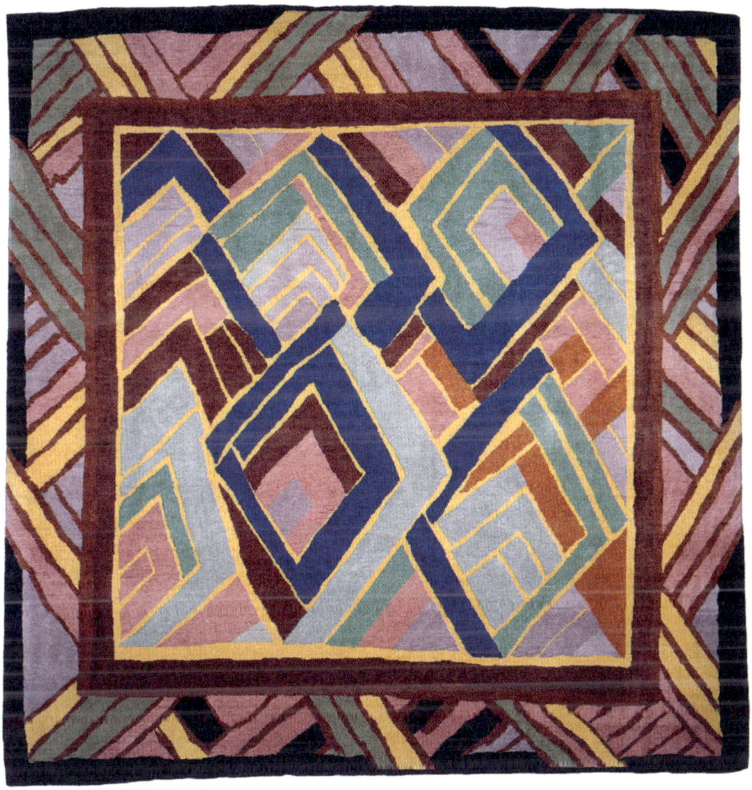

Some of the Omega Workshops rugs were put back into production in 2012 by Christopher Farr, using original artwork held by the Courtauld Gallery. This design is attributed to either Vanessa Bell or Duncan Grant.

a selection of artificial flowers, and the cross-stitch designed by Duncan and made by Vanessa of a cat playing with a butterfly on a cabbage. And certainly, the organisation was vague; seldom were the artists told what to do, and nobody criticised what was produced. With everybody's minds on the higher purpose of art, the administration, too, was chaotic: a dressing table the writer Arnold Bennett ordered for his mistress was accidentally delivered to his wife.[16] But it was a huge undertaking, and neither Roger, Vanessa nor Duncan had ever run a business. Roger described himself to Goldie as being 'bagman: I go out into smart society and advertize my scheme',[17] but he was far more besides. And, although he had stopped lecturing at the Slade, he continued to write reviews and was still editor of *The Burlington Magazine*. Nonetheless, the year closed with a successful Omega exhibition of a fully realised bedroom and nursery with panels painted by Vanessa in 'Indian' and 'African'-style, a ceiling by Winifred Gill (a Slade student, also a Quaker, who had once done secretarial work for Roger's sister), wooden toys designed by Roger based on those he'd once made for Julian and Pamela, and a dolls' house (now in the V&A) which looked a lot like Durbins and was filled with scaled-down Omega furniture.

1914 began with a second Grafton Group exhibition at the Alpine Club, on this occasion with names attached. London-based artists – Vanessa, Duncan, Roger, Gaudier-Brzeska, Winifred Gill and Nina Hamnett – were exhibited alongside works by Henri Doucet, Jean Marchand, André Lhote, Othon Friesz and photographs of recent constructions by Picasso that, fashioned from materials that included cardboard and string, were too fragile to travel. 'I really think it is the best exhibition we have organised yet,' Roger wrote to Charles Vildrac, the poet and dealer who had helped him put together the show at the Galerie Barbazanges in Paris in 1912, and sent the French works over for the show

> It strikes me for the first time that the French pictures do not stand out from ours. That is to say I believe our mutual understanding has been so greatly to our advantage that now we are beginning to construct real pictures. I am very proud of it. But we must always be strengthening the bonds between us to help the true aesthetic to emerge here where they really only like the romantic and sentimental.[18]

Roger's landscapes, with their penetrating palettes and bold emphasis on form, were particularly complimented in write-ups, and works sold; Roger's sister, Margery, bought one of Duncan's paintings.

While the show was running, Roger and Vanessa began another Omega undertaking. In 1905, Roger had written about Wedgwood china for *The Athenaeum*, describing it as 'beyond praise', but at the same time suggesting the manufacturer had

> probably contributed to the final destruction of the art, as an art, in England, since it set a standard ... which to this day prevents the trade from accepting any work in which the natural beauties of the material are not carefully obliterated by mechanical means.[19]

While the Arts and Crafts movement had included William De Morgan, the Ruskin Pottery and Mary Watts' Potters' Art Guild at Compton, just outside Guildford, pottery hadn't enjoyed the same success as other revived practices. Roger and Vanessa, in a bid to discover an alternative to 'mechanical perfection', began making their own ceramics in Mitcham, Surrey, under the tutelage of an eighty-one-year-old maker of 'flower pots', George Schenck. Roger described the beginning to Duncan as

> fearfully exciting at first: the clay was too stiff and V. very nearly bust the effort to control its wobbliness – and in vain; then

> we got softer clay and both of us turned out some quite nice things – little ones only mostly, but they'll make quite nice little bowls and pots.[20]

Mitcham became a regular destination for Roger, as he explored a new means of aesthetic expression.

At the same time, Roger, Duncan and Vanessa were beginning to push further at the boundaries of painting, taking abstraction beyond Omega decorations. Roger had seen Wassily Kandinsky's work at the Sonderbund show in Cologne and described it, in *The Nation*, as 'pure visual music … I cannot doubt any longer the

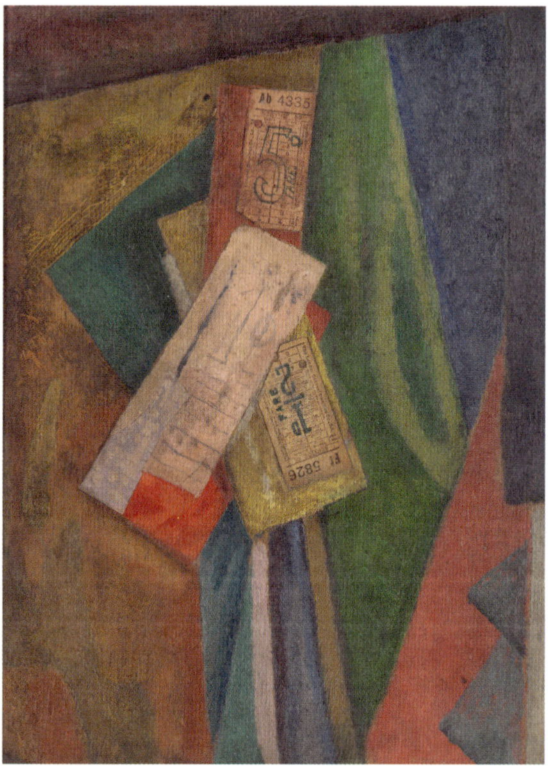

Roger Fry, *Essay in Abstract Design*, 1914 or 1915. Roger made at least three works with this title, but the others have not survived. This painting is now in the Tate's collection.

possibility of emotional expression by such abstract visual signs'.[21] He included some of Kandinsky's paintings in the anonymous Grafton Group show of 1913. Roger's own *Essay in Abstract Design*[22] (now in the Tate) features oblong and triangular forms of red, yellow, green and blue to which he collaged two bus tickets, including one to Mitcham. And Duncan created *Abstract Kinetic Collage Painting with Sound* (also now in the Tate), a fourteen-foot scroll decorated with arrangements of falling, coloured rectangles that he intended to be viewed to the accompaniment of music by J.S. Bach, further underlining the influence of Kandinsky who had, in 1911, painted *Impression III (Concert)* (now in the Lenbachhaus Museum in Munich) in direct reference to Arnold Schoenberg's music. There were parallel developments in philosophy. Bertrand Russell – ever a significant voice in Bloomsbury circles, and now two years into the affair with Ottoline Morrell that had ended his marriage – argued that to describe an object purely according to its visual appearance does not give adequate knowledge of the object; for that, the other senses too must be engaged.

Alongside this, popular taste was evolving. Although the doctrine and practice of the NEAC still presented 'all that was most typical of modern art in England',[23] some works by the Grafton Group had been exhibited in Leicester early in 1913, and, when Roger had gone to talk there, he'd discovered 'an extraordinary interest'.[24] And in February 1914, after Roger, unable to find time for it, passed the commission on, Clive published a book, *Art*, restating the Post-Impressionist cause by way of his – and to an extent, Roger's – ideas, and coining the term 'significant form'.

Against this backdrop the Omega commissions flowed in. Lady Hamilton requested the decoration of three rooms in her house on Hyde Park Gardens, which included stone pots by Gaudier-Brzeska, a mosaic by Vanessa and stained glass by Roger. There was a room for Henry Harris in Bloomsbury, Ethel Sands's dining room in

Chelsea, and the Cadena Café on Westbourne Grove. Eighty-five pieces were sent to the Whitechapel Art Gallery's exhibition of twentieth-century art that opened in May 1914, which also showed work by the London Group and Wyndham Lewis's Rebel Art Centre. French and German manufacturers were placing orders, and more artists joined the Omega, including the recent Slade graduate Paul Nash.

But none of this was enough to make the Omega Workshops financially viable, and in March 1914 Roger wrote again to George Bernard Shaw, to tell him that they had used up all the initial capital. The letter back from Shaw offers a critique of the venture: he had bought Duncan's marquetry elephant tray, and

> I regret to say that the artificer, not having had the opportunity of being apprenticed to the people who did the intarsia work at Bergamo cathedral, does not know all the secrets of the trade. His beautiful surfaces are beginning to burst up as if a traction engine has gone over them.

It was a problem that had been experienced by other customers too, along with paint, varnish and even legs falling off various items (there was little danger of Roger's project accidentally straying into that tedious – as he saw it – cult of perfection).

Shaw's letter also demonstrates that Omega wasn't all to everyone's taste. He praised the fabrics and carpets, 'but the painted table tops and one or two other efforts in the same direction seemed to me simply foolish'. He suggested that the whole be 'pulled together … as business will have to be done mainly with the more fastidious sort of millionaire'. And, although dancing figures had been hung in the niches above the door – which Shaw did not like – there was no shop window. 'It is all very well to … look like an Orthopaedic Institute, but the price you pay is that your business remains the secret of a clique.'[25] However, he sent the Omega another £500 – which Roger matched from his own purse. Joseph Storrs Fry II, Roger's uncle who had been running the chocolate firm J.S. Fry & Sons, had died in July 1913 and left a fortune. Among the beneficiaries were every one of his employees (the amount was related to their length of service), numerous philanthropic institutions, his brothers and sisters, and his thirty-seven nieces and nephews. It's believed[26] Roger's share brought in an income of about £1,000 a year.

The romantic relationship between Roger and Vanessa was also facing challenges. One was their incompatible reserves of energy. From their Italian holiday just before the workshops opened to the public in 1913, Vanessa had written to Virginia:

> Roger is up with the lark, does many sketches, sees all the sights, and he and Clive are indefatigable in their attributions and historical discoveries … after Padua I struck at sightseeing and now refuse to see more than one thing a day. I find that Duncan sympathises with me and if he and I had the conduct of the party in our hands we should settle down somewhere for a month and spend most of our time loafing.[27]

Their being together so much at the Omega also meant that Vanessa saw much more of Roger – and often found him quite exasperating in his dealings.[28] Roger could feel her pulling away, but they went to France together, with Clive too, in the spring of 1914, and together with Gertrude Stein visited both Picasso and Matisse in their studios. They toured the dealers, where Vanessa and Clive bought another Vlaminck, and they talked about the autumn show at the Grafton Galleries.

But, on August 4, following weeks of building tension and Germany's invasion of Belgium, Britain joined the war. Most of the country rallied behind what they saw as a just cause; there was an optimistic idea that it would be a quick clash, and young men driven by a keen sense of duty volunteered to fight.

The feelings among Bloomsbury were more nuanced, and there was no race among them to uphold establishment interests. Several were not only fervent pacifists but had felt that their quest for the creation of a more liberal and rational society should have made war an impossibility. For Goldie, it was 'a paralysing shock'. He had 'staked everything on the belief that human beings were fundamentally reasonable, that the appeal to reason must find a response'.[29] Roger invited him to stay at Durbins, and worried immensely about him. 'I think he might commit suicide if this depression goes on indefinitely,' he wrote to Vanessa.

Roger himself felt more inured. He described the war as being akin to living in a bad dream, but 'I've known since Helen that the world was made for the worst conceivable horrors,'[30] and he was, possibly, more preoccupied by the now definite end of his relationship with Vanessa, who had fallen in love with Duncan. Vanessa had been his 'ideal companion', had given him 'some of the most perfect happiness' he'd ever experienced, and, in comparison to the tragedy of Helen, it had been a happiness in which he'd felt secure of a future, particularly as it's thought they had discussed having a child together.[31] 'Nessa it's just fate and not a bit your fault,'[32] he wrote to her, but he stayed away from her and Duncan, and Asheham.

Duncan's relationship with Vanessa's brother, Adrian, had ended, the latter having become engaged to Mary Berenson's daughter Karin Costelloe, a Fellow at Newnham College, Cambridge. Vanessa perhaps inferred that homosexuality was not necessarily a permanent state, though Duncan was now at the beginning of an affair with the writer David (Bunny) Garnett. It meant life wasn't easy for Vanessa either, as she explained to Roger. She suggested that she therefore understood how Roger felt, but Roger didn't quite agree that their situations were comparable. He pointed out that she worked with Duncan: he was her 'constant pal' and if she wanted she could spend a week in the country alone with him. 'He gives you everything except love & I'm pushed away into any place & only wanted when there's nothing better on. All my work I have to do alone without any help or encouragement or interest.'[33]

And it was work that was immediately perceived by Roger, and others of Bloomsbury, as the best defence against the uncertainty wrought by the war.

SIX

WORK AND WAR

THE WAR IMMEDIATELY MADE A MARK ON THE Omega, bringing disruption, uncertainty, and loss. Gaudier-Brzeska and Henri Doucet both enlisted with the French army. Other young artists, who'd been in the workshops or exhibited alongside the Grafton Group, also enrolled. Boris Anrep returned to Russia, Richard Nevinson joined an ambulance brigade, Stanley Spencer volunteered for the Royal Army Medical Corps, and late in 1915 David Bomberg went to the Royal Engineers. Staff at the pottery in Mitcham departed, and it changed hands. Many of the Omega's clients left London, including the Morrells who went to their new house near Oxford, Garsington Manor, and Princess Lichnowsky, whose husband had been the German ambassador to Britain. (A British military guard of honour saluted Prince Lichnowksy's departure; he had been the only German diplomat to raise objections to Germany's provoking of the Austro-Serbian war and had implored in vain the German government to accept an offer of British mediation in that dispute.)

Belgian refugees began arriving in London, bringing with them traditions that included folk-dancing and *bal-musette* music. An 'Omega Art Circle' was set up as a means of connecting with them, and to provide a refuge for free discussion. Belgian musicians were invited to perform, and there was a production of Debussy's *La Boîte à joujoux*, a ballet whose first production had been postponed on account of the war, using Omega-made marionettes instead of dancers.[1] Winifred Gill took over the running of the workshops, and following requests, Vanessa began using Omega fabrics in dress designs, which quickly became a successful and profitable part of the business and were worn by Ottoline and others. The first of the Omega books was published, with woodcuts by Nina Hamnett's husband, the Norwegian artist Roald Kristian.

And Winifred Gill introduced Roger – who had, since the changes at Mitcham, been attending ceramics classes at Camberwell School of Arts and Crafts – to the Carter family, who owned a pottery in Poole (now Poole Pottery). As Roger's throwing skills improved and he gained in confidence, he developed more complex shapes, mostly using earthenware. He created tea and dinner services, as well as decorative pieces, all with 'expressive character'.[2] Moulds were made, so that the designs, satisfyingly honest in their solidity and bearing the marks of human touch, could be produced

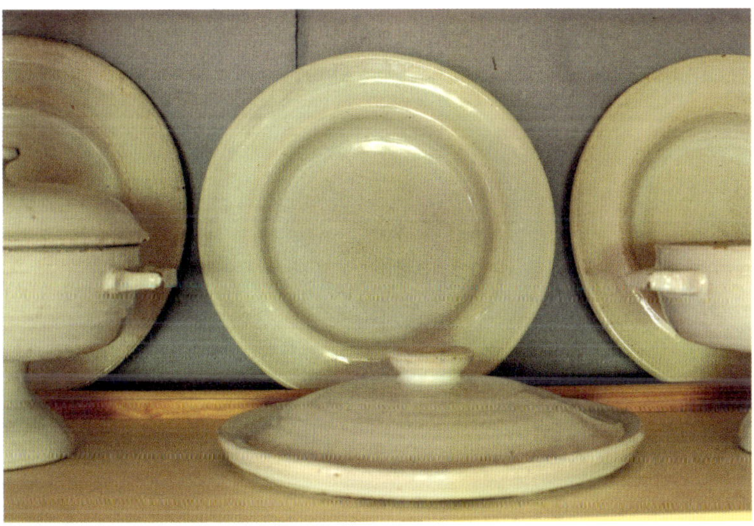

Some of Roger's most successful pottery for the Omega Workshops, made in Poole, and now in the kitchen at Charleston.

in number. They were glazed in white, turquoise, green (an attempt to emulate the Far Eastern celadon glaze), dark blue or black, or painted with abstract patterns by Vanessa or Duncan. To Roger's gratification, in December 1914 the head of pottery at the British Museum applauded the efforts as being better than any other modern examples he had seen.

But, despite such successes, the reality was inescapable. In the spring of 1915, Roger went out to France, where his sister Margery was helping organise the Quaker War Victims' Relief Fund in the *départements* of Marne and Meuse, the battlefields of the autumn offensives. Initially, Roger assisted with the building of temporary huts and repairing of farm machinery, but he didn't stick at it (conceivably, he found it difficult not being in charge). Instead, he borrowed a bicycle and set off for a tour of what was essentially repeat encounters with ruin, amid a landscape scarred by trenches, wire and craters caused by artillery fire. 'If not a single man had been killed, the cruelty of the material destruction would still be incalculable when you spell it out in terms of … destroyed hopes and bitter disillusionment,'[3] he wrote to Princess Lichnowsky, not knowing if the letter would get through to Germany.

Though there was, of course, death. 'My dear Doucet,' the artist who had stayed at Durbins and Asheham and painted Pamela, and with whom Roger had been on a painting holiday to Avignon in 1913, was killed at Ypres in March. Rupert Brooke, 'the best of our young poets', died from sepsis caused by a mosquito bite while on his way to the landings at Gallipoli in April. (His poem, *The Soldier*, with its oft-repeated lines describing a corner of foreign field being forever England, was published posthumously.) So when Roger received a letter from Rose Vildrac, asking him to try to see her husband Charles, who was stationed, Rose thought, nearby, Roger sought advice from the local mayor and determined to reach him.

Equipped with a military permit on account of his relief work, Roger made his way to the front lines at Auzéville where he enquired as to his friend's whereabouts – though without knowing what regiment he was in. Concern developed that Roger was a spy, and he was sent 'under guard to the Colonel of the eighty-ninth regiment, who did his best to interrogate me'. There were a couple more handovers, which culminated in his being passed into custody of the police, and an uncomfortable night sleeping in a stable with several others. Eventually, he was escorted back to Meuse, whereupon he bought the *gendarme* a café au lait at the station before he was eventually set free.

After spending a few days in Paris, during which he visited Doucet's widow, he set off for the South of France, to stay with Dorothy (née Strachey) and Simon Bussy, the artist he'd swapped work with in 1909, in their villa in Roquebrune-Cap-Martin that looked out across the sea to Monaco.

Others were there too, including Philippa Strachey, Lytton's sister, whom Roger painted. The Belgian artist Jan Vanden Eeckhoudt, a friend of the Bussys and of Matisse, was staying nearby, and he encouraged Roger to adopt a brighter palette for the landscapes he was working on from the terrace, where the views seemed 'just right, the right kinds of colours and shapes everywhere,' as Roger wrote to Winifred Gill.[4] Roger was with the Bussys when Gaudier-Brzeska was killed in a charge at Neuville-Saint-Vaast in June. Roger continued along the coast, and painted the harbour at Saint-Tropez, placing vermillion-trimmed boats in a teal-blue sea, and bathing the mountains on the horizon in a violet light.

The South of France seascapes were exhibited at the Alpine Club in November 1915, alongside Omega pottery, landscapes and three of Roger's abstract paintings, all titled *Essay in Abstract Design*. Among the first abstract works by a British artist ever to be shown publicly, they did not receive an enthusiastic reception. Walter Sickert reviewed the show in *The Burlington Magazine*:

> Now Mr. Fry has undoubtedly gifts as a painter. It remains, nevertheless, surprising that a painter who has the double advantage of power and erudition should continue to treat seriously fumisteries à la Picasso.[5]

But thirty to forty people came each day, and paid, and there were critics who were more receptive, including the art historian and former Keeper of the Wallace Collection, Sir Claude Phillips, who had stamped on his catalogue at *Manet and the Post-Impressionists*. He gave the show a positive write-up in *The Telegraph* – though he did qualify it by saying that Roger's best work was that which was

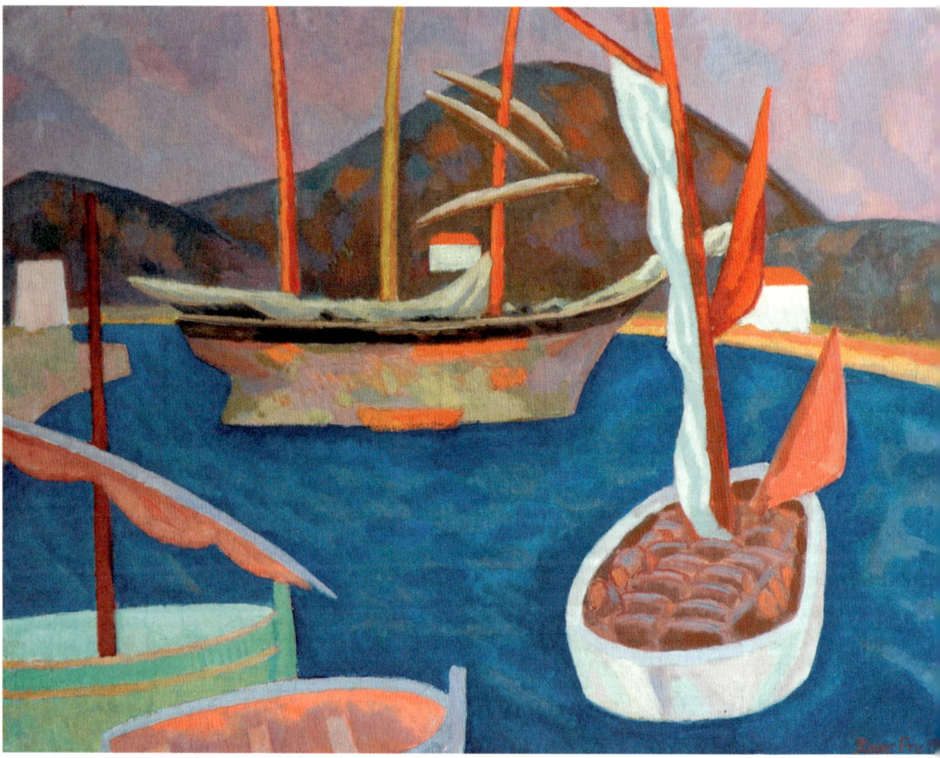

Roger Fry, *Boats in a Harbour (St-Tropez)*, 1915. This painting was exhibited at the Alpine Club exhibition in 1915 and is now in the collection of the Hepworth Wakefield.

inspired by reality. And one particular picture was widely singled out: *Three Men in Long Military Cloaks* or, as it is more often known, *German General Staff*. It used collage to reproduce a newspaper image of Kaiser Wilhelm II and two of his generals surveying the land, their feet hidden from sight. Roger had added a quote from Nietzsche in the catalogue: 'I cannot tolerate the neighbourhood of this race ... which has no sense of its feet and doesn't even know how to walk.'[6] It had begun, for Roger, as a sort of joke. It was perceived by many as a welcome gesture of patriotism.

In January 1916 the conscription act was passed. Roger, now in his late forties, was too old to be called up, and even if he hadn't been, he would have been excused on the grounds of still, technically, being a Quaker. Clive, who, the previous year had published an anti-war pamphlet, *Peace at Once*, that argued for an immediate settlement with Germany (copies had been seized and destroyed) was a conscientious objector, a stance shared by Duncan and others of their circle. COs had to present their reasons for not fighting to local tribunals and find an alternative worthy pursuit. To that end, Ottoline Morrell invited Clive, Lytton Strachey, T.S. Eliot and others to Garsington to do nationally important work on the farm there. (She also invited Siegfried Sassoon to recuperate there in the summer of 1916 after he'd been wounded – which perhaps impacted his developing anti-war views.) Vanessa, who preferred not to read newspapers or think about the war – at a dinner at Garsington, she famously asked the man sitting next to her if he was interested in politics; it was Herbert Asquith, the Prime Minister[7] – was keen to find somewhere she could live with Duncan and his lover, Bunny Garnett, while they too worked the land. To all their relief, Duncan discovered the recent death of one of his aunts had left an empty farmhouse in Suffolk, with six acres in need of cultivation. They moved in with Vanessa's children, their nursemaid and a cook.

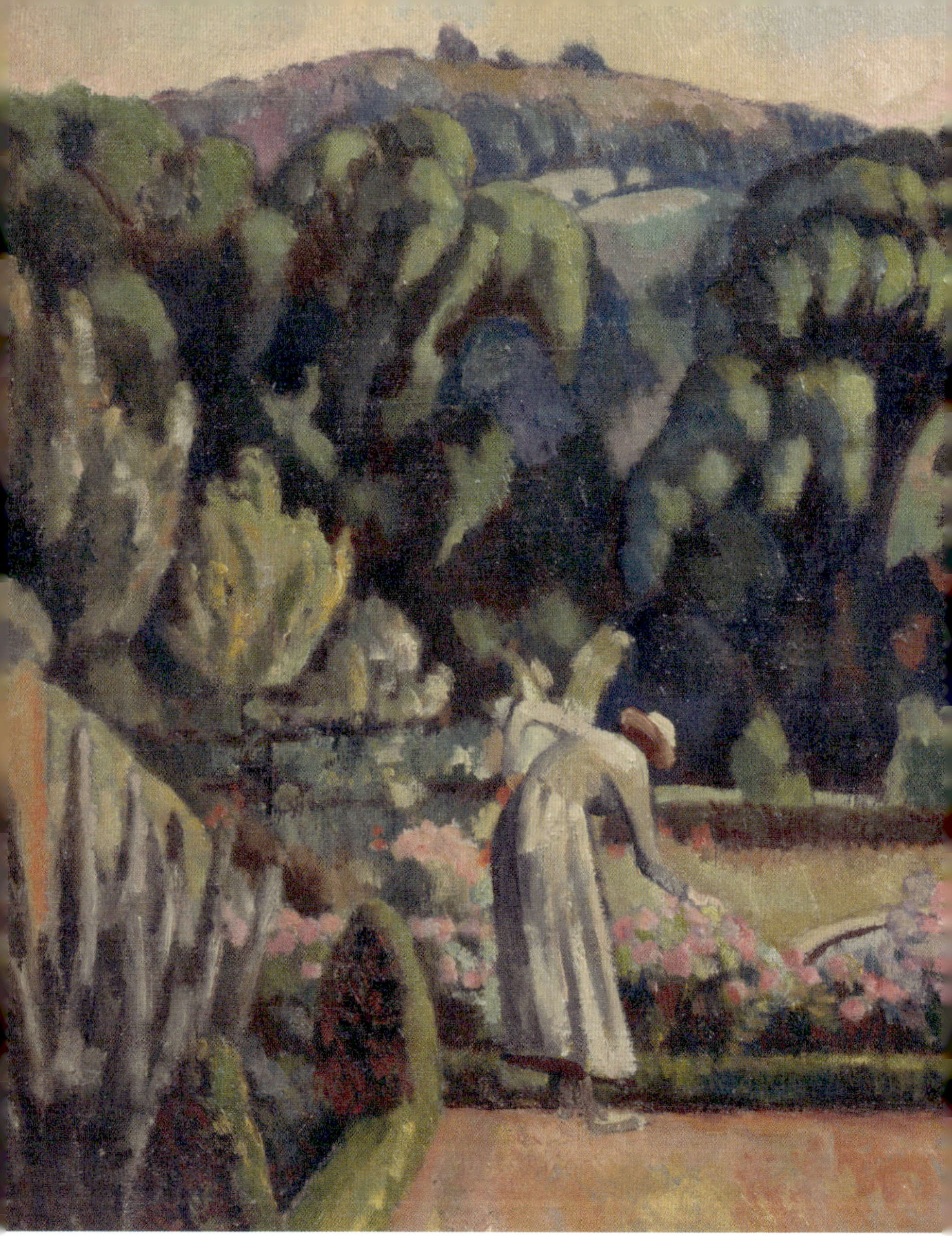

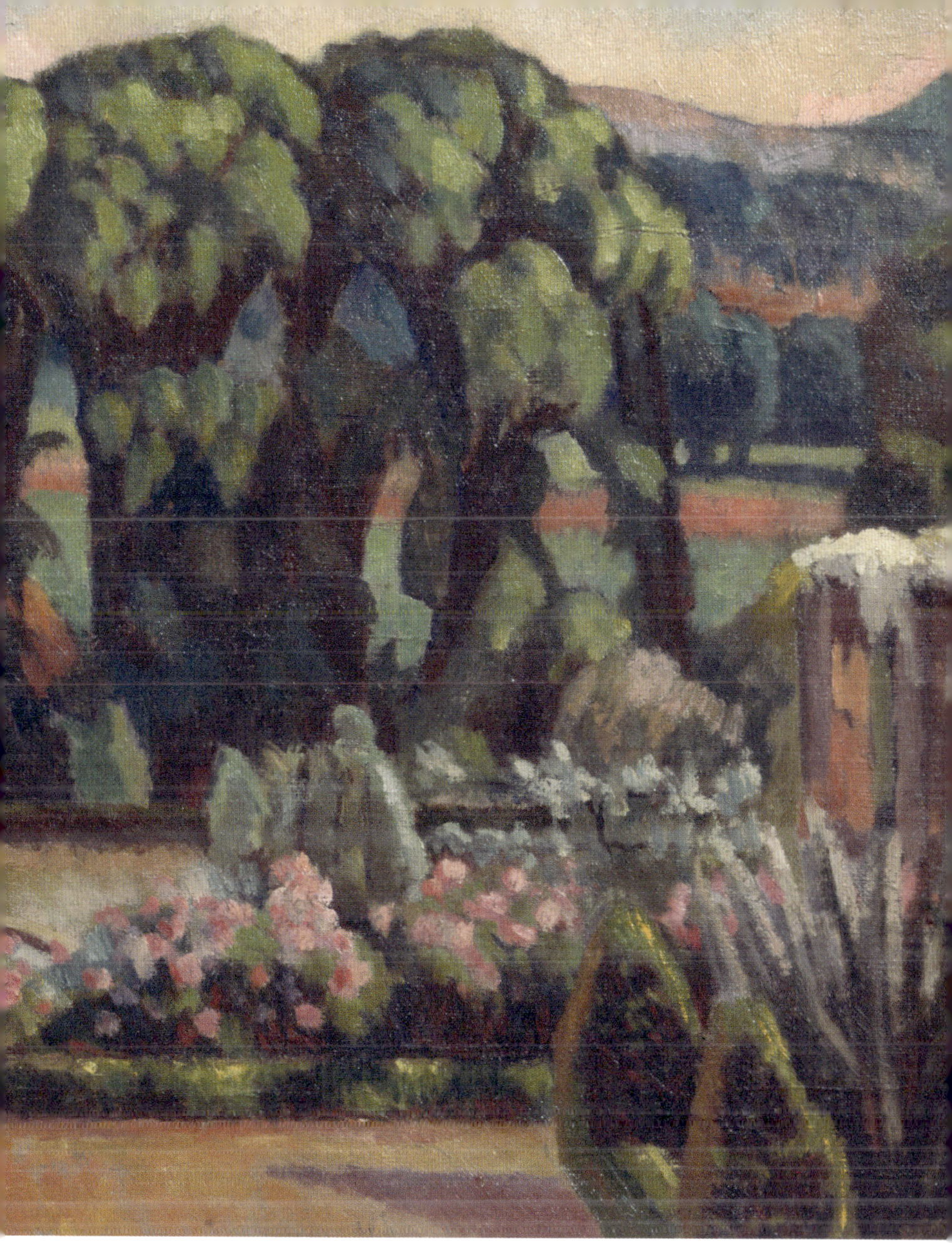

Roger Fry, *The Artist's Garden at Durbins*, c. 1915, showing the terraces designed by Gertrude Jekyll and the view to the hills beyond.

The departures added to the bleakness of the city, where there were coal shortages, air raids and blackouts, and where the parks had been repurposed. The lake in St James's Park was drained and Ministry of Shipping buildings erected in the lake beds, Hampstead Heath was crisscrossed with trenches and sandbags for military training, and parts of Hyde Park were ploughed up for vegetable production. Maynard Keynes, also a CO, took a lease on rooms at Vanessa and Clive's Gordon Square address, but was fully occupied with his work at the Treasury. And Virginia and Leonard Woolf, who was exempt from military service for medical reasons, had moved to Richmond, where in 1917 they established the Hogarth Press. Roger's letters indicate an alternating mood: 'There is no more future,' he wrote to Charles Vildrac, and then two paragraphs later, 'Possibly I shall go to America. I see it would be the only way to ensure the survival of our artistic movement.'[8] There were other possible destinations: 'Now the war must end and we shall begin the other work. I think we must establish a centre at Geneva where intellectuals of all Europe can come together. I have a good mind to settle there with my children.'[9]

Roger's friendship with Philippa Strachey had deepened, and there were romantically worded letters. However, Roger believed he needed his primary relationship to be with an artist, that he needed to be able to discuss his work with somebody who understood. He was also still in love with Vanessa, who moreover explained that she still needed him: 'Duncan and I can't give each other all the help and criticism we both want in our work, and you are the only other person we know who can be of use in that way.'[10] But in spite of her entreaties, Roger was not ready, then, for a place in a relationship akin to Clive's intimate, though secondary, role. 'Nessa and Duncan have taken to working so entirely together and ... I find it difficult to take a place on the outside of the circle instead of being, as I once was, rather central,'[11] he wrote – to Clive.

And so Roger went up and down to the pottery at Poole, where his experiments in form continued, spent occasional days at Durbins which he'd let to the Strachey family for a year – Pamela and Julian were away at school, and his sister Joan had moved into a nearby cottage – and others in London. He worked on various Omega commissions, including rooms in Berkeley Square, and dealt with *The Burlington Magazine*, which was still being published according to schedule, despite occasional paper shortages. Most afternoons he retreated to his Fitzroy Street studio, which consisted of a pair of first-floor rooms where he also ate and slept. The floor was strewn with papers, plates were as likely to hold salad as scrapings of paint, Omega samples littered surfaces – and there were staged scenes of objects, protected from the woman who cleaned for him by signs saying 'Do not touch', and described by

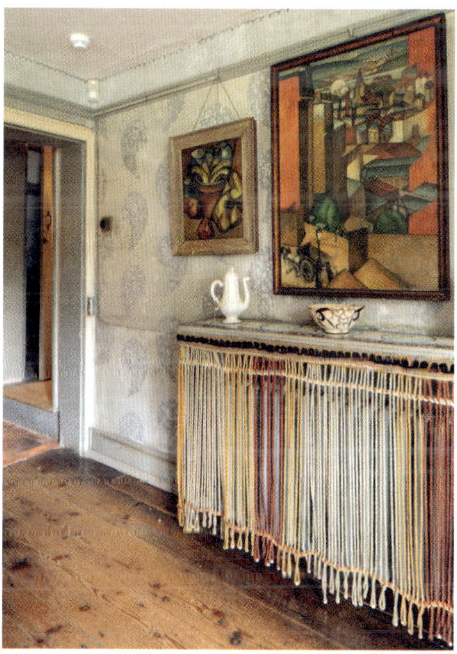

Jean Marchand in the garden room at Charleston. On the left, *Still Life with Fruit and Flower Pot*, c. 1912, was once owned by Roger. On the right, *Vue de Ville*, c. 1912, was in the *Second Post-Impressionist Exhibition*.

Virginia as 'tokens of a spiritual reality immune from destruction, the immortal apples, the eternal eggs'.[12] Without ready access to countryside, and having seen landscape shattered by war, Roger was applying himself to still lifes.

There'd been work by the French artist Jean Marchand in the *Second Post-Impressionist Exhibition*, and in the Grafton Group exhibition of 1914. Among other paintings by him, Roger owned *Still Life with Fruit and Flower Pot* (it now hangs at Charleston). In 1915, some of Marchand's works had been shown at the Carfax Gallery, and Roger had written of his 'solid and unfaltering' construction, admiring how 'without the slightest suggestion of emphasis … the material becomes expressive.'[13] Now, Roger wrote to Vanessa, he was himself 'getting back to a sort of idea of construction'.[14] At the same time, he was interested in 'plasticity': the ability of an artwork to create an illusion of three-dimensional form and depth, and the evoking of it through flat volumes, rather than by the academic means of chiaroscuro.

In June 1916, Roger managed to get to Paris with Lalla Vandervelde, the British-born wife of a Belgian politician who had commissioned the Omega to decorate her Chelsea apartment. After crossing the Channel on an unlit ship ('rather exciting … once we nearly ran into another boat but managed to pull up and turn aside in time'[15]), Mme Vandervelde's connections ensured they were rushed past the long queues for passports and customs. Roger saw Picasso, shopped for reproductions of Seurat – who he'd suddenly decided they had all overlooked in the Post-Impressionist exhibitions – and met Diego Rivera whom he described as 'a great, fat Mexican … very good natured and amusing'.[16] He also went to see Matisse in his studio, showing him photographs of a room decorated by the Omega and his own painting of the Germans, and was gratified by confirmation that they all seemed to be 'going for just the same things'.[17]

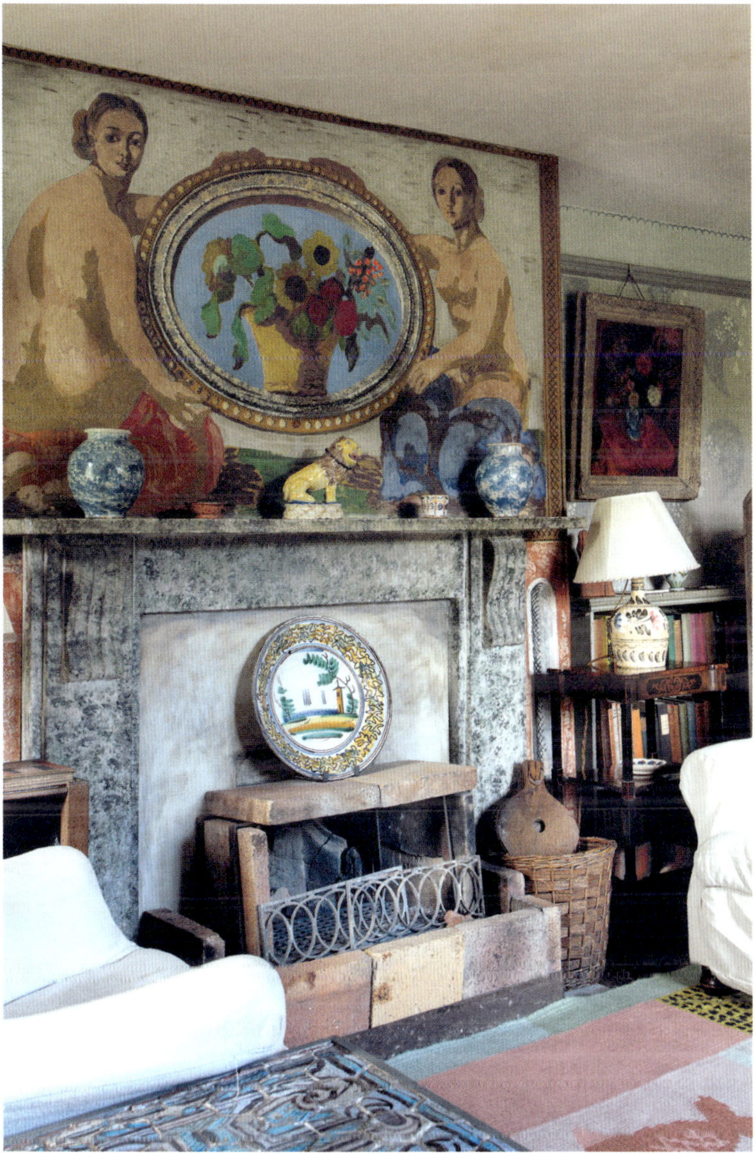

The garden room at Charleston is one of the rooms in which Roger created a fireplace construction that would help retain heat. The murals above the fireplace are by Duncan Grant.

On his return he took the children on holiday to the south coast, outside Chichester. Pamela, to his delight, enjoyed drawing and painting and poking about in shops; and while he was there he saw the artists Mark Gertler and Dora Carrington, as well as others on the Bloomsbury fringe. Goldie joined them for a few days, taking a break from his public campaigning for a 'league of nations', an intergovernmental organisation to promote international cooperation and prevent future wars.

A directive had been issued that forbade conscientious objectors from being self-employed farmhands, which spelled the end for Vanessa, Duncan and Bunny's Suffolk sojourn. That autumn, they took a lease on Charleston Farmhouse, a solid, completely unmodernised – though Georgianised – seventeenth-century house amid a patchwork of hedgerowed fields in the lea of the South Downs escarpment in East Sussex, where Duncan and Bunny could work for someone else's farm and Vanessa could create a home for their unconventional ménage. Roger – now more adjusted to the situation – was one of their first guests. Ever keen to look after Vanessa, he applied his scientific mind to the freezing conditions and refashioned the fireplaces in the main rooms to maximise the retention of heat.

Helping Roger in his acceptance of Vanessa and Duncan's relationship was his nascent entanglement with the Omega artist Nina Hamnett, who had a bedsit-studio in the same house as him on Fitzroy Street. Nina had studied in Paris, where she'd had an affair with Amedeo Modigliani, and had modelled for Walter Sickert and a series of nude bronzes by Henri Gaudier-Brzeska. She was married: her husband was the Norwegian Roald Kristian who had done woodcuts for the Omega, but since then he'd been imprisoned as an unregistered alien and deported. Nina was a fellow Francophile, confident and forthright with a Bloomsbury-appropriate disregard for social convention – she had affairs with women, too – and was tall, slim, attractive and a talented artist. Their relationship initially pleased them both; she'd visit Durbins with him, and for a time Roger adopted her use of a rougher canvas in his work. In 1917, he painted two portraits of her, combining his ideas on form with 'something personal', as he explained to Charles Vildrac.[18]

Roger was still finding new young artists and was making use of the workshops to promote them: a Chilean artist named Álvaro Guevara was given a solo show. There was an exhibition of children's drawings, which came via a connection of Roger's sister Margery who had studied maths at Somerville College, Oxford, and, before

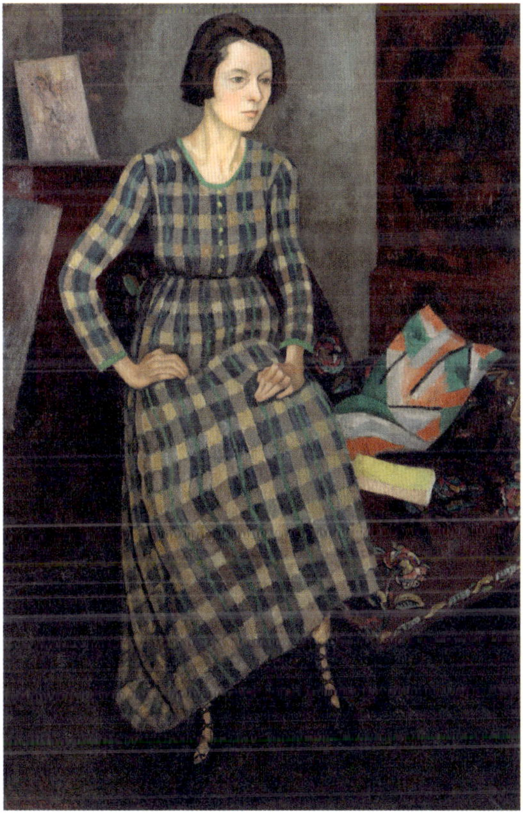

Roger Fry, *Nina Hamnett*, 1917. Nina is wearing an Omega-designed dress, and the cushion on the chair is also in an Omega fabric.

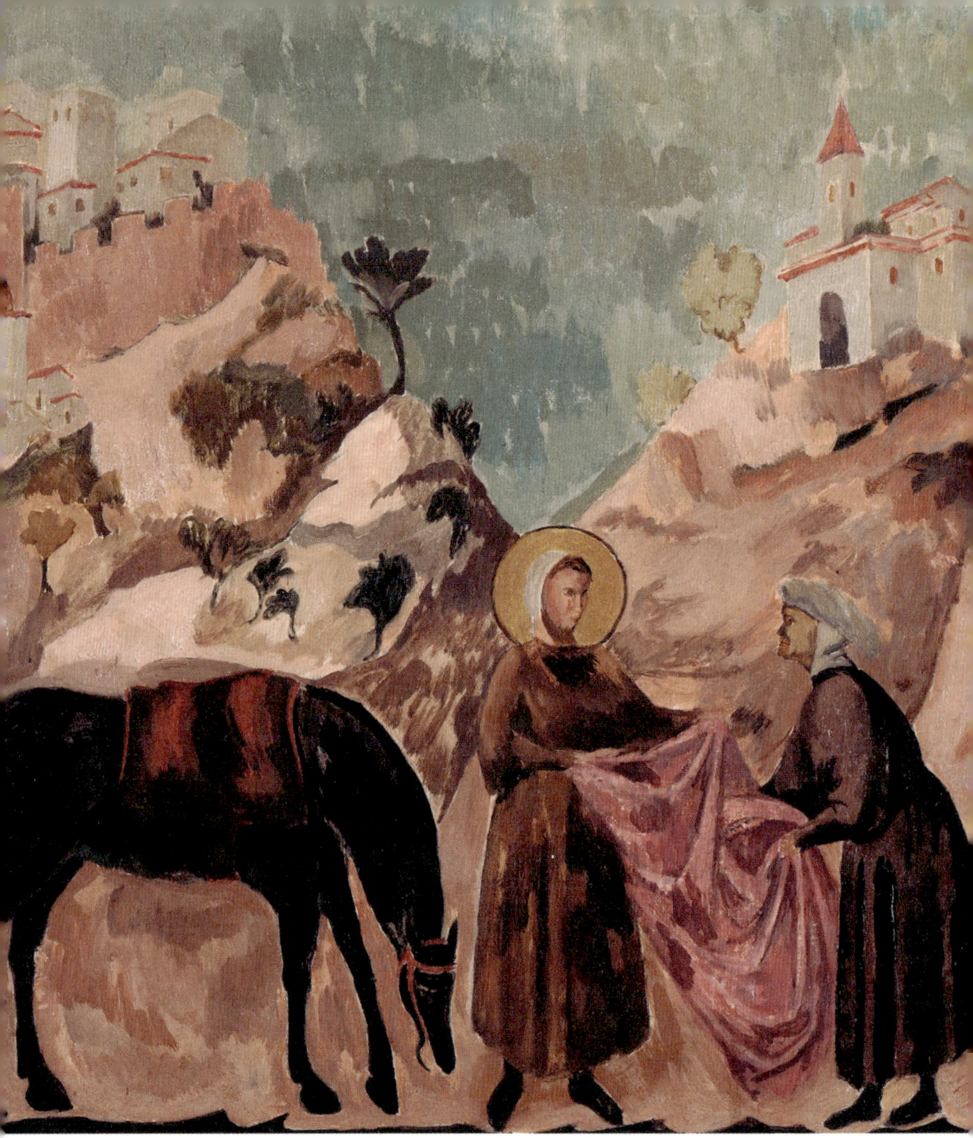

Roger's *St Francis giving his cloak to a destitute nobleman*, after Giotto, 1917; it was included in the *Copies and Translations* exhibition at the Omega Workshops.

the war, been Warden of the women's residence at the University of Birmingham. One of her pupils had gone on to teach at a school in the Black Country for 'quite poor children', Roger reported,[19] and the paintings were theirs. Roger was so impressed by their imagination and innate talent – he likened it to non-Western art, and 'Primitivism' – that he invited the Minister of Education to see the show, in the hopes that he would do something to encourage art education in schools.

Alongside, he instigated an evening club at the Omega, where those who were in town could congregate weekly. There weren't enough chairs, so pillows made from sacking and stuffed with straw were put against the walls. Among the attendees were Arnold Bennett and W.B. Yeats, who bought fabrics for his cottage in Ireland.[20] A pacifist play by Goldie entitled *War and Peace: A Dramatic Fantasia* was performed using puppets made by Winifred Gill and Duncan.

The next exhibition at the Omega, in May 1917, was entitled *Copies and Translations of Old Master Paintings*. It was an idea that Roger had had before, and one that he, Vanessa and Duncan were all well versed in (Vanessa had painted Fra Angelico scenes on the walls of the Suffolk farmhouse). It reflected Roger's ideas about form, its place in the tradition of art history and his belief in the merit of copies. Twenty-three works were offered for sale, including Roger's *St Francis giving his cloak to a destitute nobleman*, after the same in Giotto's fresco cycle in the Basilica of St Francis in Assisi, and *St Francis*, from Cimabue's *Maestà di Assisi*.

It was not what anybody would have described as a success, though Maynard Keynes bought two of Duncan's paintings, and, after a lunch with the Anglican priest Bernard Walke,[21] whose wife Annie Walke was a member of the Newlyn School, Roger made another version of his Cimabue *St Francis* for the Church of St Hilary, near Penzance in Cornwall (it is still there).

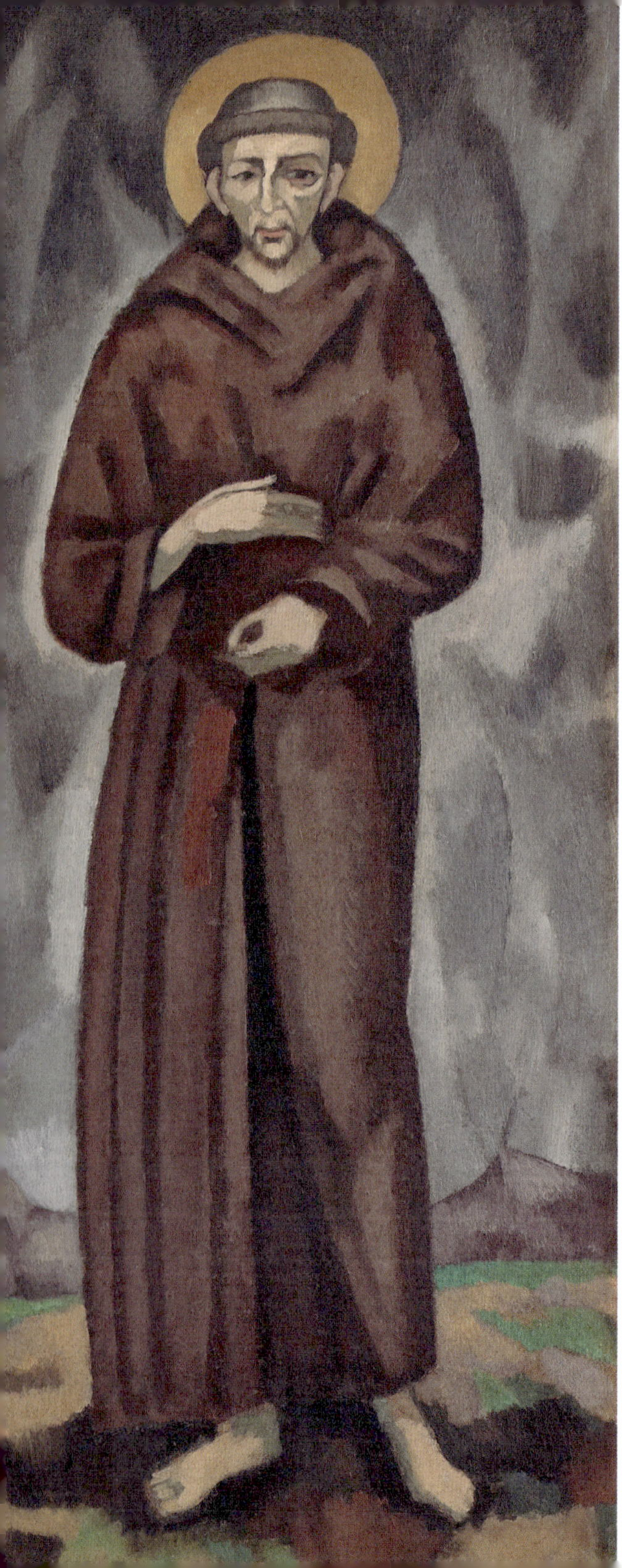

Roger Fry, *St Francis of Assisi*, 1918. Another version hangs at the church of St Hilary, near Penzance.

But, despite being busy with the Omega, Roger harboured frustration over the pausing of the Grafton Galleries shows, and the near impossibility of importing paintings. Intent on finding a means of showing the contemporary advancements in Post-Impressionism, he managed, by drawing significantly on his own collection, to put together *The New Movement in Art*, which took place in 1917 in Birmingham, and then in London, where it was one of the first exhibitions to be held at the new Mansard Gallery at Heal's furniture store (Ambrose Heal was, like Roger, keen to promote the most innovative art of the period). There were paintings by Roger, Vanessa, Duncan and Mark Gertler, as well as Derain and Jean Metzinger. In the catalogue Roger urged the viewers not to try to understand the works, but to

> allow your senses to have full play, dwell as long as possible in the contemplation of colour and form without making any judgements whatever, and discover by this process what happens to you.[22]

It was a success for Heal's, which also offered the space to the London Group, to which – a larger body than the Grafton Group – Roger had just been elected.

The still lifes and flowers that Roger had been painting were exhibited in a solo show at the Carfax Gallery in November 1917. To Roger's surprise, they sold well and fast. Walter Sickert praised them in *The Burlington Magazine* as 'serious and thoughtful work, full of feeling for the possible dignity in this branch of still life'.[23] Roger and Nina Hamnett drew each other, naked, and he invited her and Mark Gertler to stay at Durbins for the weekend. Vanessa, too, was coming over to Durbins to paint with Roger; on another occasion, Clive and his mistress Mary Hutchinson visited, and Clive suggested that Roger might do a historical portrait of

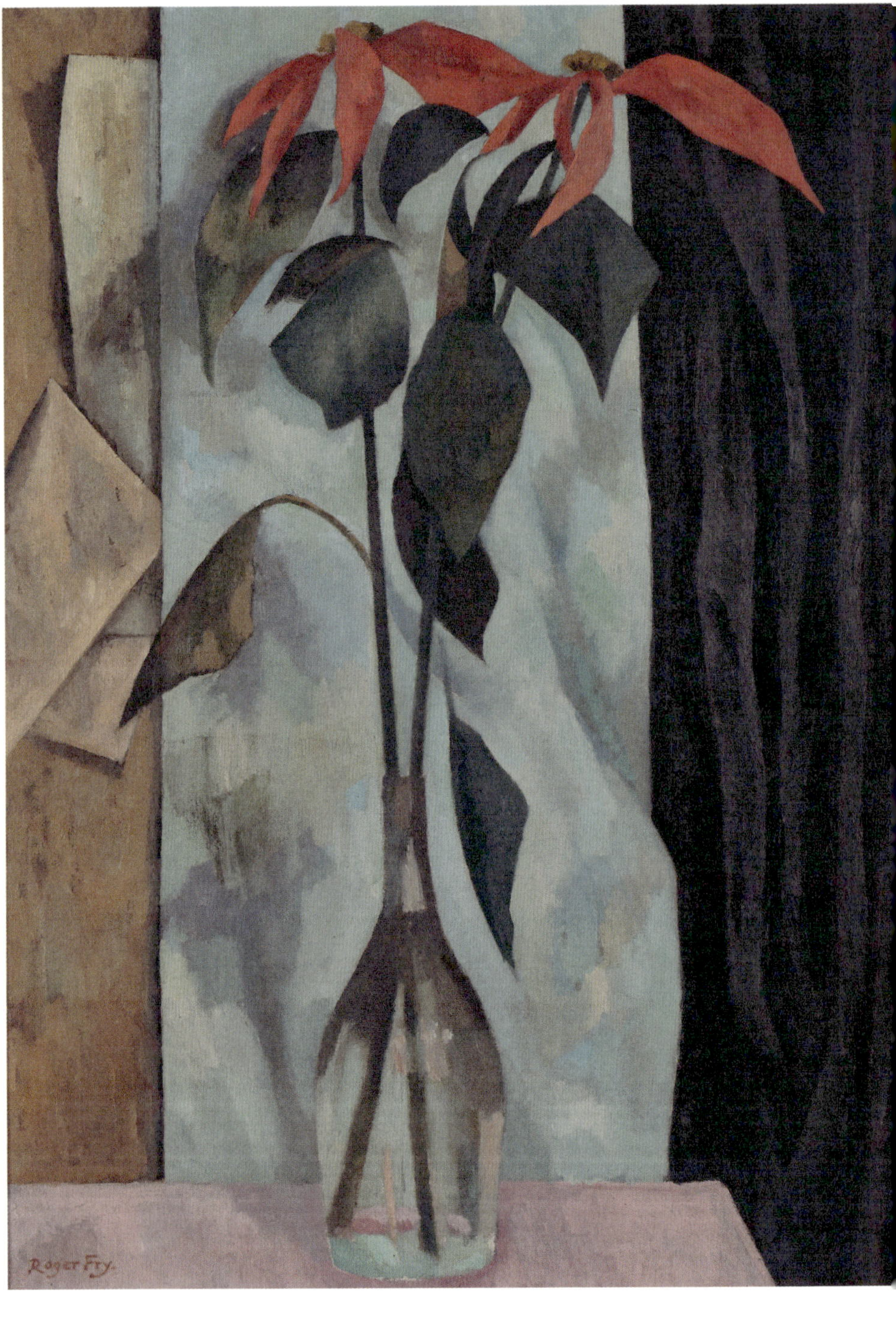

Roger Fry, *Poinsettias in a Vase*, 1914–15.

Bloomsbury. In a letter to Vanessa, Roger imagined a line-up of Lytton Strachey, Maynard Keynes, Clive, Duncan, himself, Virginia, Mary Hutchison, Desmond and Molly MacCarthy, and 'P'raps Walter Sickert coming in at the door and looking at us all with a kind of benevolent cynicism'.[24]

Roger's affair with Nina Hamnett came to an abrupt finish in January 1918 when he arrived at Fitzroy Street one day to discover that she had 'picked up a young man of 18, a drunken sodomite of pleasant manners and weak character' – and, more than that, moved him in. He was disappointed to lose the 'intimate companionship … which my domestic nature longs for,'[25] but didn't linger on it. He continued with the restoration of the Mantegna *Picture Bearers* at Hampton Court. He painted virginals for Arnold Dolmetsch, the instrument-maker for whom his wife, Helen, had once painted a harpsichord and a clavichord. And at the Omega, he designed the scenery and furniture for a play by Israel Zangwill, *Too Much Money*, using Vanessa's screen with the camping scene, which he had bought, as a prop.

It was in Roger's London studio, at the beginning of 1918, that Duncan Grant came across a catalogue for the sale of Edgar Degas' collection, the artist having died the previous September. Duncan told Maynard Keynes, and urged him to approach the Treasury, where he was working. Maynard successfully argued that he'd be able to acquire valuable paintings at discounted prices, and in March 1918, he and Charles Holmes, who was now Director of the National Gallery, set off to Paris with £20,000 of government funds. It was a dangerous time to make the journey, and a bomb fell near the train they were travelling on. But they were determined: Holmes had shaved off his moustache, was wearing glasses and even affected a French accent in an attempt at disguising himself lest his attendance encourage other attendees to bid higher. Their efforts proved worthwhile. Holmes triumphantly returned to the National Gallery with works by Manet (*The Execution of Maximilian*), Ingres, Delacroix, Corot – and Gauguin, whose pictures, only eight years earlier, had been ridiculed when Roger showed them at the Grafton Galleries. Maynard tried to persuade Holmes to buy a Cézanne of seven apples in a fruit bowl, but, although Holmes still had £5,000 of his budget left, it was a Post-Impressionist too far. Maynard bought it himself, for £500, and took it straight to Charleston, where it was briefly stashed in a hedge on the side of what is now the A27 on account of Maynard having too much to carry.

There was excitement among Bloomsbury over suddenly having a Cézanne in their midst. The once impossibility of it mirrored a growing feeling, in some quarters, that the war might end soon, and optimism began to steal through the streets. Virginia recalled running into Roger one day in April 1918, in

> his wideawake hat with four or five yellow French books under his arm. He is the centre of a whirlwind to me. Under this influence I was blown straight into a book shop, persuaded to lay out 3/7 on a French novel, *Et Cie*, by a Jew, made to fix a day for coming to Durbins, invited to a play & fairly overwhelmed – made to bristle all over with ideas, questions, possibilities which couldn't develop in the Charing Cross Rd. Of course he was in a hurry to keep an appointment at the Burlington & to produce one or two plays somewhere else – ill too, so he said.[26]

Roger's visits to Charleston had continued, he'd take Julian and Pamela with him if they weren't at school, and that spring he redesigned the walled garden, mapping a rectangular lawn and gravel paths between beds that he suggested Vanessa plant with red hot pokers and artichokes on account of their being interesting to paint. In June, Roger rented Bo-Peep Farmhouse in Alciston, a

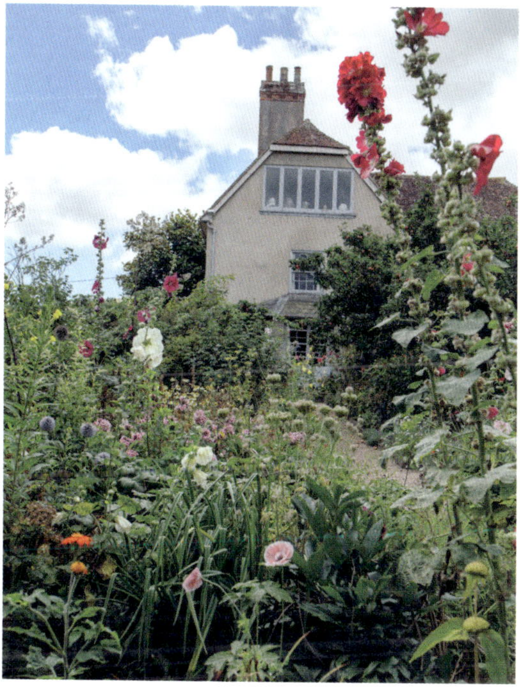

Charleston Farmhouse, viewed from the garden which Roger designed in 1918.

mile away, hoping Vanessa would spend significant time with him, away from Duncan.

It was an almost unmitigated disaster. Vanessa was pregnant with Duncan's child, absorbed in her life with him and the domestic difficulties caused by her cook leaving to get married, and emotions ran high. At one point Vanessa suggested that she and Roger never see each other again, which terrified him. He wrote to her when he returned to Durbins, explaining that it would be a pity to terminate relations

> when we had so nearly pulled through to a kind of friendship that wasn't too painful to me and didn't seem to worry you and did satisfy a lot of wants and interests we share.

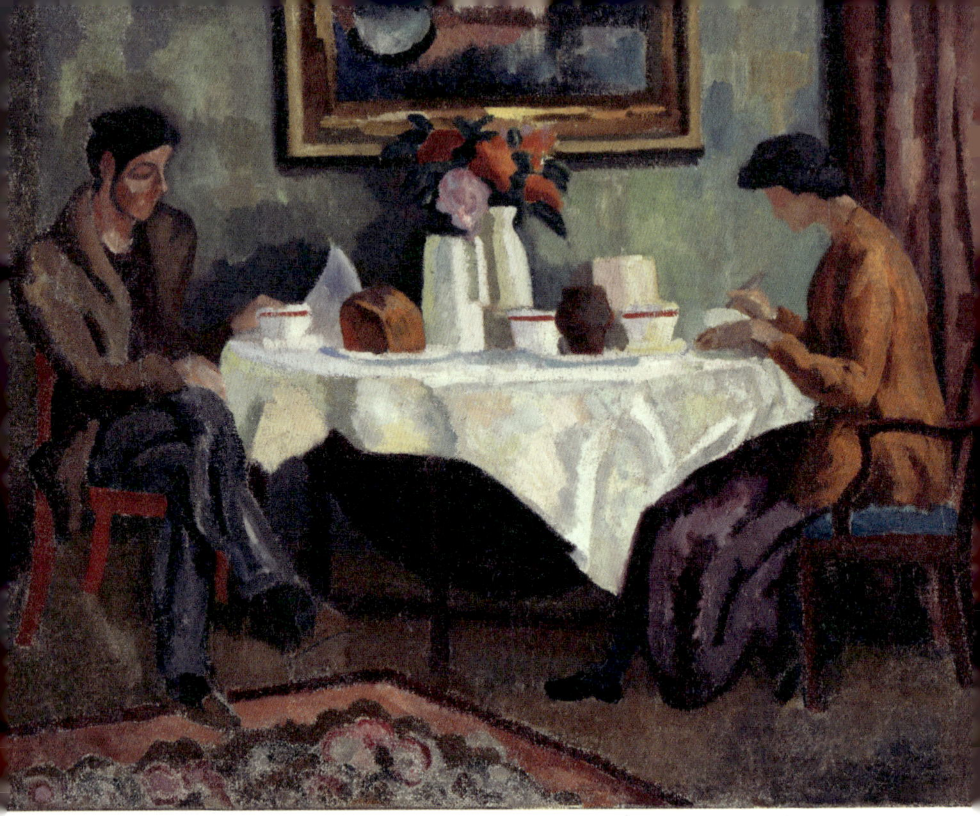

Roger Fry, *The Breakfast Table*, c. 1918; the sitters are Roger's children, Julian and Pamela, and the setting is Charleston.

He confessed to feeling

> lonely and at sea with the prospect of remaking my life. You see, my real life is with you and always has been since I got to know you. In comparison nothing else has counted.[27]

But there were distractions, and the mood of optimism held. Roger met the writer André Gide, who was also a friend of Charles Vildrac's, and they immediately found common ground in their appreciation of art, music and poetry; Roger had begun translating the work of the Symbolist poet Stéphane Mallarmé, who had influenced the Cubists. Gide was invited to Durbins; 'I never guessed there was anyone who so exactly corresponded mentally to what I want,' Roger wrote to Philippa Strachey.

> It's fearfully exciting, and when he sat down to the virginals and played all the old Italian things as no one's ever played them before and as I've always dreamt they might be played, it seemed too good to be true.[28]

There was another Omega book, featuring fourteen woodcuts by seven artists including himself, Vanessa, Duncan and Dora Carrington. He was painting Lalla Vandervelde, who'd taken him to Paris in 1916, and he was entertained by the associated whispered remarks that were part and parcel of Bloomsbury. 'How interested they are in us and how entirely uninteresting they seem to us,'[29] he wrote to Vanessa.

And, in a further portent of hope, in September 1918 the Ballets Russes returned to London after a four-year hiatus. Roger saw the Polovtsian Dances from Alexander Borodin's opera *Prince Igor*, and was even more enthused by *Le Soleil de Nuit*, with set designs and costumes by Mikhail Larionov, whose work he had shown in the 1912 *Second Post-Impressionism Exhibition*. There was a new dancer, Lydia Lopokova, whom all of Bloomsbury were enchanted with – she promised to sit for Roger, in costume – and Roger met Diaghilev several times, hoping the Omega might be commissioned to do some work for a new ballet. Some of the younger artists who had once been part of the Omega, including Paul Nash, were working on commissions for the British War Memorials Committee. But, at the workshops, there was as little sign of the conflict as ever, and the next exhibition included a portrait by Roger of his new friend André Gide and a study of Charleston, as well as works by Vanessa and Duncan, Nina Hamnett, Sickert, Gertler, the late Guadier-Brzeska

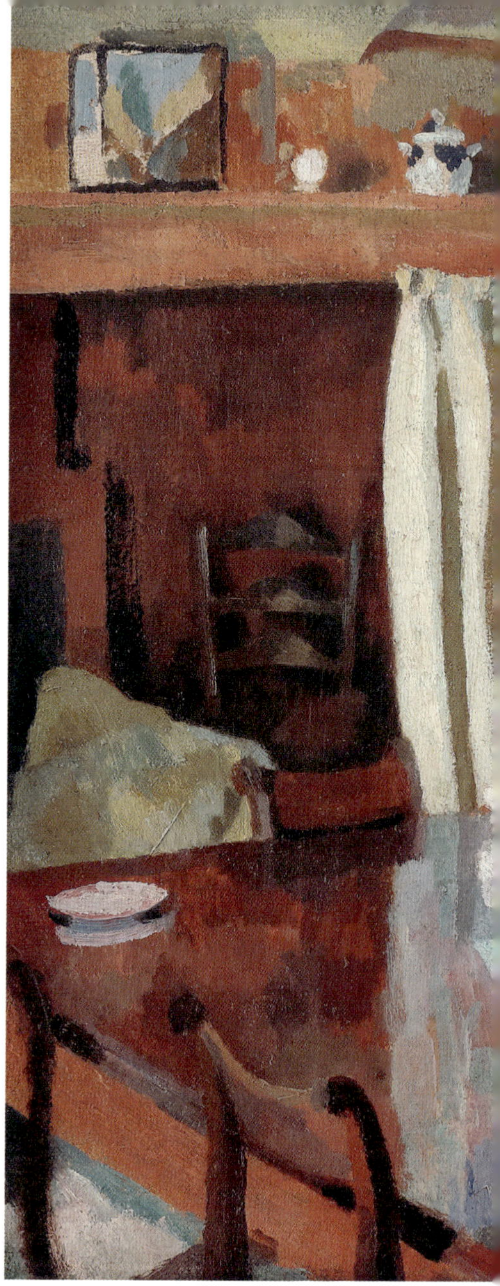

and others. 'It is a tribute to [Fry's] talent that the Omega has managed to last through times so troublous and so polemic,' wrote John Salis in the *New Witness*,[30] on November 8.

Finally, on November 11, 1918, peace was declared. Sir Edward Fry had died three weeks previously, and it's likely Roger wasn't in London to witness the 'wandering emotion'[31] of the crowds who gathered in the streets, decked in flags and oblivious of the falling rain, existing in some liminal space between exhaustion, grief, relief and jubilation. Certainly, there is no record of his being at the party at the Adelphi thrown by Montague Shearman, an art collector who owned works by Duncan as well as Sickert, Gertler and Matisse. But most of the rest of Bloomsbury were there, the women wore Omega dresses, Augustus John turned up in uniform with a land girl on each arm, and everybody danced – the more so when Diaghilev, his choreographer Léonide Massine and the

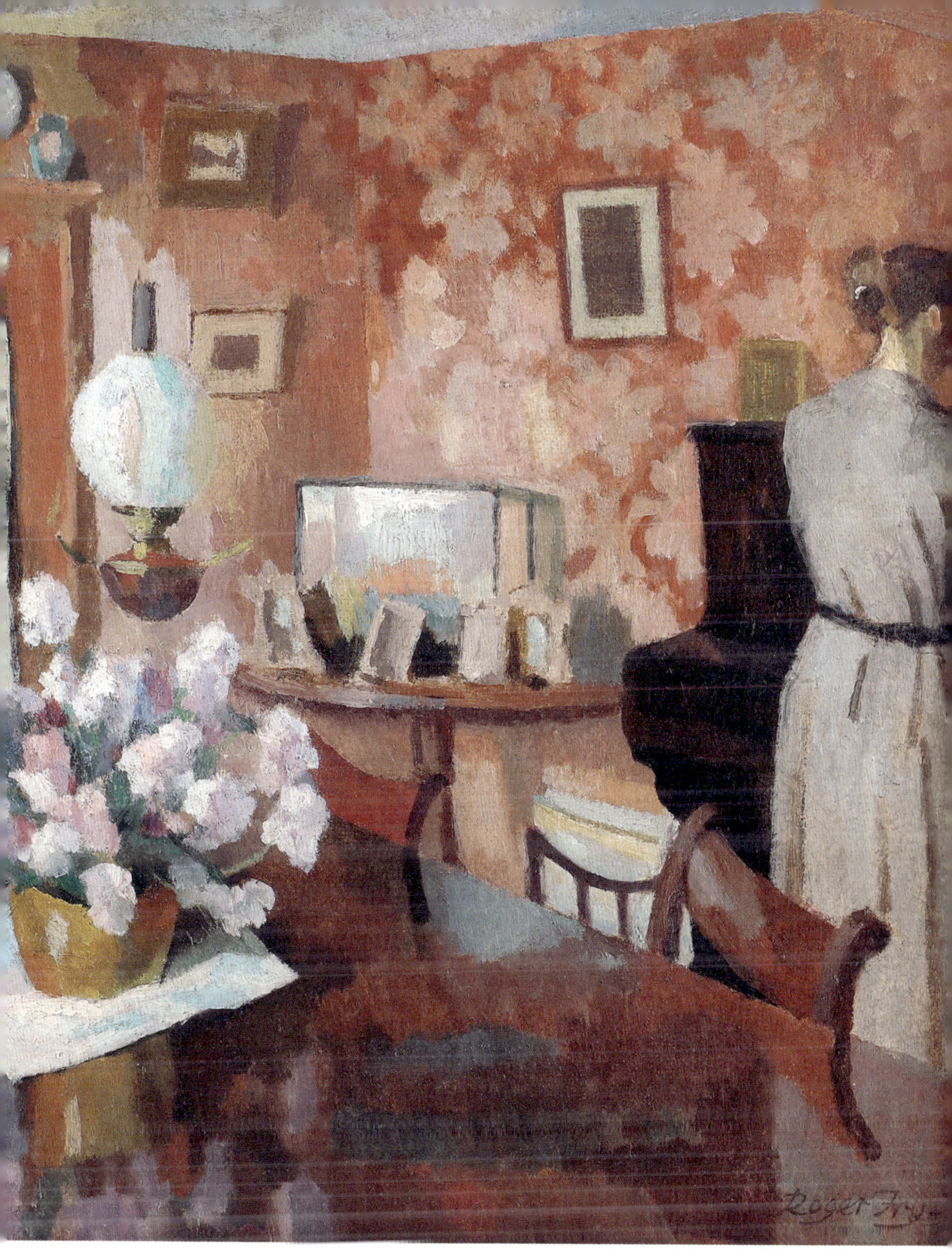

Roger Fry, *Interior at Bo Peep House*, c. 1919.

dancer Lopokova arrived after that evening's performance. In the weeks after, there were more trips to the ballet and more parties, including a Ballets Russes costume party to which Roger wore Omega pyjamas, and took Pamela.

But the glimpse of euphoria was followed by the stark reality of the post-war economic landscape. Durbins had become too expensive to run, and Roger decided to put it into a trust, and let it, though it was photographed for *Vogue* (which had launched in Britain in 1916) before he packed up. He found a house on Dalmeny Avenue in the then-unfashionable Camden for himself, Julian and Pamela, and his sister Margery, who had become the Honorary Secretary of the Penal Reform League. It looked straight out at Holloway Prison but had 'a garden that stretches away for ever'. On a tight budget – he was, he confessed to Vanessa, overdrawn at the bank and owed money for Helen's facility and Pamela's school fees – he swapped his studio on Fitzroy Street for smaller rooms in the attic. Acknowledging he would have to sell something, in almost the same breath he arranged to buy one of Vanessa's paintings: 'However many pictures of yours I have, I can't help wanting them more than almost any others.'[32]

He had been hoping that the Omega Workshops might pick up, which he had been funding to the tune of £500 a year since the war had started. Unable to get furniture made – the war had depleted supplies of wood, and there was a shortage of skilled labour – he bought up any bit of old furniture he could find to be painted, Omega style. He organised a solo show of Mikhail Larionov's marionette designs and enthused on them in *The Burlington Magazine*, and there was another exhibition of children's drawings. But on the heels of peace came the Spanish Flu epidemic, which claimed the life of Harold Gilman, President of the London Group. The Omega employees fell sick one after the other, Nina Hamnett disappeared, and Roger found he was mostly painting the furniture himself. He dropped hints about investing in the company to Arnold Bennett, for whose play *Judith* he was designing sets and costumes, but nothing was forthcoming.

And so in June 1919 – two months after the opening of the Bauhaus in Weimar, which operated according to Walter Gropius's vision for uniting artists, designers and craftspeople to create a unified, modern world – there was a very well-attended Omega Workshops clearance sale. It drew inevitable commentary: 'maybe he can't live with his own wallpapers?'[33] But its end, Roger felt, was a pity, and he was enormously sorry for his friends who had invested money in it.

Looking at it from over a hundred years on, the brevity of the Omega's existence does not negate its triumphs. The endeavour involved a number of the most significant artists of the twentieth century, whose fame and diversity of style can make one regret the ideal of anonymity. It did, however, encourage the experimentation that Roger believed it would, and for some, that went beyond the workshops. Duncan believed that designing for the Omega was of benefit to his own studio work, as it generated ideas and opened his mind to new possibilities. And, aesthetically, the effects of Omega were lasting. Although Roger's personal endeavours in pottery ceased, he had established the framework for an emerging British studio pottery movement (Bernard Leach established his pottery in St Ives in 1920). Vanessa and Duncan, for their part, continued to paint murals and help furnish the residences of various friends, which included Monk's House in Rodmell, East Sussex (now owned by the National Trust) which Virginia and Leonard Woolf bought in 1919.

And there is Charleston (now managed by the Charleston Trust) where the Omega look that Roger had begun at Durbins in collaboration with Vanessa and Duncan, was most fully continued. Roger might have told Vanessa that he wished she 'wouldn't always paint your best things just to decorate odd corners of your house,'[34] but that famed interior, which has come to embody the Bloomsbury look, continues to inspire and enliven new generations of artists and designers, across disciplines.

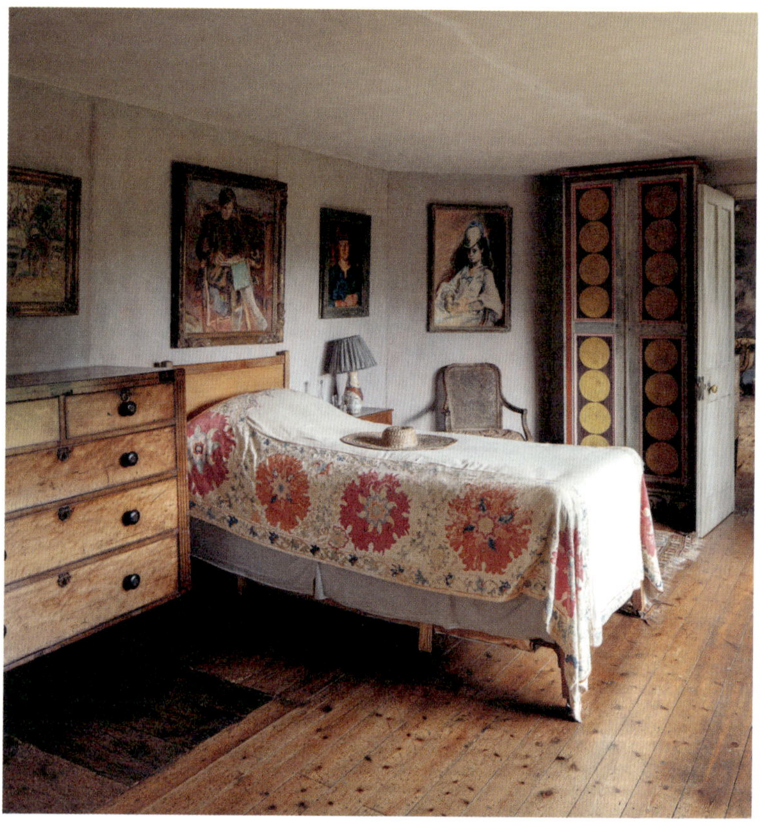

Vanessa's downstairs bedroom at Charleston, with a bedspread that was brought back from Turkey in 1911, the holiday during which she and Roger fell in love.

SEVEN

A RETURN TO ORDER

'IT IS AS DANGEROUS TO BE POLITICAL IN ART AS IT is to be artistic in politics,'[1] wrote Roger to his friend, Charles Vildrac, shortly before peace came. Rather, he opined, art's 'real use is a direct result of its detachment from any actual goal. It is there we must drink our fill of the absolute and not in matters concerning society.' But politics in the post-war period were unavoidable, with the early months of 1919 marked by social unrest. The Russian Revolution had sent waves across Europe, and January saw a mutiny of over two thousand British troops at Folkestone who, exhausted after years of fighting that had left so many dead, refused to board ships, fearing they'd be used to quell uprisings on the Continent. A week later, a thousand soldiers marched on Downing Street, demanding quicker demobilisation and better living conditions. And in February strikes broke out in Glasgow and Belfast, involving one hundred thousand engineering workers clamouring for a reduction to the fifty-four-hour week.

In January, the Paris Peace Conference began, with Maynard Keynes attending on behalf of the Treasury. The League of Nations that Goldie had advocated for came to fruition, but it was coupled with crippling reparations for Germany where Allied blockades had already caused major food shortages, leading to a country-wide famine. Maynard, on his return, resigned from the Treasury, and wrote, in two months, *The Economic Consequences of the Peace*, outlining his fears regarding European economic instability, the rise of extremist ideologies, and further conflict. When it was published in November, it quickly became an orthodoxy in academic circles; Roger described it as 'a book of the first importance in the present world' and recommended it to his friends in France, too.[2] There, swathes of the country lay in ruins, necessitating extensive rebuilding efforts. Roger's sister, Joan, had moved to Berlin to head the Quaker relief effort. And in Britain, the Addison Act was being debated in parliament, which was to establish the foundations for council housing. As moods oscillated between hope and disillusion, there was a collective drive for the tangible and the rational – and Roger, clearing out Durbins, threw out his radical pre- and early-war experiments in abstraction.

Picasso and Derain, neither of whom Roger had seen since his brief trips to Paris in the early years of the war, came to London in the spring of 1919. Picasso had recently married the Ballets Russes dancer Olga Khokhlova and was designing the set and costumes for the company's *El sombrero de tres picos*. By now widely considered a genius, and with a bank balance that could afford to indulge his wife's love of luxury, he put up at the Savoy. Derain, who was also working for the Ballets Russes – his sets and costumes were for *La Boutique fantasque* – stayed at Vanessa's flat, an arrangement secured by Roger. Vanessa had given birth to Angelica, her daughter with Duncan, in December. Though, outside of Bloomsbury, Clive was named as Angelica's father, and Angelica grew up thinking the same.

Roger and Derain, whom Roger described as 'perfectly charming – a great lazy giant, very intelligent and not at all "the great man",' went around 'looking at pictures,' and Derain regularly joined Roger at his new house in Camden. Decorating on a budget, Roger had created an approximation of panelling in the main rooms from strips of wallpaper, painted on the reverse and dotted with a complementary colour chosen to present his pictures to their best effect: a deep blue on yellow ochre, vermillion on pea green. Derain admired Vanessa's *Nativity* and was presumably gratified to see his own work on the walls, and they talked into the night about art and ideas; Picasso joined them at least once – but whereas 'tu' was an imaginable development with Derain, it remained 'vous' with Picasso. Both artists visited the Omega before it closed – Picasso commended the pottery in particular – and Derain visited that year's London Group exhibition at the Mansard Gallery at Heal's, where he admired Roger's paintings without knowing whose they were, and was, generally, 'tremendously encouraging'.[3]

The presence of these two famous men in London revitalised the interest in modern French art, and in August Osbert and Sacheverell Sitwell organised an exhibition with a Parisian–Polish dealer, Léopold Zborowski. Focussing on the period 1914–1919, it too took place at the Mansard Gallery, and as well as work by Picasso and Derain there were paintings by Matisse, Modigliani and Utrillo, as well as a handful of younger artists. Roger, so excited that he arrived while the show was still being hung, reviewed it for *The Athenaeum*. He observed the stream of influence that was 'Naturalist, though not of course the Naturalism of the nineteenth century'. A shifting away from the preceding years' avant-garde extremism, experiments in Cubism, Futurism and Abstraction had given way to a readily identifiable subject matter, though viewed through a modernist lens. Picasso was segueing to Neoclassicism. It was the beginning of what became known as the *retour à l'ordre*, a post-turmoil emphasis on balance, order, reason and form. Still sufficiently cutting-edge to draw almost as much contemptuous ire as Roger's pre-war Post-Impressionist exhibitions, it confirmed, for Roger, his own direction. Describing Derain as 'one of the definite centres of radiation', he enthused on the vitality of the modern movement, and the power it still had to 'set free the expression of individual sentiment'.[4]

Roger's emphasis on freedom reflected his own desired state of being. Almost suddenly – though to some extent by design – he was less encumbered than he'd been in years. His children were older, and once he'd sorted out his debts he had, thanks to the public's appetite for chocolate, sufficient income for his comparatively modest wants, particularly as he would no longer have to fund the Omega. He was out of millionaires to service, as J.P. Morgan had died in 1913 and John G. Johnson in 1917. He'd finally almost finished his lengthy restoration of Mantegna's *The Picture Bearers* at Hampton Court, which had involved quantities of repainting in which he'd been assisted by Paul Nash and Dora Carrington. (It was not an unqualified success – not least in the changing of the race of one of the standard-bearers – and he labelled it one of his 'maddest follies'.) And in May, he'd even resigned from editing *The Burlington Magazine*. Nominally, his departure was due to a disagreement over editorial policy, though he'd weathered worse in the past. But he was itching to return to France, and, in the event, booked his passage before he'd even cleared out the workshops; his sister Margery oversaw their final emptying.

Feeling akin to someone returning from exile, he went straight to Paris. The trains were crowded and chaotic and there were shortages of various essentials, but nothing could mar his thrill at being back in the city that always bowled him over with its beauty. He likened the burgeoning art scene to Renaissance Florence, as artists flocked in, reclaiming the city as an international centre of creativity, helped by the presence of major collectors of modern and contemporary art such as the Steins.

Roger was travelling – and having what was a fleeting affair – with an artist called Angela Lavelli, who'd initially got in contact with him hoping to work for the Omega. They spent several evenings with the Vildracs, and Roger went to the Louvre – which was only partly reopened after being hit by artillery shells in 1918, and very badly arranged, 'all the pictures in little cubicles with a side light' – and to the dealer Paul Guillaume to see his collection of African sculpture. He helped Elspeth Champcommunal, the editor of British *Vogue*, to go through her late husband Joseph's paintings and select works for the section in that year's Salon d'Automne devoted to artists who had been killed in the war. He visited Derain at home and in his reassuringly unpretentious studio, 'just an old garret with a top light',[5] and he bought, from a dealer, a little sketch by Derain that he compared to a Fra Angelico.

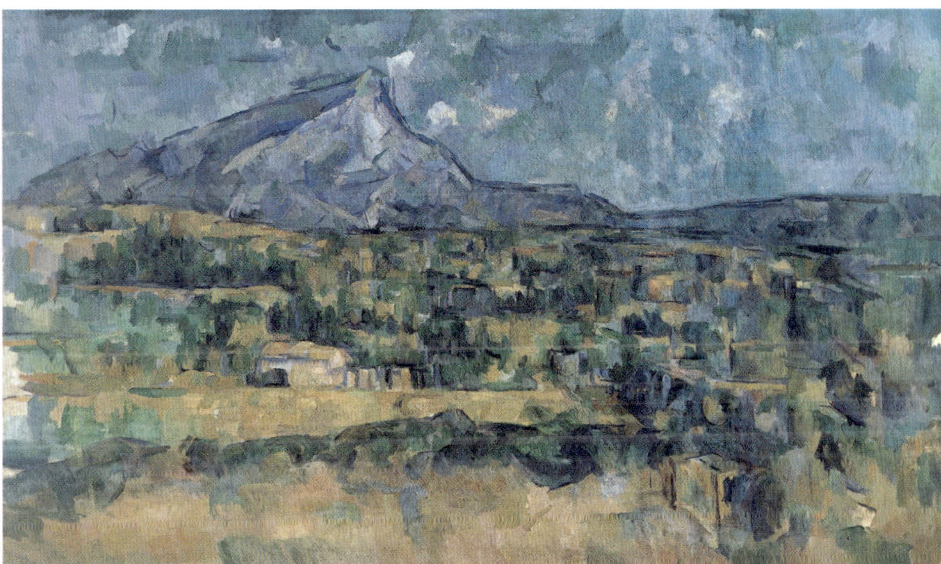

Paul Cézanne, *Mont Sainte-Victoire*, 1902–6.

From Paris he and Angela headed south of Avignon, to landscape unblighted by war, where Roger had painted with Henri Doucet in 1914. His pleasure in the colouring, in every bit of old wall and every tiled roof, was so great that he was almost immune to the fly-ridden filth and discomfort of the rooms (one for painting, one for sleeping) that he'd found in the medieval village of Aramon. He set off by bicycle each morning for a particular valley where he painted from first light until the last, with Angela – whom he felt no compulsion to look after as he would have done Vanessa – walking to join him with their lunch. The locals all wanted their portraits drawn, and in the evenings sat for him in the inn's café. When Angela departed for Italy, he progressed to Les Baux where, following a fortuitous encounter with a young couple, Marie and Charles Mauron (he was studying at the Faculty of Science at Marseilles) Roger spent an evening entranced by Provençal songs sung by the local countrymen. The following day, Marie and Charles took him to visit a man Roger described as 'the great poet of Provence', who lived in a single-roomed house, had translated Homer into Provençal and was now working on Dante. 'I can't give you the curious delight of finding that one can spend an evening with these peasants with much greater ease and happiness than, let us say, Osbert H. Sitwell,'[6] Roger tried to explain to Vanessa.

Next, his itinerary took him on a pilgrimage to Cézanne's house, where he persuaded the gardener (who had never heard of the artist) to allow him to explore. He painted Mont Sainte-Victoire, though from a different perspective to his deity, and using a more muted palette of greys and browns to evoke the shifts in depth. Months later he explained to Marie Mauron that his aim was to 'express the emotions that the contemplation of forms' produced in him, to 'extract fundamental relationships from the multiple, more or less chaotic and discordant shapes of Nature,'[7] something he compared to music, and which tones with Cézanne's well-known dictum, 'I

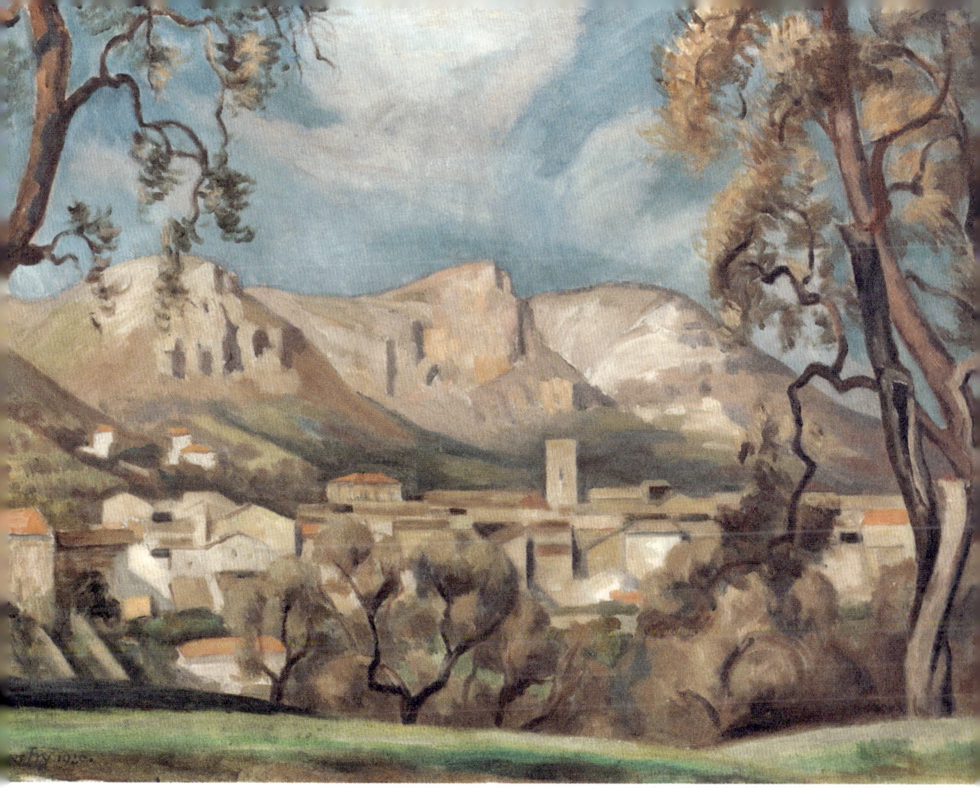

Roger Fry, *Autumnal Landscape, South of France*, 1920.

have not tried to reproduce nature: I have represented it.' There followed ten days at Cagnes-sur-Mer with Jean Marchand, five of whose paintings he owned, but whom he had never met. 'Our tastes are very alike … He possesses that austerity and that solidity of construction which, for me, are the great qualities of the French tradition from Poussin to Cézanne.'[8] He had hoped to meet Renoir, too, when in Cagnes-sur-Mer, but the older artist – who was then seventy-eight – died while Roger was there.

And then, reluctantly – though he conceded that he missed Vanessa and Pamela; Julian was now at his own alma mater of King's College, Cambridge, and having tea with Goldie once a

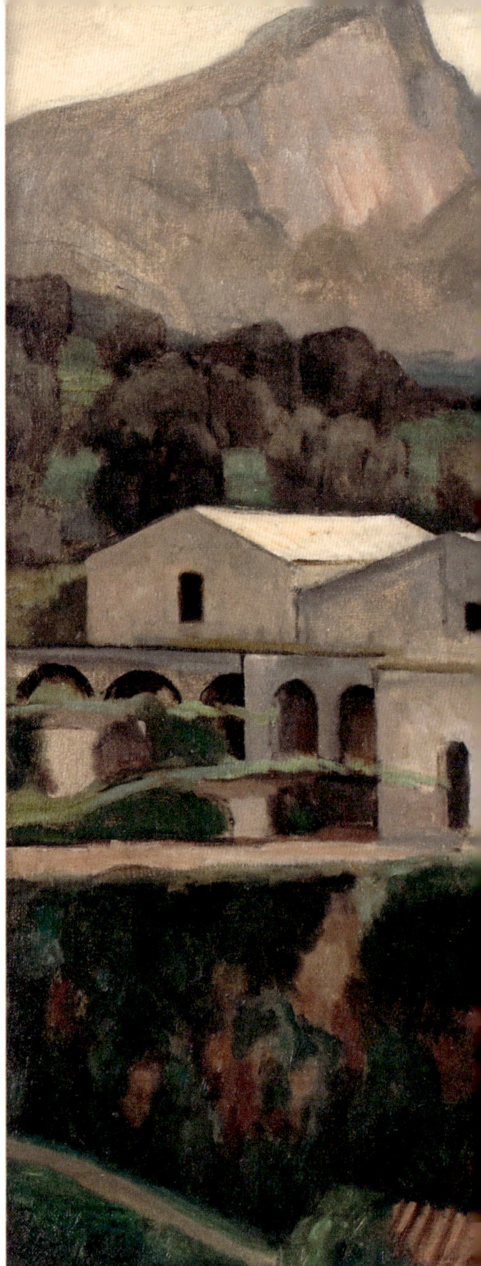

week – Roger headed back to Britain. He went via Paris to drop off some of his paintings with dealers and visit more artists, and again he observed the extraordinary and febrile atmosphere, the opening up of artistic possibilities, and renewed his determination to spend more time on his own painting, which he still viewed as being the most important strand of his career. Through his study of Cézanne, he had concluded that form became most significant in art when it resulted from intense encounters with things seen.[9] Roger's preferred place for those encounters was, without question, Provence. His pattern of splitting his time between France and England resumed.

That spring he hung an exhibition of his, Duncan's and Vanessa's work at Charles Vildrac's gallery in Paris. He met Natalia Goncharova and Mikail Larionov, who were among the many Russian artists and intellectuals who had moved to Paris on account of the Russian Revolution. Roger had shown

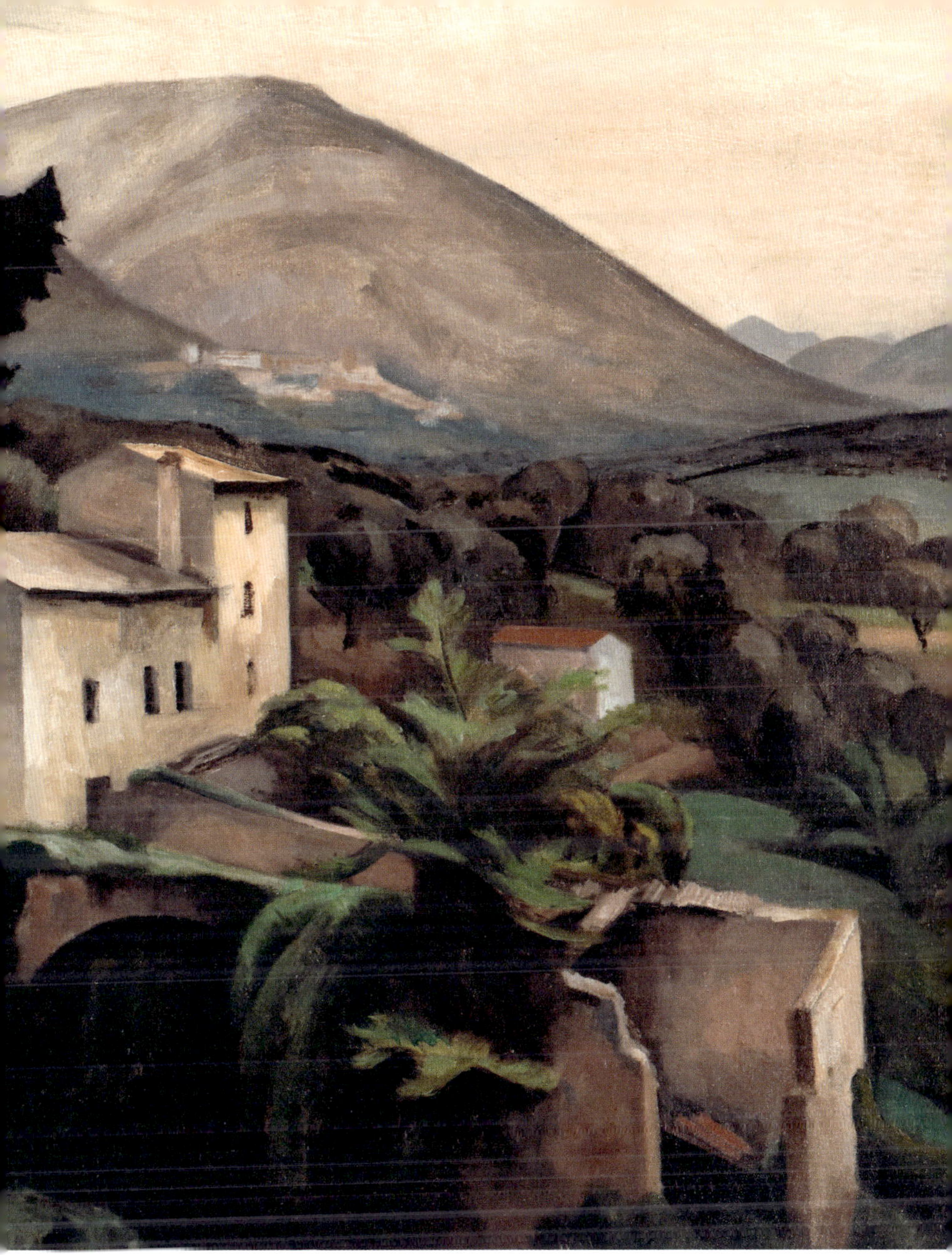

Roger Fry, *Moulin de la Lubiane, Vençe*, 1920. Roger was painting in Vence with Jean Marchand, and this work was likely exhibited at the Independent Gallery on Grafton Street in June 1920 – a show that almost entirely failed.

both their works in the *Second Post-Impressionist Exhibition*, and Larionov's theatre designs had been exhibited at the Omega. Now, Larionov produced a Cubist-style collage, *Homage à Roger Fry*, that had Roger's name incorporated into the design, and Goncharova tried to keep up with translating his excited Russian into French so that a conversation could take place. She was supplementing their income by teaching children, and Roger arranged for her to give lessons to Pamela.

But a solo exhibition of Roger's work, held in June 1920 at the Independent Gallery on Grafton Steet and consisting of eighty-one paintings – predominantly landscapes he'd painted just before the show in an intense bout of productivity in Vence, once more with Jean Marchand – almost entirely failed. It was a depressing moment, and vowing never to exhibit again, he set off with Margery and Pamela for Brittany, where the Vildracs were staying nearby.

There, immediately contradicting his vow, he worked on a vast canvas, over a metre and a half wide, and a metre high, for exhibition at the Salon d'Automne. The subject was a view of sailing boats on the estuary, seen through the towering pines that line the water's edge. When *In the Morbihan* was hung at the Salon, the flash of red sail amid the dark greens and turquoise blues and the gratifyingly solid forms of the painting were widely praised, including by Matisse and Clive – though Clive downgraded his appreciation on the second viewing. But the initial acclamation, especially from Matisse, revived Roger. Goldie wrote to him in October from Italy, suggesting that they find a villa, and spend the rest of their lives together. Roger liked the idea, but it was, he felt, 'for one's later years',[10] and in his mid-fifties he was not yet old enough. Concluding that he was more appreciated in France than in England, he attributed his paintings' failure there to his writings.

> I have defended artists like Picasso and Matisse who are more extraordinary. I am taken for a sort of Bolshevik and then they find that I paint more like Claude Lorrain or Poussin and they are completely baffled.[11]

His observation reflected the popularity of his writing in Britain and how widely his reviews and essays were read. The numbers only increased following the publication, in November 1920, of *Vision and Design*. Persuaded by Margery, he had selected twenty-four of what he considered his most important articles including those on Cézanne, his friend Jean Marchand and the Post-Impressionists; and on Giotto, the Florentine Renaissance and non-Western art of other cultures – Aboriginal, Ancient American, Islamic and African. He expanded some, cut others, and wrote a conclusion in which he traced the development of his aesthetic taste. His uniting message was, again, to 'look at form'. Although the critics didn't award the book entirely universal approbation, it quickly became an essential text for anyone who considered themselves cultured, while the catholicity of subject matter opened new areas of interest. The twenty-two-year-old Henry Moore, a student at Leeds School of Art, described himself led by the chapters on African and Ancient American art to the British Museum, and thence to other non-Western cultures.[12]

The book further solidified Roger's reputation as Britain's leading art critic. Clive – waspish, and professionally competitive with Roger – muttered to Vanessa that among their mutual friends in Paris, where new movements such as Dada were gaining traction, there were some who thought Roger's views a little old-fashioned. But Roger's ideas were still considered by many of the British public to be sufficiently fanatical as to be worthy of satire. John Galsworthy's *The Forsyte Saga* had Soames Forsyte buy a Gauguin because it was in fashion; it became 'the sorest point of his collection'.[13] Mary Hutchison, Clive's mistress, commissioned Tonks to produce a series of cartoons that culminate in Roger holding up a dead cat, with Clive standing next to him proclaiming 'Cezannah!' And in 1921, the Tate Gallery declined a loan of one of Cézanne's paintings, declaring it too modern. Roger, in *The Burlington Magazine*, proclaimed the omission comparable to 'a gallery of Florentine art without Giotto'.[14]

Moreover, Post-Impressionism continued to be a significant influence on painters working in Britain, its impact visible in every exhibition of the London Group – to which Vanessa and Duncan had been elected in 1919, joining Roger, as well as Walter Sickert, Paul Nash, David Bomberg and others. Roger, though he refused all official titles within the group, was widely recognised as a dominant force, and skilfully negotiated the continued success of what was the most progressive exhibiting platform of the time. Alongside, he curated other shows: an exhibition of French art from the past hundred years at the Burlington Gallery, and in 1921, the *Nameless Exhibition of Modern British Painting* at the Grosvenor Gallery, where the anonymity of Roger's 1913 Grafton Group show was revisited on a larger scale. With Tonks and Charles Sims, Keeper of the Royal Academy, Roger brought together works from all the modern movements, including paintings by Royal Academicians. It irritated the press, who thought it was a game played against them, and mixed up pictures by Vanessa and Duncan.

But it was Roger's own paintings that he so wanted to succeed. He and his sister Margery spent the early autumn at Elspeth Champcommunal's house in Saint-Tropez, where Roger rigged up sheets around their beds to evade the mosquitos. There were other artists in the town, and Roger would occasionally join their picnic parties in less-discovered bays, during which they swam 'more or less naked'[15] and discussed art. In October, Margery left, Roger moved into an apartment, and Vanessa, Duncan and the children came out and stayed nearby. Roger reverted to sometimes painting with them, and noticed he was moving in a different direction. He felt he'd got somewhere 'no one else in England'[16] had – not that he thought that would help his pictures succeed there. But it was a happy time, with Sundays on the beach watching Angelica frolic in the waves, shrieking and retreating by turn, while Roger met and embarked on an affair with the Polish painter Mela Muter[17] who was on the selection committee of the Salon d'Automne; several of his paintings featured that year, though Roger observed that the only notice he received was 'slight and not very friendly'. Meanwhile, at the London Group exhibition, everybody had sold except him. He didn't understand what he described as his 'total failure', particularly as he felt so certain of his work. 'I no longer have the feeling that I wish I'd done Duncan's pictures which I always used to have,' he wrote to Margery. 'I'd rather have done my own.'[18] And yet nobody seemed to like them, including Vanessa, who found them 'a dead drab affair',[19] but held back from telling him.

In Paris in the spring of 1922, he saw Picasso, attended, with André Gide, a 'dismal tea party' of Sybil Colefax's in the back room of a hotel,[20] visited more galleries, and examined the Poussins in the Louvre, looking at them with Cézanne-aware eyes. Back in London, a little book of twelve of his woodcuts, published with the Hogarth Press, sold well enough to necessitate another printing.

But a second solo show at the Independent Gallery, where he exhibited recent portraits – Mela Muter, Bertrand Russell (now in the National Portrait Gallery), the Ballets Russes dancer Lydia Lopokova with whom Maynard Keynes had fallen absolutely in love (and was to marry) – fared badly, again. There were accusations of a lack of spontaneity and of laboriousness, and the gallery owner advised Roger to give up painting altogether.

To add to the sense of dismay, Roger's health since the war had been less than perfect. He suffered from internal pains that sometimes kept him awake for hours at night, and his toing and froing was punctuated by trips to doctors in London and Paris, who X-rayed him and diagnosed nervous spasms. He was given strong injections of atropine, and a reduced diet was recommended and followed. In November 1922, he even travelled from Saint-Tropez, where he was spending another autumn painting, to Nancy to see a psychologist. Émile Coué was on the cusp of becoming renowned for his prescribed affirmation, 'Day by day in every way I'm getting better and better' – an exercise Roger found reassuring.

But the illness, and disappointment over the reception of his pictures, didn't noticeably hold Roger back. He continued with his translations of Mallarmé, read Baudelaire, went to the theatre – he described Chekhov's *Uncle Vanya* as 'a very impressionist idea of art'[21] – gave lectures to appreciative audiences, and wrote.

Duncan was gaining in prominence, and in 1923 the Hogarth Press published a book on him written by Roger. 'There are no pangs of jealousy or envy when I see someone else doing good work. It gives me pure delight,'[22] he once said to Virginia, and now he praised Duncan's work for virtues his own paintings had been accused of lacking: 'so spontaneous, so unconstrained, so entirely natural and unaffected'. He described Duncan's designs for the Omega Workshops as having reached 'the high-water mark of applied design in England',[23] delighted in his and Vanessa's continued Omega-like decoration of rooms, and argued that Duncan should be given more commissions for costume and set design (Duncan had collaborated with the French theatre director, Jacques Copeau, for a production in Paris in 1914).

He bought a Matisse odalisque at a Bernheim-Jeune show in Paris, and wrote to Vanessa: 'He seems to go on inventing one melody after another and each more exactly right than the last.

He's a kind of Mozart in colour.'[24] He went back to Spain, where he met Vanessa and Duncan, marvelled at the vast, flat plains, green with corn, that abruptly turned to desert where the irrigation canals stopped, spent days in the Prado looking at paintings by Velázquez, and gathered his sketches and observations into a book, *A Sample of Castille*, also published by the Hogarth Press.

He was called back to Paris in September 1923, to give evidence in the notorious Hahn v. Duveen trial, against the American version of *La Belle Ferronnière* whose owner, Andrée Hahn, claimed it to be the real version of a Leonardo da Vinci in the Louvre. Joseph Duveen, the renowned dealer, had professed it a fake without even seeing it, thus blocking its sale to a museum. Roger, Charles Holmes, and various other Old Master experts were assembled in a private room in the Louvre where the two paintings were placed side-by-side, before they were each questioned in the American Chamber of Commerce. Roger's four hours on the stand became an approximation of one of his lectures, the subject being fifteenth- and sixteenth-century painting technique in Italy. Nevertheless he concluded that Hahn's lawyer was cleverer than Duveen's and indeed, despite every expert opinion, the jury eventually returned an open verdict, and Duveen paid a $60,000 settlement. The painting is now believed to be by a follower of Leonardo.

Watching Roger, even though she didn't speak English, was a young woman called Josette Coatmellec whom he had met in Nancy, where she had gone for her tuberculosis. They were together in Paris in the spring, too, when Roger bought more art, including a Bonnard nude, while simultaneously shopping for the Contemporary Art Society, who got a Matthew Smith and a Roderic O'Connor. The organisation was becoming more influential, mounting exhibitions as well as purchasing art for the nation. Its choices of work to donate to galleries – which was, inevitably, influenced by Roger – increased demand among other institutions for the same artists. Deciding that the Contemporary Art Society needed to be looking abroad too, Roger successfully argued for the creation of a parallel 'foreign fund'. But now, he and Josette argued over an African mask that Roger had bought and showed her, which she had found frightening. Her mental health was delicate in any case, and before she had received the letter that Roger wrote her when he got home to London, explaining that he hadn't intended to alarm her with it, she had shot herself. The whole business left Roger shaken and reminded of the worst times with Helen. He designed Josette's tombstone, and despairing that he'd never find happiness, set off for another season in Provence.

There, countering his mood, his paintings began to regain some of the colour they had lost in the aftermath of the war. It was the beginning of a subtle shift in axis – and, proving Vanessa right in her faintly unfeeling summation that he'd recover from the Josette business,[25] that winter he embarked on the relationship that was to grant him, finally, the 'domestic happiness'[26] which had so long eluded him.

EIGHT

THE FUTURE

It began with a party at Vanessa Bell's Fitzroy Street studio. Helen Anrep, née Maitland, was twenty years younger than Roger. She had spent her later childhood and early adulthood travelling around Europe with her mother, while taking singing and violin lessons. Duncan met her in Florence when she was twenty, and declared her his ideal of feminine beauty. After a brief tour with a small opera company, she moved to Paris, where she had an affair with Henry Lamb, and met Augustus John and his mistress Dorelia McNeill, with whom she developed a close friendship. In 1908, Boris Anrep – who was to be the curator of the Russian section at the 1912 *Second Post-Impressionist Exhibition* – began at the Académie Julien, and met and fell in love with Helen, teaching himself the piano to impress her. They lived together in Britain from 1911 and married in 1918 having had two children, Anastasia and Igor. But it wasn't an easy relationship. Boris had joined the Russian army when the war broke out and embarked on an intense affair in St Petersburg with the poet Anna Akhmatova, who wrote a suite of poems about their relationship. And when he returned to London in 1917, having been made Military Secretary to the Russian Government Committee, he brought with him a young Russian girl who was a distant relation, and became, in effect, a second wife. To begin with, Helen accepted this (Augustus John had lived with his wife and his mistress for while) but Boris was also controlling and jealous.

When Helen – who wore long, flowery dresses and shawls that she pinned at her bosom with a brooch, and white stockings with black shoes, giving her the air of having 'stepped out of a picture by Goya or Manet'[1] – spent almost the entire evening of this party talking to Roger, Boris was furious. He issued threats and recriminations when they got home, and Helen, exhausted by the devotion expected of her for such little return, returned to Fitzroy Street and knocked on the door of Roger's studio.[2] A short time later, so the story goes, Roger was seen dashing across the street back to Vanessa's studio, to seek her advice.

The evolution of the relationship, however, was drawn out. Both were married, and Helen Anrep had two children to consider. Nor did Roger want to embarrass his mother. And so he counselled patience; but the fledgling days proved an uplifting distraction from another disastrous solo show, at the Brummer Gallery in New York. Nothing sold, and Roger incurred £200 in expenses. He perhaps knew of the parallel situation with Picasso's 1923 show in New York; either way, 'comical isn't it?'[3] he commented, and carried on his varied activities, which then included designing a studio for Vanessa and Duncan at Charleston. Having decided to keep the house on after the war, they had recently renewed the lease (for a moment, Vanessa thought they'd have to move and had found a possible replacement in Essex). Roger put together the plans and elevations while working with the shapes of the existing flint walls and reusing the tiles from the existing sheds and outhouses: the aim was to keep the costs as low as possible, which appealed to Roger almost as much as if it were his own money he was saving.

Meanwhile, new artistic movements in France and elsewhere on the Continent were becoming impossible to ignore. In the spring of 1925 Roger was again in Paris, where the *International Exhibition of Modern Decorative and Industrial Arts* had taken over

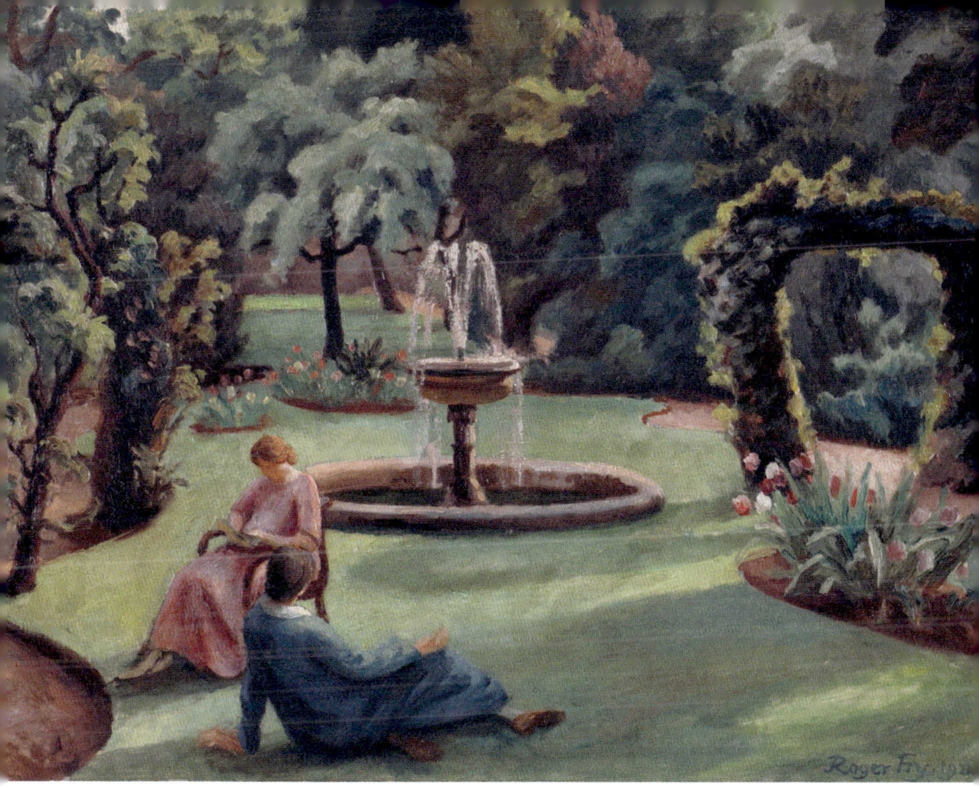

Roger Fry, *Roger Fry's Garden at no. 7 Dalmeny Avenue*, 1924.

seventy-two acres of the city centre, and was introducing, via a succession of pavilions, the style that became known as Art Deco. Roger saw examples of paintings by the Surrealists, whose manifesto had been published in November, and met the *avant-avant-garde* Dada poet Tristan Tzara at a dinner. Wanting to understand, Roger succeeded in getting the Dada writer Jacques Viot alone, and drew him out on his stance and reasoning, which he repeated in a letter to Helen.

> We spent our youth at the war – that has made us more serious than the old … We seek to dislocate everything to stir up trouble for trouble's sake … If we have art at all it must be in order to destroy all existing forms.

There was no beauty in it for Roger, no relatable tradition in the absurdity, and it was too political. He lamented

> the arrivisme, the mercantilisme of the art world here. It has fallen very low and it seems to me all the young are given over to the determination to arrive and attract attention.

He spent most of his days in the Louvre, looking at everything 'as though I'd never seen it before,' and then again 'in blank adoration of Poussin',[4] admiring his clarity and logic and emphasis of line over colour. There was more Poussin when Vanessa joined him in May, as well as Corot and Cézanne.

However, the financial plight of his fellow creatives was ever at the forefront of Roger's mind, and he seldom missed an opportunity to commission a young, 'hard-up' artist to paint him or one of his children. Other pictures by the newer generation were stacking up in the downstairs loo at Dalmeny Avenue, from where they were rescued if a visit by that artist was imminent. Roger had begun advising the industrialist Samuel Courtauld, who was buying French Post-Impressionists; Roger would send him long letters from Paris dealers, describing paintings by Gauguin and Cézanne, and promising him that the exorbitant prices would seem cheap in twenty years' time. At Roger's instigation, Courtauld and Maynard Keynes set up the London Artists' Association. It aimed to assist artists by giving them a small but regular income, taken from the financial guarantors of organised exhibitions, for which those guarantors would have first refusal at buying the works. Importantly, the artists would be paid even if nothing sold. The first exhibition was held in the spring of 1926 and included paintings by Vanessa and Duncan.

There were also ten paintings by Roger, most of which had been made the summer before, in Provence. He had agreed to

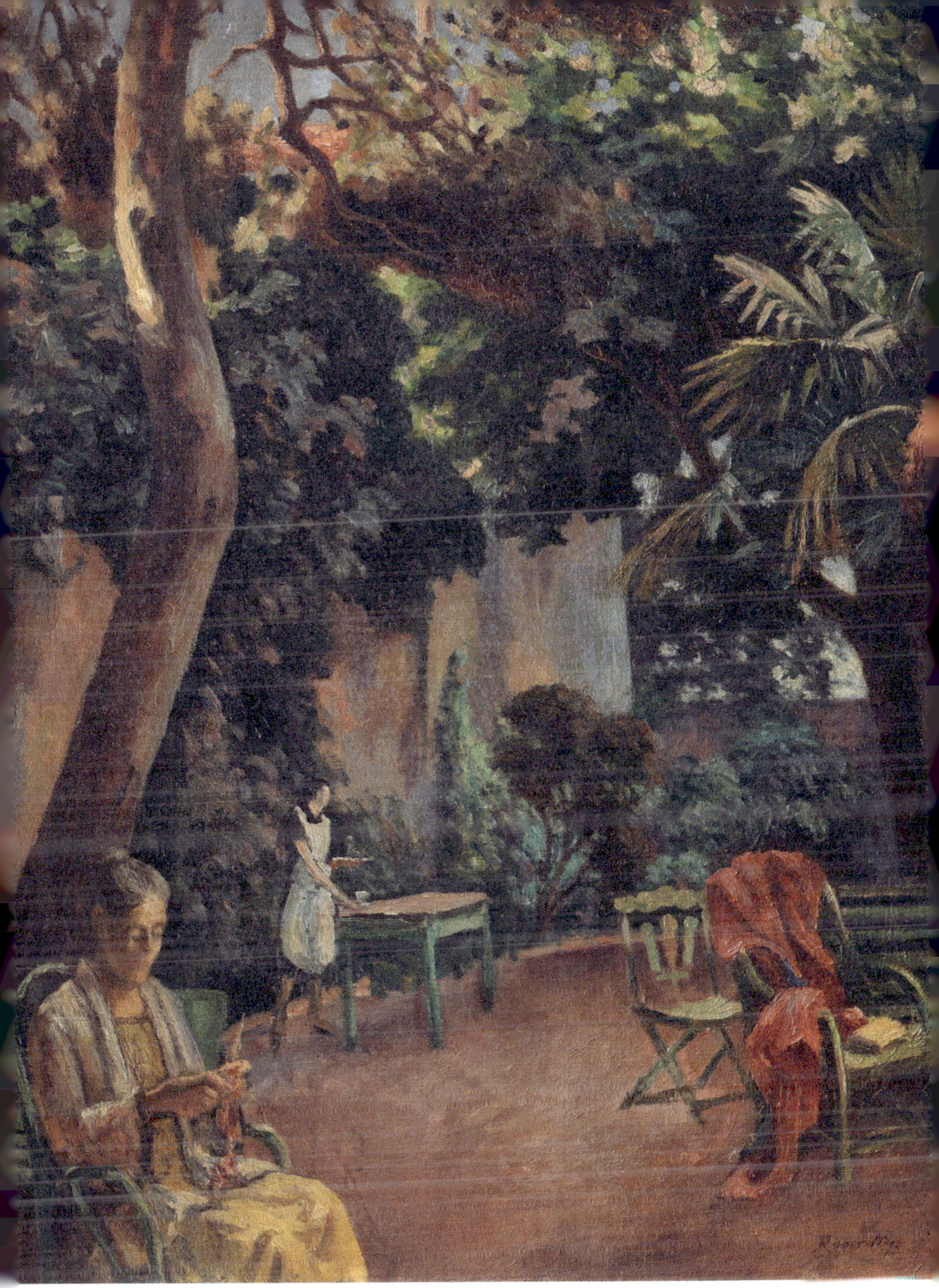

Roger Fry, *Garden at Cassis*, 1925.

forego his 'salary' to get the enterprise off the ground, and hadn't necessarily expected the pictures to sell – but they did. Moreover, the critics professed their admiration. 'Mr Roger Fry never painted as well as now. His large picture, entitled Cassis, baffles criticism. It illustrates his wonderful power of bringing everything in the scene before him into harmonious relationship with the whole,' declared *The Daily Telegraph*.[5] Roger's works were also to be found in the British Pavilion at that year's Venice Biennale – along with Vanessa's, Duncan's, and a host of other British artists, the exhibition having been organised by Frank Dobson, who was then President of the London Group, and Paul George Konody whose Ideal Home Show recommendations had inadvertently caused the Omega fracas.

Further increasing Roger's sense of fulfilment, that summer of 1926 he and Helen moved into a house on Bernard Street, back in WC1, where Roger again arranged his Omega furniture, African carvings, ever-changing collection of paintings, 'rare Persian china and the cheap peasant pottery that he had picked up for a farthing at a fair'.[6] The area was as happily hugger-mugger Bloomsbury as ever, and Roger and Helen shared a cook with Vanessa and Duncan, who did lunch for one household, and supper for the other at their Fitzroy Street studios.[7] Maynard Keynes and his now-wife, Lydia, threw parties at their Gordon Square house that included theatrical revues – one involved a chorus of artists made up of Roger, Duncan and Walter Sickert.[8] Roger too organised gatherings, drawing together friends from across his worlds, bringing together the young French chemist Charles Mauron, whom he had met on that first post-war return to France – and who had been translating Forster's *A Passage to India* into French – with Goldie, Stracheys, Woolfs and Bells, for 'a good old Cambridge Apostolic discussion about existence, whether good was absolute or not'.[9] Helen integrated easily and accepted Roger's declaration that while his passion for

Vanessa had been 'the intensest thing in my life', she, Helen, was 'infinitely better as my wife than [Vanessa] would have been'. He compared Vanessa's intensity and concentrated vision to Helen's 'rich and full'[10] spirit. Of course, Helen wasn't an artist, which Roger had always thought he'd needed; but it transpired that he'd been wrong.

And Helen was a helpful editor; in 1926, Roger published a second set of essays, under the title *Transformations*. The following year, he extended an essay he'd written in French on Cézanne for a publication called *L'Amour de l'art* into a book, published by the Hogarth Press, titled *Cézanne: A Study of His Development*. The National Gallery had, finally, bought a painting by the artist in 1925 (his *Self-Portrait* of c 1880 – acquired at Samuel Courtauld's insistence and with his financial support) and Roger's book was the first critical evaluation of his work in Britain. It was widely acclaimed, as was, in 1930, his book on Matisse. Alongside, he was continually in demand by *The Burlington Magazine,* where he was still a director, *Vogue* and *The Nation and Athenaeum*,[11] where Leonard Woolf was literary editor, who all wanted essays on a broad range of types and periods of art. And in January 1927, when the Royal Academy began putting on a highly successful series of lectures by Roger that tied into a programme of exhibitions of art from different countries, several of them were published.

Other lectures, sponsored by the National Art Collections Fund, were given at Queen's Hall.[12] Its capacity of 2,000 regularly sold out '[to] people from all classes and callings'[13] for his two hour-long discourses, for which he attired himself in evening dress. Sickert was a regular attendee, as was Kenneth Clark, who, in the late 1920s, having recently graduated from Oxford, was assisting Bernard Berenson with research; Clark so admired Roger that he bought one of his paintings. And in 1929 the BBC began broadcasting, on the radio, a series of Roger's lectures entitled *The*

Meaning of Pictures, for which the works Roger discussed were published ahead of time in the corporation's broadcast guide, *The Listener*. All the while, Roger refined and reformed his opinions, turning over his ideas, eventually concluding that contrary to his earlier thoughts, representational content could play an equal role to form. It was something of a volte-face, but as he laid out in a letter to Helen in December 1928, 'One runs a theory as long as one can and then too many difficulties in its application – too many strained explanations accumulate and you have to break the mould and start afresh.'[14]

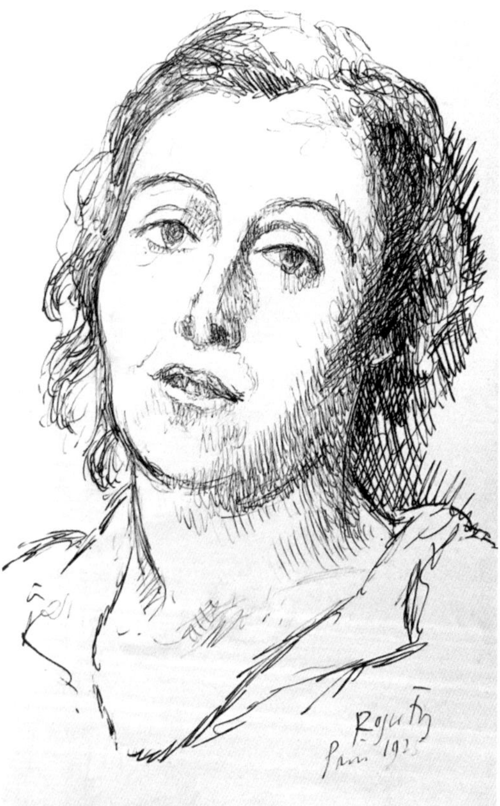

Roger's pen drawing of Helen Anrep, signed with his name and Paris 1925.

It is feasible that Roger's relationship with Helen improved his friendship with Vanessa, serving to balance it, though it still retained elements of the intimacy they had once shared. Vanessa's daughter Angelica noticed that Roger always treated Vanessa with a particular consideration, and listened to her as if hoping, still, 'for a message that had gone astray'.[15] Other relationships also prospered. Angelica was close in age to Helen's children, and, with her brothers Julian and Quentin, viewed Roger as a grandfather figure. There were real grandchildren, too: Pamela had married, becoming Pamela Diamand, and had two daughters: Annabel and Betty. Julian had moved to Canada but came back to visit; he also married, and had two sons, Roger and Alan.

Roger, now in his sixties, would turn up with surprises, teach knots, and make paper birds that flew. He dressed up as Lewis Carroll's White Knight for Angelica's birthday party, and, for another tea, fashioned faux baked potatoes from cardboard that, when cut open, were packed with hundreds and thousands. At Charleston, he played chess with the boys and helped them dredge the pond. One afternoon there, wrapped up by the fire in the dining room, convinced a bout of flu was going to kill him, he noticed that the fireplace didn't look quite right, and requested a hammer and chisel. There were immense quantities of dust – but he uncovered the original inglenook fireplace.

Occasionally, in a mark of his contentedness, Roger talked of retiring. At the same time he hoped, in 1927, for the Slade post at Oxford (he didn't get it, though so many people had wanted him to that there was talk of a petition) and wondered if he might take on the directorship of the National Gallery when Charles Holmes resigned in 1929 (the job went to Augustus Moore Daniel, with whom Roger had travelled to Italy in the 1890s). The problem was that he was, in London, frequently swamped by telephone calls and other correspondence. A letter to Virginia Woolf contained a vignette:

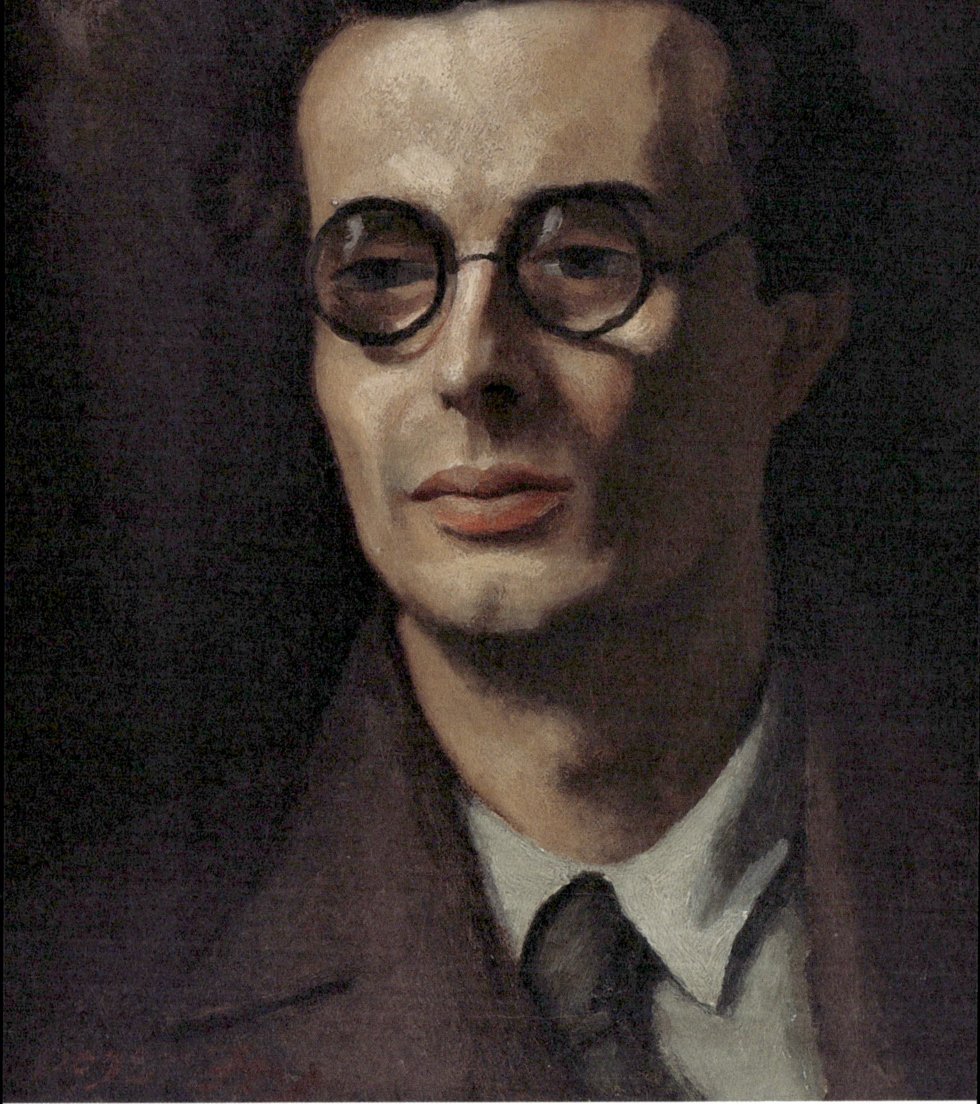

Roger Fry, *Aldous Huxley*, 1931. Vanessa Bell was painting Huxley at the same time, and there was much distracting conversation. Vanessa's version is in the National Portrait Gallery with Huxley sporting an orange tie – Roger painted the orange out.

> Miss — wishes to know if she may come and look at my Matisse. Mr — wants advice on a lot of old masters … A. wants to borrow my Vlaminck. B. came to consult me about his son's education as an art student.

Naturally, he said yes – as well as to the 'hordes of school marms from the USA armed with note-books seeking information' who wanted to look around his rooms, and the 'very intelligent young man from Manchester'[16] who was interested in Chinese pottery.

It necessitated regular escape. In 1927, Roger was made a Fellow of King's College, Cambridge, which gave him a role and a base there, and in 1928 Helen bought a house in Suffolk as somewhere to take her children when they weren't at school, and because the light there reminded Roger of Holland. In possession of a second-hand Citroën, whose mechanics he would attempt to improve himself using rubber bands, string and anything else that came to hand, Roger drove the East Anglian lanes, passing churches and sights he'd sketched with Charles Ashbee while a student at Cambridge.

Travel abroad continued, and with it the same dedication to studying all day in churches and museums, re-evaluating earlier assessments of paintings – and looking at their content as well as their form – whether in Germany, Italy, France or Greece, and whether with Helen, Goldie, Margery, Vanessa and Duncan, or Virginia and Leonard. His enthusiasm never faltered as he wrote to whoever wasn't with him of the splendour of Giorgione, or the divineness of Bellini. There were the dealers to be visited – and the Renoir that Roger bought; 'I never dreamed [it was] within the range of my powers,'[17] he declared to Samuel Courtauld, before explaining that it was cheap, as it wasn't one of the more attractive paintings, but 'the head of an old lady'. He took up lithography, and in 1930, he published a collection of the prints – most being the interiors of French churches – as *Ten Architectural Lithographs*.

And following the death of his mother at the age of ninety-six in 1930 and the ensuing sale of Failands, Roger found an old farmhouse house just outside Saint-Rémy-de-Provence, which he shared with the Maurons and furnished economically from the local town. He made his bed himself from four sections of plane trees, sawn across,[18] and did his own housework, bought his own food, and with Charles Mauron, whose eyesight was failing, played chess and discussed scientific matters, as he once had with his father. It gave him a regular base in the landscape he loved painting, and he'd set up under the pine trees, his head swathed in veils against the mosquitoes. A series of works capture the light and shade and earthy beauty of the olive groves and garrigue, and the calm wrought by the simple form of houses.

Alongside, his interest in portraiture was reawakened, and he began taking commissions, for which he charged about £100, and executed a series of self-portraits. He designed a pair of curtains for Kenneth Clark, who was now Keeper at the Ashmolean Museum in Oxford.

In 1931, the Cooling Galleries, in association with the London Artists' Association, gave Roger a retrospective, in which hung landscapes, still lifes and portraiture from throughout his career, going as far back as *Edward Carpenter*, painted in 1894 (page 41). It was a moment of consolidation – and Roger was pleased with what he saw.

But there were reminders of mortality. 1932 was marked by the deaths of first Lytton Strachey, from stomach cancer, and then in August – on account of bodged care following the removal of his prostate gland – Goldie. Roger had been recuperating from an operation himself, and losing the friend he had once described as being like 'bedrock to anchor on'[19] left him distraught. Memorial services were held in London and in the King's College Chapel at Cambridge. Roger wrote an obituary for the *King's College Memoirs*, while Morgan Forster addressed Goldie's biography.

Bringing some ballast, October saw the opening of the Courtauld Institute in Portman Square as part of the University of London, and the first academic centre in Britain specifically devoted to the serious study of art history. Roger, who had long been exasperated by the residual nineteenth-century attitude that regarded 'any attempt to think or talk seriously about Art as ridiculous',[20] welcomed and celebrated the Institute's existence in *The Burlington Magazine*. Samuel Courtauld, whom Roger had been advising, was one of its founders – and although almost in parallel, the London Artists' Association, which Roger had suggested Courtauld set up with Maynard Keynes, closed, it did so having provided assistance to artists including Ivon Hitchens, Henry Moore and Paul Nash, and having given William Coldstream and Victor Pasmore their first solo shows.

And, in 1933, Roger was finally awarded the long-desired post of Slade Professor at Cambridge, whose earlier holder had inspired such passion in him. Roger was in Spain with Helen when he found out, and in a letter to Margery, glibly put it down to the English worship of antiquity, while taking immense gratification in the appointment. Between hanging a solo show at Agnew's of paintings related to his recent travels and putting together another volume of essays, *Reflections on British Painting*, he set to work preparing the twenty-four lectures he was to give.

Typically, the Slade Professor had a specialist subject. Roger approached the role differently, applying his theories of aesthetics to the visual arts of the whole world, and looking at ideas they shared – 'sensibility', 'vitality' – as well as non-Western artistic styles from Ancient Egypt to China. Cambridge was always a place of conversation and exchange (something of Goldie's spirit lived on in the Lowes Dickinson society, formed by undergraduates to discuss how best peace could be preserved) and Roger was immediately popular among the students. 'He always took one's ideas seriously enough to discuss them, and contradicted them if he disagreed …

He made one share his pleasure in thinking,'[21] explained Julian Bell, Vanessa's son, who was at King's College at the time.

But in September 1934, only half-way through his Slade Professorship, Roger fell while getting ready to go out to dinner in London with Kenneth Clark. Helen called Clark, who came over, and Roger was taken to the Royal Free Hospital. He slipped into a coma, and two days later, died of heart failure.

Vanessa was at Virginia and Leonard's Sussex home, Monk's House, when she was told, and she fainted. The following day, her daughter Angelica heard anguished howling coming from behind her closed bedroom door, and for weeks afterwards Vanessa seemed, to Virginia, 'infinitely mournful & struck, like a statue, something frozen about her'. For Virginia herself, 'the substance has gone out of everything,' she wrote in her diary.[22]

There was a simple funeral at Golder's Green Crematorium on September 13. Roger's coffin was covered in an old red brocade, an organist played Bach's Chorales and Frescobaldi's Fugue in G minor, and not a word was spoken. A larger memorial service at King's College, Cambridge included a passage from his book, *Transformations*, in which Roger wrote of Baudelaire's comparing great names to lighthouses lining the track of time.

> But the lighthouses of art do not burn with so fixed and unvarying a lustre. The light they give is always changing insensibly with each generation, now brighter, now dimmer ... We sometimes forget that the lights have to be tended or they grow faint and may expire altogether. For them to burn brightly they must be fed by the devotion of some few spirits in each generation.[23]

At the end, his ashes, in a casket decorated by Vanessa, were placed in the vault of the soaring spired chapel that he'd once attended daily, in the place that had changed the direction of his whole life.

Roger's will stipulated that paintings by Seurat, Renoir and Bonnard were to be given to the nation. A Matisse landscape was to go to Vanessa, Pamela was to have a landscape by her mother Helen, whom Roger had been writing to weekly, and who survived him (she died in 1937). Helen Anrep was to have anything she wanted from the houses they'd shared, and the same went for his children, Julian and Pamela, and his sisters. Then there was a list of names[24] of non-relations whom he wanted to be able to choose paintings by him, with asterisks indicating those who might have 'a proportionately larger remembrance'. Vanessa and Duncan had two asterisks each. The Maurons also had two, showing how fond he'd become of them – and Charles Mauron helped Julian Bell publish, with the Hogarth Press, Roger's translations of Mallarmé's poems, which he and Roger had redone just before Roger died, after Roger had lost the first draft in a railway station. Clive got a single asterisk with a suggestion of 'books'. The Bell children, Helen Anrep's children and Philippa Strachey all got an asterisk. The MacCarthys were listed, and so was Morgan Forster, Simon Bussy, Bertrand Russell, Kenneth Clark and Charles Ashbee. Anything left, Roger specified, was not to be sold, but to be distributed among institutions who desired works, in this country and abroad.

Most of the rest of his collection went to the Courtauld, awarding it one of the most extensive groupings of Bloomsbury art, as well as one of the finest collections of French Post-Impressionism anywhere in the world. Other major museums and galleries in America and Britain contain paintings that Roger acquired directly or advised on. And the numbers increase when we consider the organisations he founded, and that are proving their essential worth by still fulfilling their original aims. Art Fund, set up as the National Art Collections Fund, has, at the time of writing in 2025, saved over 860,000 works of art for the nation. The Contemporary Art Society has placed 10,500 works in British public collections (others have gone to Commonwealth countries), including – thanks to the foreign fund that Roger instigated and that ran until 1965 – the Tate's first Picasso, which was given to the gallery in 1933. And while we're on the survival of enterprises he founded, *The Burlington Magazine* is still renowned as one of the foremost publications of its type in the world.

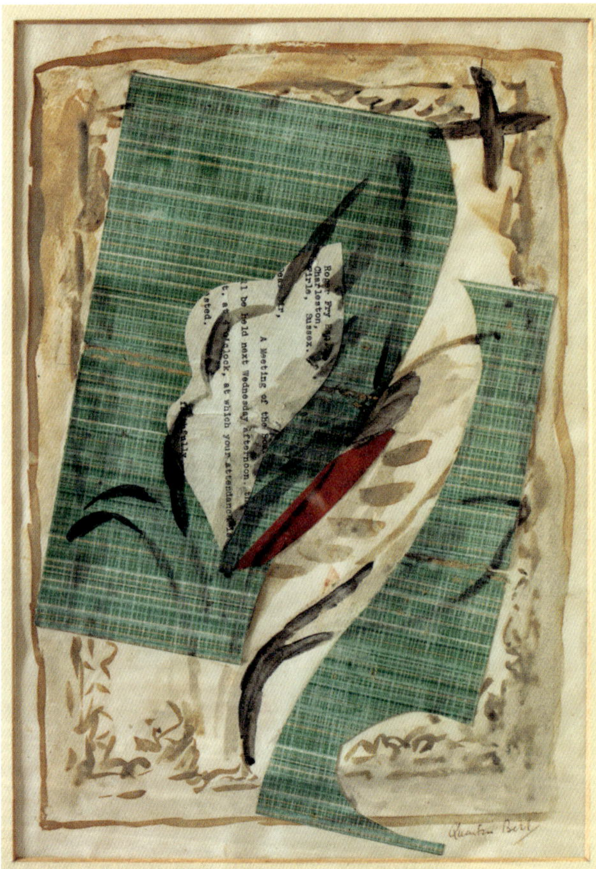

This collage by Quentin Bell hangs at Charleston and was made c. 1934–5. It includes a fragment of a letter addressed to Roger at Charleston.

While alive, Roger set himself against Joshua Reynolds, whose *Discourses* he had re-introduced in the 1890s, declaring

> my highest ambition would be to be able to claim that I have striven to carry on his work in his spirit by bringing it into line with the artistic situation of our own day.[25]

Arguably, he surpassed Reynolds; and the belief he placed in the purity of form gave rise to some of the most significant developments of the twentieth century. Rooted within his writings is not only the appreciation for non-Classical art that so inspired Henry Moore, Barbara Hepworth and others, but the beginnings of English abstraction. As pertinent are Roger's ideas regarding the coupling of art and design: the British studio pottery movement is ongoing, and so is the practice of artists designing fabrics, wallpapers

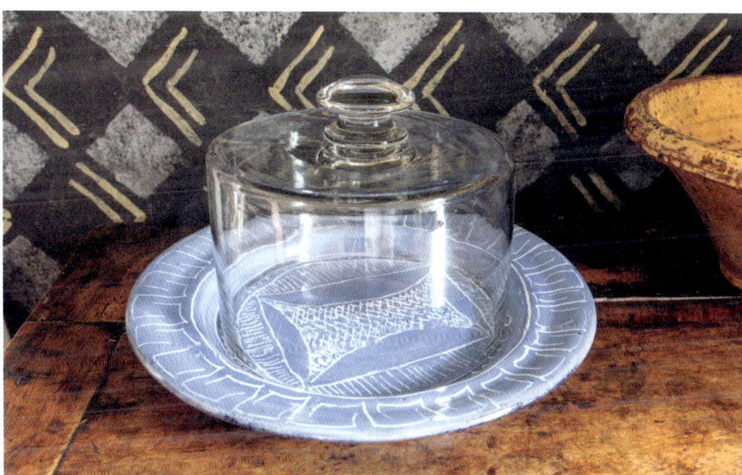

In 1936, Quentin Bell took some Omega Workshops ceramics to Stoke-on-Trent. This charger, in the dining room at Charleston, is a direct copy of one of Roger's designs, and is marked with the Omega symbol, and S.O. 1936.

and more. Art's place in everyday life has not only prevailed, but flourished.

Today, Britain's best universities offer History of Art as a subject, including Cambridge. Alongside, the popularity of our museums and galleries reflects our appreciation for works by the masters of the Italian Renaissance, by Cézanne, Gauguin, Matisse and Van Gogh, by the artists of the modern movements that came after, and by contemporary artists whose approach we might at first struggle to understand but are nonetheless keen to encounter. Roger's exhortation to see and believe in the beauty of art, that it might prove as immeasurably enriching an addition to our lives as it did to his, resounds across the decades.

OVERLEAF: Roger Fry, *Mountainous Landscape near St Remy*, c. 1930.

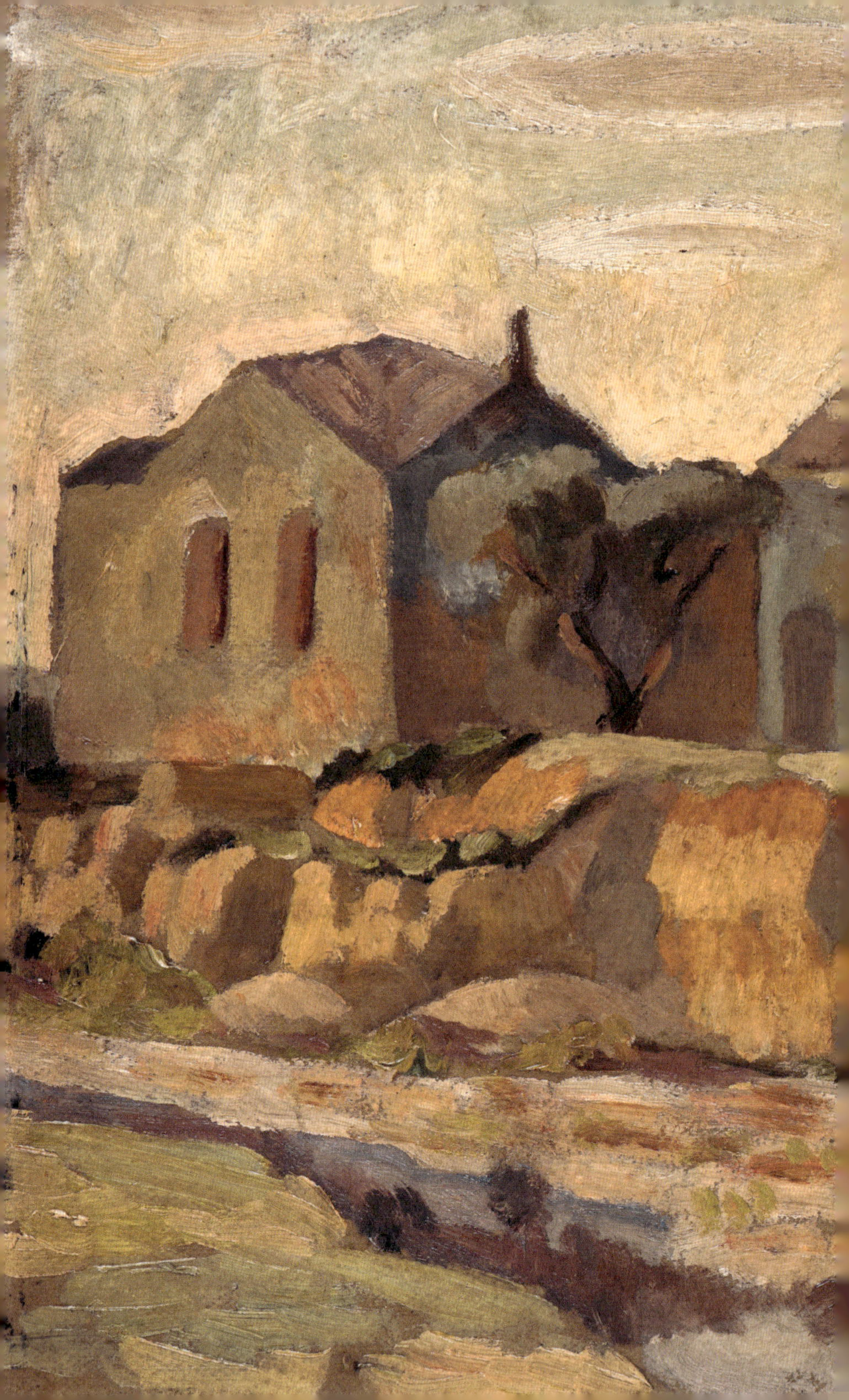

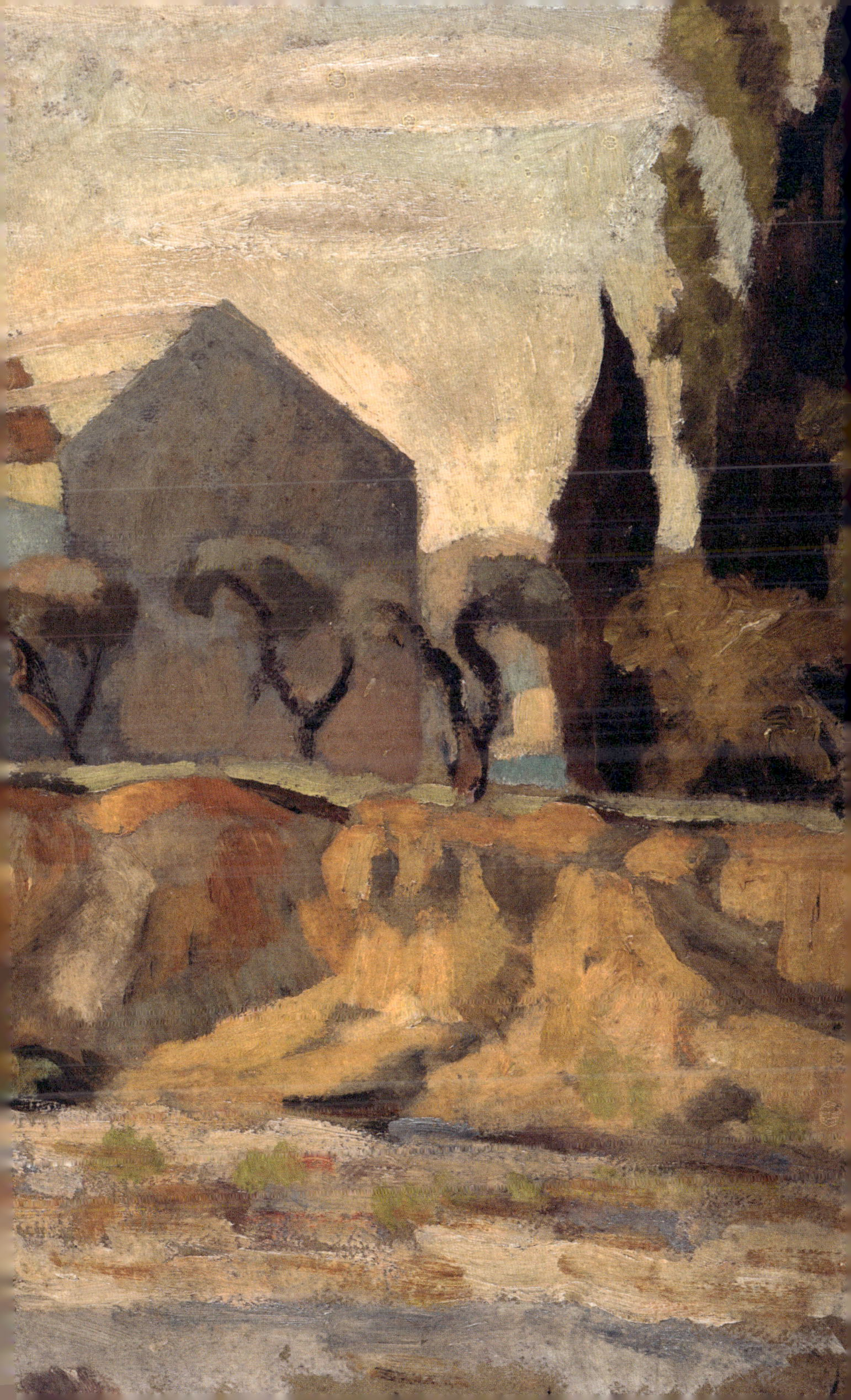

Acknowledgements

THIS BOOK WAS RESEARCHED AND WRITTEN IN AN intense period of excitement interspersed with occasional moments of self-doubt – and I frequently reminded myself of the short time frame Roger gave himself for his books on Bellini, Cézanne and Matisse.

I am indebted to earlier research and published writings, particularly those by Frances Spalding, Richard Shone and Denys Sutton. *The Burlington Magazine* archive has, similarly, been a much-appreciated resource.

Alongside are experts and enthusiasts who have kindly shared their knowledge: Patricia McGuire and Tom Davies at the King's College Archives; Nathaniel Hepburn, Darren Clarke, Polly Jones and Kathy Crisp at Charleston Trust; Barnaby Wright at the Courtauld; Philip Mould and Ellie Smith at Philip Mould & Company; Tania Adams at the Contemporary Art Society; David Herbert; and Richard Shone (again), who knew Duncan Grant.

First-hand accounts also came from Virginia Woolf's diaries and her biography of Roger (written at the behest of Helen Anrep and Roger's sister Margery, and undertaken not entirely willingly, though 'someone will be certain to write about Roger – so it had better be by us'[1]); Vanessa Bell's letters edited by Regina Marler; the myriad Bloomsbury memoirs; conversation with Juliet Nicolson; and autobiographies by other artists of the day. And I am so grateful to Roger's great granddaughters, Rachel Cole and Margery Diamand, for talking me through Fry family history.

A picture tells a thousand words – and we wouldn't have been able to include as many as we have were it not for the generosity of Philip Mould & Company, Piano Nobile, Harry Moore-Gwyn Fine Art, Christie's, Bonham's and the Fry family. I am also delighted to have been able to include colour images of the murals that Roger, Vanessa and Duncan painted at Durbins; thank you to Victoria Wormsley at French-Brooks Interiors, and Philipp Lukas.

There are friends, family, colleagues, and fellow writers who have been enthusiastic and supportive, provided introductions and information and suggested threads to follow. They are many, but I owe particular thanks to Sara Langham, Hatta Byng, Virginia Clark, Rose Washbourn, Susan Deliss, Laura Freeman, Robin Muir, Laura Mitchell, Noel Stewart, Marcus Crofton, Yasmin Hyder, Christopher Thompson-Royds, Robert and Kate McKenzie Johnston and Andrew Steel.

Finally, I am beholden to Henry Howard's and Mike Turner's thorough editing, Tetragon's elegant design and to all at Triglyph Books for having given me the opportunity to write about Roger; Clive Aslet, whose excellent books on Sir Edwin Lutyens and H.M. The King this follows, Dylan Thomas, Kate Turner, India Brooker and Devon Harvey, who did so much picture research, and made the whole process a memorable joy.

Any mistakes are my own.

Cast

(in approximate order of appearance)

FRY FAMILY

Sir Edward Fry – Roger's father; Lord Justice of Appeal
Mariabella Fry – Roger's mother
Portsmouth, Mariabella, Joan, Alice, Agnes, Isabel, Margery, Ruth Fry – Roger's siblings
Joseph Storrs Fry II – Roger's paternal uncle, who ran the family chocolate business, J.S. Fry & Sons
Alfred Waterhouse – Roger's maternal uncle by marriage; renowned Arts and Crafts architect
Helen Fry (née Coombe) – Roger's wife, artist
Julian and Pamela Fry – Roger and Helen's children

CAMBRIDGE

John M.E. McTaggart – Roger's schoolfriend from Clifton College; a Cambridge Apostle; one of the most respected of the English idealist metaphysicians
Charles Robert Ashbee – architect, designer, and founder of the Guild and School of Handicraft
Goldsworthy Lowes Dickinson (Goldie) – Cambridge Apostle; political scientist and philosopher who conceived the idea of the League of Nations

George Bernard Shaw – critic, playwright, winner of the Nobel Prize for Literature for 1925; funded the Omega Workshops

LONDON IN THE 1890S

Francis Bate – Roger's art teacher; secretary of the New English Art Club (NEAC)

Walter Sickert – member of the NEAC; gave Roger evening classes; later founded the Camden Town Group, and then the London Group

Ida and Cecilia Widdrington – Roger proposed to Ida, and had an affair with her mother Cecilia

William Rothenstein – artist, exhibited with the NEAC; he and Roger attended the Académie Julian together, and Walter Sickert's evening classes

Robert (Bob) Trevelyan – Cambridge Apostle; poet; Roger and he shared a house together; collected Roger's work

Bertrand Russell – Cambridge Apostle; philosopher; Roger designed bookplates for him and curtains for his wife Alys; had a long-term relationship with Ottoline Morrell

Henry Tonks – artist; surgeon; taught at the Slade School of Art; NEAC committee member

Edward Marsh – Cambridge Apostle; collector (of Roger's work and Bloomsbury's); committee member of the Contemporary Art Society

Arthur Heygate Mackmurdo – co-founder of the Century Guild of Artists, with whom Roger's wife, Helen, was associated

Arnold Dolmetsch – musician and instrument maker

THE OLD MASTER WORLD, AND OTHER ART ASSOCIATES

Augustus Moore Daniel – a Cambridge contemporary; travelled to Italy with Roger in the 1890s; became Director of the National Gallery in 1929

Bernard Berenson – Florence-based art historian and writer; advised Isabella Stewart Gardner on acquisitions for her museum in Boston; co-founder of *The Burlington Magazine*

Herbert Horne – co-founder of the Century Guild of Artists with Arthur Heygate Mackmurdo; art historian; co-founder of *The Burlington Magazine*; Botticelli expert

Charles Holmes – critic; co-founder of *The Burlington Magazine*; editor of *The Burlington Magazine* 1904–09; Director of the National Portrait Gallery 1909–16; committee member for *Manet and the Post-Impressionists*; Director of the National Gallery 1916–28

Dugald Sutherland MacColl – artist and member of the NEAC; critic; co-founder of the National Art Collections Fund and the Contemporary Art Society; Keeper of the Tate 1906-1911, and the Wallace Collection 1911-1924

Joseph Duveen – major transatlantic art dealer

John Pierpont (J.P.) Morgan – financier and investment banker; President of the Metropolitan Museum of Art

John G. Johnson – corporate lawyer (including for J.P. Morgan); collector

THE FRENCH ART SCENE

The Nabis – influenced Roger in the 1890s and examples of their work were included in *Manet and the Post-Impressionists* and the *Second Post-Impressionist Exhibition*; artists include Pierre Bonnard, Félix Vallotton, Maurice Denis, Édouard Vuillard

Leo and Gertrude Stein – brother and sister; collectors, friends of Picasso and Matisse; Gertrude was a writer

Simon Bussy – artist; married Dorothy Strachey (sister of Lytton Strachey); Roger stayed at their house in the South of France during the war

The Post-Impressionist masters – Paul Cézanne, Paul Gauguin, Vincent van Gogh, Georges Seurat (all deceased by the time of *Manet and the Post-Impressionists*)

Henri Matisse, André Derain – Fauvist artists, included in the *Manet and the Post-Impressionists* and the *Second Post-Impressionist Exhibition*; both became friends of Roger's, particularly Derain who also designed for the Ballets Russes and spent the summer of 1919 in London

Pablo Picasso – Pioneer of Cubism; included in *Manet and the Post-Impressionists* and the *Second Post-Impressionist Exhibition;* became a friend of Roger's, also designed for the Ballets Russes and spent the summer of 1919 in London

Charles Vildrac – poet and art dealer; ran the Galerie Barbazanges, where Roger, Vanessa Bell and Duncan Grant showed their work in Paris; Roger was arrested while trying to reach him at the Front during the war

Henri Doucet – artist; friend of Roger's who stayed at Durbins and at Asheham, included in the *Second Post-Impressionist Exhibition* and exhibited with the Grafton Group, designed for the Omega Workshops; Roger painted with him in the South of France before the war

Jean Marchand – artist; included in the *Second Post-Impressionist Exhibition* and exhibited with the Grafton Group, he and Roger painted together in France after the war

BLOOMSBURY

Vanessa Bell, née Stephen – artist; she and Roger had an affair 1911–14

Clive Bell – Vanessa's husband and father of two children with Vanessa, Julian and Quentin; art critic, author of *Art*

Thoby and Adrian Stephen – brothers of Vanessa Bell and Virginia Woolf; Thoby died tragically young

Virginia Woolf, née Stephen – Vanessa's younger sister; writer (including of Roger's biography); married Leonard Woolf; founder (with Leonard) of The Hogarth Press

Leonard Woolf – writer, editor, political theorist; founder (with Virginia) of The Hogarth Press

Duncan Grant – artist; long-term partner of Vanessa from 1914 and father of Vanessa's daughter Angelica; had other (male) lovers alongside, notably David (Bunny) Garnett

John Maynard Keynes – economist and author of *The Economic Consequences of the Peace*; art collector, Duncan's greatest friend (and former lover); after the war married Ballets Russes dancer Lydia Lopokova

Lytton Strachey – writer and critic; cousin and former lover of Duncan Grant; lived with Dora Carrington, who was in love with him

Philippa Strachey – Lytton's sister; close friend to Roger

(Edward) Morgan (E.M.) Forster – writer

Desmond MacCarthy – critic and writer; secretary for *Manet and the Post-Impressionists*

Ottoline Morrell – patron of the arts; married to Liberal MP Philip Morrell; had a brief affair with Roger and a longer affair with Bertrand Russell

Julian, Quentin and Angelica Bell – Vanessa's children, the first two fathered by her husband, Clive; Angelica was Duncan's daughter

THE LONDON PRE-WAR ART SCENE

Robbie Ross – gallerist and critic; Oscar Wilde's former lover and literary executor; gave Roger exhibitions; slammed *Manet and the Post-Impressionists;* became art advisor to the British War Memorials Committee

The Ballets Russes – founded by Serge Diaghilev in Paris, but performed in London – and elsewhere around the world

Boris Anrep – Russian mosaicist who curated the Russian section of the *Second Post-Impressionist Exhibition*, bringing to London works by Mikhail Larionov and Natalia Goncharova

Paul George Konody – art critic; inadvertently caused a rift between Roger and Wyndham Lewis at the Omega Workshops; co-organised the British Pavilion at the Venice Biennale where Roger, Vanessa and Duncan's work was shown

(Percy) Wyndham Lewis – part of the Grafton Group and the Omega Workshops; after a public argument with Roger founded the Rebel Art Centre and the Vorticists

Nina Hamnett – artist, part of the Omega Workshops; had an affair with Roger during the war

Winifred Gill – artist (no relation to Eric Gill); ran the Omega Workshops during the war

Paul Nash and Dora Carrington – artists; met Roger as young Slade students, worked at the Omega Workshops, helped him with the restoration of the Mantegna *Picture Bearers* at Hampton Court; Carrington fell in love with Lytton Strachey

THE WAR, AND AFTER

André Gide – writer, won the Nobel Prize for Literature in 1947; friend of Roger's and stayed at Durbins

Marie and Charles Mauron – a young couple Roger met and befriended by chance; Charles Mauron was a scientist; Roger shared a house with them in Provence; Charles helped Roger with his translations of Mallarmé's poems

Mikhail Larionov and Natalia Goncharova – avant-garde Russian artists included in the *Second Post Impressionist Exhibition*; Larionov designed for the Ballets Russes; Roger gave him an exhibition at the Omega Workshops, and sold Goncharova's embroideries there

Helen Anrep – wife of Boris Anrep; left him for Roger

Kenneth Clark – art historian, museum director; met Roger when Clark was still a student; published Roger's *Last Lectures* after he died

London Art Groups

The New English Art Club (NEAC) – formed in the 1880s as opposition to the Royal Academy; Roger was a member in the 1890s and early 1900s and exhibited with them; Vanessa Bell and Duncan Grant also exhibited with them in the 1900s

The Friday Club – set up by Vanessa Bell in 1905; she and Duncan Grant both exhibited with them until c. 1913; members included Henry Lamb, Mark Gertler, Frederick Etchells, C.R.W. (Richard) Nevinson and David Bomberg

'The Last Crisis of Brilliance' – not a group, but the name given by their teacher Henry Tonks to an exceptional group of artists who met at the Slade School of Art in the pre-war years and had access to lectures by Roger. They include Stanley Spencer, Mark Gertler, Dora Carrington, Paul Nash, David Bomberg, Edward Wadsworth, Ben Nicholson and C.R.W. Nevinson

The Camden Town Group – 1911–13; members included Walter Sickert, Spencer Gore, Lucien Pissarro, Augustus John, Henry Lamb, Wyndham Lewis and Duncan Grant

The Grafton Group – 1913–14; members included Roger, Vanessa Bell, Duncan Grant, Frederick Etchells, Jessie Etchells, Wyndham Lewis, Henri Doucet, Henri Gaudier-Brzeska, Edward Wadsworth and Nina Hamnett

The London Group – formed in 1913 from an amalgamation between the Camden Town Group and the English Cubists; members included all those from the former, as well as Henri

Gaudier-Brzeska, Jacob Epstein, Ethel Sands, and later Roger, Vanessa Bell and Duncan Grant

The Omega Workshops – not an art group *per se* and there was no membership; those who spent time in the Workshops and/or exhibited there, besides Roger, Vanessa Bell and Duncan Grant, include Wyndham Lewis, Henri Gaudier-Brzeska, Nina Hamnett, Eric Gill, Edward Wadsworth, Cuthbert Hamilton, William Roberts, Paul Nash, Jessie Etchells, Frederick Etchells, Spencer Gore, Henri Doucet, Winifred Gill, Edward Wolfe, Dora Carrington, Mark Gertler and David Bomberg

The Rebel Art Centre/the Vorticists – the Rebel Art Centre was formed in 1914, Vorticism was conceived the same year, and was over by the end of the war. Members included Wyndham Lewis, Frederick Etchells, Edward Wadsworth, Cuthbert Hamilton and C.R.W. Nevinson. Duncan Grant exhibited with the Vorticists in 1915

Endnotes

EPIGRAPH

1 Letter from Virginia Woolf to Vanessa Bell, December 1928, reproduced in S.P. Rosenbaum (ed.), *The Bloomsbury Group: A Collection of Memoirs and Commentary* (London: University of Toronto Press, 1995), p.63.
2 Roger Fry, *The Last Lectures*, introduction by Kenneth Clark (Cambridge: Cambridge University Press, 1939), p.ix.

INTRODUCTION

1 *The Listener*, February 1, 1945.
2 Clive Bell, *Old Friends: Personal Recollections* (Chatto & Windus, 1956), p.77.
3 Paul Nash, *Outline* (London: Faber & Faber, 1949), pp.162–163.
4 Roger Fry, *Cézanne: A Study of His Development* (London: Hogarth Press, 1927), pp. 1–7; the point was first made by Christopher Green in *Art Made Modern: Roger Fry's Vision of Art* (London: Courtauld Institute Gallery, 2000), p.22.
5 William Rothenstein, *Men and Memories: 1872–1938*, ed. and abridged Mary Lago (London: University of Missouri Press, 1978), p.80.
6 Virginia Woolf, *Roger Fry: A Biography* (Columbia, SC: McAllister Editions, 2016; first publ. 1940), p.60.
7 Frances Spalding, *Roger Fry: Art and Life* (London: Black Dog Books, 1999; first publ. 1980), p.138.
8 Letter to Marie Mauron, December 1919, in *Letters of Roger Fry*, ed. and intro. Denys Sutton (New York: Random House, 1972), p.475.
9 Virginia Woolf, *Old Bloomsbury*, written for the Memoir Club, reproduced in Rosenbaum, *The Bloomsbury Group: A Collection of Memoirs and Commentary*, p.55.
10 Woolf, *Roger Fry: A Biography*, pp.109–110.
11 Woolf, *Old Bloomsbury,* p.55.
12 August 1933, reproduced in Woolf, *Roger Fry: A Biography*, pp.215–216.
13 Ibid., p.131.
14 Martin Ferguson Smith, *The Artist Helen Coombe* (Bristol: Shearsman Books, 2023).

1. THE EDUCATION OF AN ARTIST

1 Roger Fry, letter to Sir Edward Fry, February 1888, in *Letters of Roger Fry*, p.120.
2 Ibid., p.2.
3 Woolf, *Roger Fry: A Biography*, p.10.

4 Ibid., p.5.
5 Ibid., p.9.
6 In Roger's letters the school is referred to as Sunninghill House.
7 Ibid., p.17.
8 Eight years younger than Roger, he started there in 1882.
9 Winston S. Churchill, *My Early Life: A Roving Commission* (London: Thornton Butterworth, 1930).
10 It was presumably brief.
11 Roger Fry, letter reproduced in Woolf, *Roger Fry: A Biography*, p.35.
12 G. Lowes Dickinson, *The Autobiography of G. Lowes Dickinson*, ed. Dennis Proctor (London: Duckworth, 1973), p.92.
13 Ibid., p.xiii (foreword by Noel Annan).
14 Ibid., p.92.
15 Fry Archive, King's College, Cambridge, REF/3/46/1.
16 In May 1887.
17 Fry, *Letters of Roger Fry*, p.633.
18 Fry Archive, King's College, Cambridge, letter from Roger to Lady Fry, August 1887, REF/3/57/24.
19 Ibid.
20 Fry, *Letters of Roger Fry*, p.121.
21 Letter to Charles Ashbee, November 1887, ibid., p.118.
22 Letter to Goldie, January 1889, ibid., p.122.
23 Woolf, *Roger Fry: A Biography*, p.44.
24 Ibid.
25 Letter to Goldie, February 1891, in Fry, *Letters of Roger Fry*, p.125.
26 Fry, *Letters of Roger Fry*, p.133.
27 Fry Archives, King's College, Cambridge, REF/3/46/3.
28 Letter to Helen Anrep, August 1929, in Fry, *Letters of Roger Fry*, p.640.
29 From Cecilia Widdrington's diary, reproduced in Celia Chance, *The Widdrington Women and their Eminent Men* (Alnwick: Wanney Books, 2010), p.129.
30 Fry Archive, King's College, Cambridge, letter from Goldsworthy Lowes Dickinson to Roger Fry, May 1891, REF/3/46/3.
31 Chance, *The Widdrington Women and their Eminent Men*, p.135.
32 Rothenstein, *Men and Memories,* p.40.
33 Ibid., pp.48–49.
34 From lecture notes given at Bangor, January 1927, reproduced in Spalding, *Roger Fry: Art and Life*, p.40.
35 Chance, *The Widdrington Women and their Eminent Men*, p.143.
36 Woolf, *Roger Fry: A Biography*, p.60.
37 Fry, *Letters of Roger Fry*, p.154.
38 Roger Fry Archive, King's College, Cambridge, letter from Roger to Goldie, May 1894, REF/3/46/5.
39 Smith, *The Artist Helen Coombe*, p.169.

2. THE MAKING OF AN OLD MASTER EXPERT

1 Woolf, *Roger Fry: A Biography*, p.62.
2 Fry, *Letters of Roger Fry*, p.160.

3 Ibid., p.161.
4 Letter to Lady Fry, 1896, ibid., p.165.
5 Ibid., p.163.
6 Roger Fry, *The Artist as Decorator*, originally published in *Colour* (1917), reproduced in *A Roger Fry Reader*, ed. and with introductory essays by Christopher Reed (Chicago: University of Chicago Press, 1996), pp.207–211.
7 St John the Evangelist, High Cross, Hertfordshire.
8 Fry Archive, King's College, Cambridge, Letter from Roger to Goldie, May 1893, REF/3/46/4.
9 A chain of possibility implied by Spalding, *Roger Fry: Art and Life*, pp.55–56.
10 Letter from Margery Fry to Dorothy Scott, August 1896, ibid., p.133.
11 Letter from Roger to Lady Fry, August 1896, ibid., p.125.
12 Letter from Margery Fry to Dorothy Scott, August 1896, ibid., p.133.
13 Ibid., p.184.
14 From the Berenson Papers, ibid., p.188.
15 Woolf, *Roger Fry: A Biography*, p.73.
16 Letter to Bob Trevelyan, September 1898, in Fry, *Letters of Roger Fry*, p.172.
17 Letter to Sir Edward Fry, June 1898, ibid., p.172.
18 Letter to Bob Trevelyan, October 1899, ibid., p.174.
19 By Dolmetsch; Smith, *The Artist Helen Coombe*, p.204
20 Vanessa Bell, when she met Helen in 1906, noticed Helen was wearing a dress Roger had designed; Spalding, *Roger Fry: Art and Life*, p.90.
21 The Fry Archive, King's College, Cambridge, REF/1/173.
22 Letter to Margery Fry, June 1904, in Fry, *Letters of Roger Fry*, p.189.
23 Woolf, *Roger Fry: A Biography*, p.91.
24 The Leonardo da Vinci was sold at Christie's for $450 million in 2017 – it had been bought by Francis Cook in 1900. The Cook family sold it in 1958 at Sotheby's for only £45, as they had believed the artist was Giovanni Antonio Boltraffio, an attribution likely made by John Charles Robinson, the V&A curator who advised Francis Cook.
25 Roger Fry, review in *The Athenaeum*, 2 August 1902, reprinted in *A Roger Fry Reader*, pp. 249–250.
26 Letter to Sir Edward Fry, October 1902, in Fry, *Letters of Roger Fry*, pp.198–199.
27 Appendix to Woolf, *Roger Fry: A Biography*, p.224 (thought to be written by Vanessa Bell and Duncan Grant).
28 Spalding, *Roger Fry: Art and Life*, p.104.
29 From an article in *The Studio*, 1945, reproduced in Spalding, *Roger Fry: Art and Life*, p.71.
30 Fry, *Letters of Roger Fry*, p. 30.
31 Fry, review in *The Athenaeum*, pp.255–258.

3. AMERICAN AND THE METROPOLITAN MUSEUM

1 Letter to Helen Fry, January 1905, in Fry, *Letters of Roger Fry*, p.227.
2 Ibid., p.228.
3 Ibid., pp.230–231.
4 Letter from Helen to Roger, December 1904, in Smith, *The Artist Helen Coombe*, p.250.
5 Letter to Helen Fry, January 1905, in Fry, *Letters of Roger Fry*, p.233.

6 Philip Hook, *Rogues' Gallery: A History of Art and its Dealers* (London: Profile Books, 2017), p.194.
7 Letter to John G. Johnson, February 1905, in Fry, *Letters of Roger Fry*, p.236.
8 Now in the Metropolitan Museum of Art, New York.
9 Fry Archive, King's College, Cambridge, REF/3/46/5.
10 Letter to Goldie, Fry Archive, King's College, Cambridge, REF/3/46/5.
11 Letter to Sir Edward Fry, March 1906, in Fry, *Letters of Roger Fry*, p.254.
12 Letter to Helen Fry, March 1906, ibid., p.258.
13 Letter to Lady Fry, 1906, ibid., p.252.
14 Letter to Helen Fry, February 1906, ibid., p.253.
15 Letter to Helen Fry, April 1906, ibid., p.262.
16 Metropolitan Museum of Art, New York, temporary exhibition list.
17 Letter to A.F. Jaccaci, June 1906, in Fry, *Letters of Roger Fry*, p.267.
18 Letter to Lady Fry, September 1906, ibid., p.269.
19 Flaminia Gennari Santori, 'European "Masterpieces for America"', in Green, *Art Made Modern: Roger Fry's Vision of Art*, pp.116–117.
20 Letter to Helen Fry, November 1906, in Fry, *Letters of Roger Fry*, p.274.
21 Ibid., p.273.
22 Smith, *The Artist Helen Coombe*, p.264.
23 Spalding, *Roger Fry: Art and Life*, p.97.
24 Fragment of Roger's autobiography, included in Woolf, *Roger Fry: A Biography*, pp.102–105.
25 Spalding, *Roger Fry: Art and Life*, p.99.
26 Letter to Helen Fry, May 1907, in Fry, *Letters of Roger Fry*, p.287.
27 Letter to Helen Fry, June 1907, ibid., p.288.
28 Letter to William Rothenstein, May 1907, ibid., p.285.
29 Letter to Lady Fry, August 1907, ibid., p.289.
30 Letter to Lady Fry, November 1907, ibid., p.292.
31 Reproduced in Spalding, *Roger Fry: Art and Life*, p.99.
32 Fry Archive, King's College, Cambridge, REF/3/58/10.
33 Letter to *The Burlington Magazine*, March 1908, in Fry, *Letters of Roger Fry*, pp.298–301.
34 Letter to Simon Bussy, January 1909, ibid., p.309.
35 Roger Fry, 'Essay in Aesthetics', first published in *The New Quarterly*, April 1909, reproduced in *Vision and Design* (London: Chatto & Windus, 1920), pp.14–27.
36 Reproduced in Spalding, *Roger Fry: Art and Life*, p.113.
37 Letter to J.P. Morgan, in Fry, *Letters of Roger Fry*, p.32.
38 Ibid.
39 Reproduced in Spalding, *Roger Fry: Art and Life*, p.100.

4. ART-QUAKE

1 Virginia Woolf, speech given in Cambridge, 1924, later published in *Mr Bennett and Mrs Brown* (London: Hogarth Press, 1924).
2 Woolf, *Old Bloomsbury*, p. 47.
3 Frances Spalding, *Vanessa Bell: Portrait of the Bloomsbury Artist* (London: Chatto & Windus, 2016), p. 63.
4 Woolf, *Old Bloomsbury*, p.54.

5 Richard Morphet, 'Roger Fry: The Nature of his Painting', *The Burlington Magazine*, vol. 122, no. 928 (July 1980), pp. 437–444.
6 Vanessa Bell, 'Notes on Bloomsbury', reproduced in Rosenbaum, *The Bloomsbury Group: A Collection of Memoirs and Commentary*, p.109.
7 Woolf, *Old Bloomsbury*, p.55.
8 Letter to Sir Edward Fry, February 1910, in Fry, *Letters of Roger Fry*, p.328.
9 Nellie Boxall and Lottie Hope, who in 1916 went to work for the Woolfs.
10 Fry Archive, King's College, Cambridge; REF/3/46/6.
11 Letter to C.J. Holmes, October 1901, in Fry, *Letters of Roger Fry*, p.337.
12 Desmond MacCarthy, *The Post-Impressionist Exhibition of 1910*, reproduced in Rosenbaum, *The Bloomsbury Group: A Collection of Memoirs and Commentary*, pp.74–78.
13 Fry Archive, King's College, Cambridge, REF/3/46/6.
14 MacCarthy, *The Post-Impressionist Exhibition of 1910*, pp.74–78.
15 Reproduced in Spalding, *Roger Fry: Art and Life*, p.128.
16 Reproduced in Woolf, *Roger Fry: A Biography*, p.113.
17 Neil Sinyard, 'Human Character Changed', lecture given at the University of Hull, online version (2018): neilsinyard.britishtelevisiondrama.org.uk/?p=580.
18 Reproduced in Spalding, *Roger Fry: Art and Life*, p.132.
19 Anecdote from Vanessa Nicolson, Vita Sackville-West's granddaughter.
20 Nash, *Outline*, p.93.
21 Letter reproduced in Woolf, *Roger Fry: A Biography*, p.115.
22 Letter to Sir Edward Fry, November 1910, in Fry, *Letters of Roger Fry*, p.338.
23 Letter from Eric Gill to William Rothenstein, reproduced in Woolf, *Roger Fry: A Biography*, p.114.
24 Vanessa Bell, fragment of memoir *Roger Fry*, 1934, reproduced in Richard Shone, *Bloomsbury Portraits* (London: Thames and Hudson, 1976), p.73.
25 Letter from Ottoline Morrell to Roger Fry, reproduced Spalding, *Roger Fry: Art and Life*, p.136.
26 Neil Sinyard, 'Human Character Changed': neilsinyard.britishtelevisiondrama.org.uk /?p=580.
27 Fry Archive, King's College Cambridge, REF/3/58/13.
28 Letter from Roger to Margery Fry, reproduced in Smith, *The Artist Helen Coombe*, p.289.
29 Letter from Dr Head to Roger, in Fry, *Letters of Roger Fry*, p.31.
30 Bell, *Old Friends*, p.83.
31 Letter to *The Burlington Magazine*, March 1908, in Fry, *Letters of Roger Fry*, pp.298–301.
32 Letter to Simon Bussy, May 1911, in Fry, *Letters of Roger Fry*, p.348.
33 Letter to Clive Bell, February 1911, ibid., p.341.
34 Woolf, *Old Bloomsbury*, p.58.
35 Letter from Vanessa Bell to Roger Fry, July 1911, in *Selected Letters of Vanessa Bell*, ed. Regina Marler (Oxford: Oxford University Press, 1998), p.105.
36 Spalding, *Roger Fry: Art and Life*, p.142.
37 Letter from Vanessa Bell to Roger Fry, reproduced in Martin Ferguson Smith, *In and Out of Bloomsbury* (Bristol: Shearsman Books, 2021), p.30.
38 Charleston Papers, King's College Cambridge, CHA/1/216/3/1.
39 Ibid.
40 Reproduced in Spalding, *Roger Fry: Art and Life*, pp.141–142.

41 The date isn't certain. It might have been the following spring of 1913, while they were preparing to open the Omega Workshops.
42 Letter from Vanessa Bell to Roger, July 1912, in *Selected Letters of Vanessa Bell,* p.121.
43 Letter to Lady Fry, June 1912, in Fry, *Letters of Roger Fry*, p.359.
44 Letter to Duncan Grant, Autumn 1912, in Fry, *Letters of Roger Fry*, p.360.
45 Leonard Woolf, *The Second Post-Impressionist Exhibition*, reproduced in Rosenbaum, *The Bloomsbury Group: A Collection of Memoirs and Commentary*, p.146.
46 From *The Observer*, reproduced in Spalding, *Roger Fry: Art and Life*, p.150.
47 Roger Fry, *The Grafton Gallery, An Apologia*, first published in *The Nation*, 9 November 1912, reproduced in *A Roger Fry Reader*, pp.112–116.
48 Woolf, *Roger Fry: A Biography*, p.132.
49 Ibid., p.133.
50 Shone, *Bloomsbury Portraits*, p.78.
51 Bell, *Old Friends*, p.84.
52 Ibid., p.85.
53 Letter to Edward McKnight Kauffer, April 1918, in Fry, *Letters of Roger Fry*, p.426.

5. INTERIOR INNOVATIONS AND THE OMEGA WORKSHOPS

1 Letter from Vanessa Bell to Clive Bell, August 1913, reproduced in Spalding, *Vanessa Bell: Portrait of the Bloomsbury Artist*, p.108.
2 Sjeng Scheijen, *The Avant-Gardists: Artists in Revolt in the Russian Empire and the Soviet Union 1917–1935* (London: Thames & Hudson, 2024), p.110.
3 Roger Fry, Omega Workshops Fundraising Letter, December 1912, reproduced in *A Roger Fry Reader*, pp. 196–197.
4 Ibid.
5 Woolf, *Roger Fry: A Biography*, p.135.
6 Letter to Goldie, May 1913, in Fry, *Letters of Roger Fry*, p.369.
7 Letter from Vanessa Bell to Virginia Woolf, May 1913, in *Selected Letters of Vanessa Bell,* pp.138–139.
8 Fiona MacCarthy, *The Omega Workshops 1913–19: Decorative Arts of Bloomsbury* (London: Thames and Hudson, 1983), p.17.
9 Letter from Vanessa Bell to Virginia Woolf, May 1913, in *Selected Letters of Vanessa Bell,* pp.138–139.
10 MacCarthy, *The Omega Workshops 1913–19,* p.14.
11 Nina Hamnett, *Laughing Torso: Reminiscences of Nina Hamnett* (London: Jonathan Cape, 1932), p.42.
12 Letter to Spencer Gore, October 1913, in Fry, *Letters of Roger Fry*, p.372.
13 Jeffrey Meyers, *The Enemy: A Biography of Wyndham Lewis* (New York: Harper & Row, 1980).
14 Reproduced in Spalding, *Roger Fry: Art and Life*, p.174.
15 Postscript in Clive Bell's hand in a letter from Vanessa Bell, October 2013, in *Selected Letters of Vanessa Bell*, p.147.
16 Fiona MacCarthy, *The Omega Workshops 1913–19: Decorative Arts of Bloomsbury*, p.20.
17 Letter to Goldie, May 1913, in Fry, *Letters of Roger Fry*, p.370.
18 Letter to Charles Vildrac, January 1914, ibid., p.377.

19 Roger Fry, *Wedgwood China*, first published in *The Athenaeum*, July 1905, reproduced in *A Roger Fry Reader*, pp.192–194.
20 Letter to Duncan, ?1914, in Fry, *Letters of Roger Fry*, pp.377–378.
21 Reproduced in Spalding, *Roger Fry: Art and Life*, p.159.
22 The Tate attributes it to either 1914 or 1915 – there were originally several, all with the same title.
23 Nash, *Outline*, p.166.
24 Letter to Goldie, February 1913, in Fry, *Letters of Roger Fry*, p.363.
25 Letter from Bernard Shaw to Roger Fry, reproduced in Spalding, *Roger Fry: Art and Life*, p.177.
26 Ibid., p.167.
27 Letter from Vanessa Bell to Virginia Woolf, May 1913, in *Selected Letters of Vanessa Bell*, p.139.
28 Spalding, *Roger Fry: Art and Life*, p.161.
29 Roger Fry, obituary of Goldsworthy Lowes Dickinson, *College Memoirs*, King's College Archives, Cambridge.
30 Letter to Vanessa Bell, August 1914, in Fry, *Letters of Roger Fry*, p.381.
31 Wendy Hitchmough, *Vanessa Bell: The Life and Art of a Bloomsbury Radical* (London: Bloomsbury Publishing, 2025), p.128.
32 Charleston Papers, King's College, Cambridge CHA/1/216.
33 Letter to Vanessa Bell, February 1915, in Fry, *Letters of Roger Fry*, p.383.

6. WORK AND WAR

1 Ben Angwin, 'Join the Club: The Omega Workshops as a Space for Private Bohemianism', in *Post-Impressionist Living: The Omega Workshops* (Charleston, 2019), p.63.
2 *Omega Catalogue*, 1914, quoted in MacCarthy, *The Omega Workshops 1913–19,* p.63.
3 Letter to Princess Lichnowsky, April 1915, in Fry, *Letters of Roger Fry*, p.384.
4 Reproduced in Spalding, *Roger Fry: Art and Life*, p.184.
5 Ibid., pp.117–118.
6 Ibid., p.186.
7 Spalding, *Vanessa Bell: Portrait of the Bloomsbury Artist*, p.149
8 Letter to Charles Vildrac, February 1916, in Fry, *Letters of Roger Fry*, p.393.
9 Letter to Charles and Rose Vildrac, May 1916, ibid., p.397.
10 Letter from Vanessa Bell to Roger, May 1915, in *Selected Letters of Vanessa Bell*, p.180.
11 Letter to Clive Bell, May 1915, in Fry, *Letters of Roger Fry*, p.385.
12 Woolf, *Roger Fry: A Biography*, p.159.
13 Fry, *Vision and Design*, p.162.
14 Letter to Vanessa Bell, June 1916, in Fry, *Letters of Roger Fry*, p.398.
15 Letter to Pamela Fry, June 1916, ibid., p.399.
16 Ibid., p.399.
17 Letter to Vanessa Bell, July 1916, ibid., p.400.
18 Letter to Charles Vildrac, November 1917, ibid., p.419.
19 Letter to Pamela Fry, March 1917, ibid., p.406.
20 Shone, *Bloomsbury Portraits,* p.169.
21 Bernard Walke, *Twenty Years at St Hilary* (London: Michael Joseph, 1935), p.109.
22 Fry, *Letters of Roger Fry*, p.56.

23 Walter Sickert (RS), review comment in *The Burlington Magazine*, vol. XXXII, Jan–June 1918, p.38.
24 Letter to Vanessa Bell, December 1917, in Fry, *Letters of Roger Fry*, p.423.
25 Charleston Papers, King's College, Cambridge, CHA/1/216/3/124.
26 Virginia Woolf, *The Diary of Virginia Woolf*, vol. 1 (London: Granta, 2023; first publ. 1953), p.172.
27 Letter from Roger to Vanessa Bell, July 1918, in Fry, *Letters of Roger Fry*, pp.430–431.
28 Letter to Philippa Strachey, September 1918, ibid., p.433.
29 Letter to Vanessa Bell, November 1918, ibid., p.439.
30 Reproduced in Shone, *Bloomsbury Portraits*, p.190.
31 Woolf, *The Diary of Virginia Woolf*, vol. 1, p.279.
32 Letter to Vanessa Bell, March 1919, in Fry, *Letters of Roger Fry*, pp.448–449.
33 Woolf, *Roger Fry: A Biography*, p.160.
34 Letter to Vanessa Bell, September 1920, in Fry, *Letters of Roger Fry*, p.489.

7. A RETURN TO ORDER

1 Letter to Charles Vildrac, October 1918, in Fry, *Letters of Roger Fry*, p.435.
2 Letter to Marie Mauron, June 1920, ibid., p.482.
3 Letter to Vanessa Bell, May 1919, ibid., p.451.
4 Roger Fry, *Modern French Art at the Mansard Gallery*, first published in *The Athenaeum*, 8 August 1919, reproduced in *A Roger Fry Reader*, pp. 339–442.
5 Letter to Vanessa Bell, October 1919, in Fry, *Letters of Roger Fry*, pp.457–459.
6 Letter to Vanessa Bell, November 1919, ibid., pp.464–466.
7 Letter to Marie Mauron, November 1920, ibid., pp.496–499.
8 Letter to Marie Mauron, December 1919, ibid., pp.474–475.
9 Letter from Roger Fry to Vanessa Bell, autumn 1919, reproduced in Christopher Green, *Into the Twentieth Century*, included in Green, *Art Made Modern: Roger Fry's Vision of Art*, pp. 23–24.
10 Fry Archive, King's College, Cambridge, REF/3/46/7.
11 Letter to Marie Mauron, June 1920, in Fry, *Letters of Roger Fry*, pp.481–483.
12 Henry Moore, *Henry Moore on Sculpture*, ed. Philip James (London: Macdonald, 1966), p.33.
13 In *To Let*, the concluding novel of *The Forsyte Saga*, published in 1921.
14 Reproduced in Barnaby Wright, *The Courtauld Cézannes* (London: Courtauld Institute Galleries, 2008), p.13.
15 Letter to Virginia Woolf, October 1921, in Fry, *Letters of Roger Fry*, p.514.
16 Letter to Margery Fry, November 1921, ibid., p.516.
17 The pseudonym of Maria Melania Mutermilch; she was the first professional Jewish painter in Poland.
18 Letter to Margery Fry, November 1921, in Fry, *Letters of Roger Fry*, p.517.
19 Letter from Vanessa Bell to Clive Bell, November 1921, in *Selected Letters of Vanessa Bell*, p. 260.
20 Letter to Virginia Woolf, May 1922, in Fry, *Letters of Roger Fry*, p.535.
21 Letter to Vanessa Bell, April 1922, ibid., p.524.
22 Virginia Woolf, Roger Fry, reproduced in Rosenbaum, *The Bloomsbury Group: A Selection of Memoirs and Commentary*, p.169.
23 Roger Fry, *Duncan Grant*, reproduced ibid., pp.209–212.

24 Letter to Vanessa Bell, May 1923, in Fry, *Letters of Roger Fry*, p.534.
25 Woolf, *The Diary of Virginia Woolf*, vol. 1, p.379.
26 Letter to André Gide, September 1927, in Fry, *Letters of Roger Fry*, p.617.

8. THE FUTURE

1 Angelica Garnett, *Deceived with Kindness* (London: Virago, 1984), p.100.
2 Spalding, *Roger Fry: Art and Life*, p.233.
3 Letter from Roger to Marie Mauron, April 1925, in Fry, *Letters of Roger Fry*, p.563.
4 Letters to Helen Anrep, April 1925, ibid., pp.565–567.
5 Reproduced in Spalding, *Roger Fry: Art and Life, pp.*236–237.
6 Woolf, *Roger Fry: A Biography*, p.201.
7 Shone, *Bloomsbury Portraits*, p.211.
8 Michael Bloch and Susan Fox, *Bloomsbury Stud: The Art of Stephen 'Tommy' Tomlin* (London: Philip Mould Gallery, 2023), p.95.
9 Woolf, *Roger Fry: A Biography*, p.201.
10 Letter to Helen Anrep, October 1926, in Fry, *Letters of Roger Fry*, p.597.
11 The two magazines had merged in 1923 – it was thereafter usually referred to as *The Nation.* It was led by a group owned by Maynard Keynes.
12 In Langham Place, London W1. It was destroyed in the Blitz.
13 Virginia Woolf, *Roger Fry*, reproduced in Rosenbaum, *The Bloomsbury Group: A Collection of Memoirs and Commentary*, p.160.
14 Spalding, *Roger Fry: Art and Life*, p.253.
15 Garnett, *Deceived with Kindness*, p.103.
16 Woolf, *Roger Fry: A Biography*, p.197.
17 Letter from Roger Fry to Samuel Courtauld, July 1929, The Courtauld Archive, London.
18 Woolf, *Roger Fry: A Biography*, p.211.
19 Fry Archives, King's College Cambridge, REF/3/46/4.
20 Fry, *The Last Lectures*, p.2.
21 Woolf, *Roger Fry: A Biography*, pp.208–209.
22 Woolf, *The Diary of Virginia Woolf*, pp.322–323.
23 Roger Fry, *Transformations* (London: Chatto & Windus, 1926), p.82.
24 King's College, Cambridge, REF/13/1A/1.
25 Roger Fry, *Reflections on British Painting* (London: Chatto & Windus, 1934), p.48.

ACKNOWLEDGEMENTS

1 Virginia Woolf, *The Diary of Virginia Woolf*, vol. 4: *1931–1935*, ed. Anne Olivier Bell (London: Hogarth Press, 1980), p.336.

Further Reading

Bell, Clive. *Old Friends: Personal Recollections* (London: Chatto & Windus, 1956)
Bell, Quentin. *Bloomsbury* (London: Chatto & Windus, 1968)
Buck, Stephanie, John House, Ernst Vegelin van Claerbergen and Barnaby Wright (eds). *The Courtauld Cézannes* (London: Courtauld Institute Galleries, 2008)
Chance, Celia. *The Widdrington Women and their Eminent Men* (Alnwick: Wanney Books, 2010)
Dickinson, G. Lowes. *The Autobiography of G. Lowes Dickinson*, ed. Dennis Proctor (London: Duckworth, 1973)
Ede, Jim. *Savage Messiah: A Biography of the Sculptor Henri Gaudier-Brzeska* (London: Faber & Faber, 1931)
Fry, Roger. *A Roger Fry Reader*, ed. and with introductory essays by Christopher Reed (Chicago: University of Chicago Press, 1996)
Fry, Roger. *Cézanne: A Study of his Development* (London: Hogarth Press, 1927)
Fry, Roger. *Letters of Roger Fry*, ed. and introduction by Denys Sutton (New York: Random House, 1972)
Fry, Roger. *Reflections on British Painting* (London: Chatto & Windus, 1934)
Fry, Roger. *The Last Lectures*, introduction by Kenneth Clark (Cambridge: Cambridge University Press, 1939)
Fry, Roger. *Transformations* (London: Chatto & Windus, 1926)
Fry, Roger. *Vision and Design* (London: Chatto & Windus, 1920)
Garnett, Angelica. *Deceived with Kindness* (London: Virago, 1984)
Green, Christopher (ed). *Art Made Modern: Roger Fry's Vision of Art* (London: Courtauld Institute Gallery, 1999)
Gruetzner Robins, Anna. *Modern Art in Britain 1910–1914* (New Haven, CT: Yale University Press, 1997)
Hamnett, Nina. *Laughing Torso: Reminiscences of Nina Hamnett* (London: Jonathan Cape, 1932)
Haycock, David Boyd. *A Crisis of Brilliance: Five Young British Artists and the Great War* (London: Old Street, 2009)
Hitchmough, Wendy. *Vanessa Bell: The Life and Art of a Bloomsbury Radical* (London: Bloomsbury Publishing, 2025)
Hook, Philip. *Rogue's Gallery: A History of Art and its Dealers* (London: Profile Books, 2017)
Humm, Maggie. *The Bloomsbury Photographs* (London: Yale University Press, 2024)
Licence, Amy. *Living in Squares, Loving in Triangles: The Lives and Loves of Virginia Woolf and the Bloomsbury Group* (London: Saqi Books, 2015)
MacCarthy, Fiona. *The Omega Workshops 1913–19: Decorative Arts of Bloomsbury* (London: Thames and Hudson, 1983)
Manet and the Post-Impressionists (London: Grafton Galleries, 1910)
Nash, Paul. *Outline* (London: Faber & Faber, 1949)

Post-Impressionist Living: The Omega Workshops (Charleston, East Sussex, 2019)
Reynolds, Joshua. *Sir Joshua Reynolds' Discourses with Introductions and Notes*, ed. Roger Fry (London: G. Bell & Sons, 1905)
Rosenbaum, S.P. (ed). *The Bloomsbury Group: A Collection of Memoirs and Commentary* (London: University of Toronto Press, 1995)
Rothenstein, William. *Men and Memories: 1872–1938*, ed. and abridged Mary Lago (London: University of Missouri Press, 1978)
Scheijen, Sjeng. *The Avant-Gardists: Artists in Revolt in the Russian Empire and the Soviet Union 1917–1935* (London: Thames & Hudson, 2024)
Shone, Richard. *Bloomsbury Portraits* (London: Thames and Hudson, 1976)
Shone, Richard. *The Art of Bloomsbury* (London: Philip Wilson Publishers, 1999)
Smith, Martin, F. *In and Out of Bloomsbury* (Bristol: Shearsman Books, 2021)
Smith, Martin, F. *The Artist Helen Coombe* (Bristol: Shearsman Books, 2023)
Spalding, Frances. *Roger Fry: Art and Life* (London: Black Dog Books, 1999; first publ. 1980)
Spalding, Frances. *The Real and the Romantic: English Art Between Two World Wars* (London: Thames & Hudson, 2022)
Spalding, Frances. *Vanessa Bell: Portrait of the Bloomsbury Artist* (London: Chatto & Windus, 2016)
The Burlington Magazine (London: The Burlington Magazine Publications, 1903–present)
Tillyard, S.K., *The Impact of Modernism: The Visual Arts in Edwardian England* (London: Routledge, 1988)
Vandenbrouk, Melanie and Miriam O'Connor Perks (eds). *Seeing Each Other: Portraits of Artists* (London: Pallant House Gallery, 2025)
Woolf, Virginia. *Roger Fry: A Biography* (Columbia, SC: McAllister Editions, 2016; first publ. 1940)
Woolf, Virginia. *The Diary of Virginia Woolf*, vol. 1 (London: Granta, 2023; first publ. 1953)

Picture Credits

Front cover: Archive Centre, King's College, Cambridge. REF/4/8/12
Endpapers: Rug CF956 produced by CF Editions
10: © Andrew Steel / Philipp Lukas, 2025
13: Private Collection. On long-term loan to The Courtauld Gallery, London.
15: Courtesy of Philip Mould & Company
20: Courtesy of the Fry Family
25: The Metropolitan Museum of Art, New York, Rogers Fund, 1908
28: Archive Centre, King's College, Cambridge. REF/4/8/2
31: The Metropolitan Museum of Art, New York, Rogers Fund, 1905
37: The Metropolitan Museum of Art, New York, Rogers Fund, 1906
39: © National Portrait Gallery, London
41: © National Portrait Gallery, London
48: The Metropolitan Museum of Art, New York, Rogers Fund, 1908
54: The Metropolitan Museum of Art, New York, Rogers Fund, 1906
56–57: Courtesy of Bonhams
64: The Metropolitan Museum of Art, New York, Rogers Fund, 1906
72: The Metropolitan Museum of Art, New York, Catharine Lorillard Wolfe Collection, Wolfe Fund, 1907
77: © Andrew Steel / Philipp Lukas, 2025
78–79: Predella Panels from the High Altarpiece of Sant'Elisabetta delle Convertite, Florence, Sandro Botticelli (Alessandro di Mariano Filipepi) (1445–1510), and Filippino Lippi (1457–1504), John G. Johnson Collection, 1917, cat. 44—4
80–81: © Photography by Dylan Thomas / Courtesy of Charleston House
83: The Metropolitan Museum of Art, New York, Gift of Dr. and Mrs. Franz H. Hirschland, 1957
90: The Metropolitan Museum of Art, New York, Gift of William Church Osborn, 1949
95: The Metropolitan Museum of Art, New York, The Walter H. and Leonore Annenberg Collection, Gift of Walter H. and Leonore Annenberg, 1996, Bequest of Walter H. Annenberg, 2002
99: *Trees by a Lake, Le Parc de Carrières-St-Denis*, 1909 (oil on canvas), Derain, Andre (1880–1954) / The Courtauld, London (Samuel Courtauld Trust) / Photo © The Courtauld / Bridgeman Images
101: Courtesy of Philip Mould & Company
104–105: Courtesy of Philip Mould & Company
107: © Photography by Dylan Thomas / Courtesy of Charleston House
108: Roger Fry, *White Road with Farm*, c. 1912, National Galleries of Scotland. Purchased 1975
110: © National Portrait Gallery, London
111: © Andrew Steel / Philipp Lukas, 2025

112: © Andrew Steel / Philipp Lukas, 2025
116: *River with Poplars*, c. 1912, Roger Fry. Tate, Presented by Mrs Pamela Diamand, the artist's daughter 1973. Photo: Tate
120: Courtesy of Charleston Trust
125: © Victoria and Albert Museum, London
127: Courtesy Piano Nobile, London
128: © Photography by Dylan Thomas / Courtesy of Charleston House
131: Rug CF973 produced by CF Editions
134: *Essays in Abstract Design*, 1914 or 1915, Roger Fry. Tate, Presented by Mrs Pamela Diamand, the artist's daughter 1975. Photo: Tate
141: © Photography by Dylan Thomas / Courtesy of Charleston House
144: Wakefield Permanent Art Collection (The Hepworth Wakefield). Gifted by the Friends of Wakefield Art Gallery and Museums, 1939. Photo: Courtesy The Hepworth Wakefield
146–147: Yale Center for British Art, Paul Mellon Fund
149: © Photography by Dylan Thomas / Courtesy of Charleston House
151: © Photography by Dylan Thomas / Courtesy of Charleston House
153: Reproduced with the permission of Cultural Collections and Galleries, Leeds University Library, Art Collection
154: Courtesy of Philip Mould & Company
156: Courtesy of Philip Mould & Company
158: Courtesy of Philip Mould & Company
161: © Photography by Dylan Thomas / Courtesy of Charleston House
162: Aberdeen Art Gallery & Museums
164–165: Courtesy of Philip Mould & Company
168: © Photography by Dylan Thomas / Courtesy of Charleston House
173: The Metropolitan Museum of Art, New York, The Walter H. and Leonore Annenberg Collection, Gift of Walter H. and Leonore Annenberg, 1994, Bequest of Walter H. Annenberg, 2002
175: Courtesy of Philip Mould & Company
176–177: Courtesy of Philip Mould & Company
187: Courtesy of Philip Mould & Company
189: Courtesy of Bonhams
192: Archive Centre, King's College, Cambridge. REF/4/8/1
194: Courtesy of Philip Mould & Company
200: Courtesy of Harry Moore-Gwyn
201: © Photography by Dylan Thomas / Courtesy of Charleston House
204–205: © Photography by Dylan Thomas / Courtesy of Charleston House

Every reasonable effort has been made to credit and acknowledge the ownership of copyright for illustrations, photography and artwork included in this book. Any errors that may have occurred are inadvertent and will be corrected in subsequent editions, provided notification is sent in writing to the publisher.

Index

FURTHER PRAISE FOR THE TRIGLYPH PEOPLE SERIES

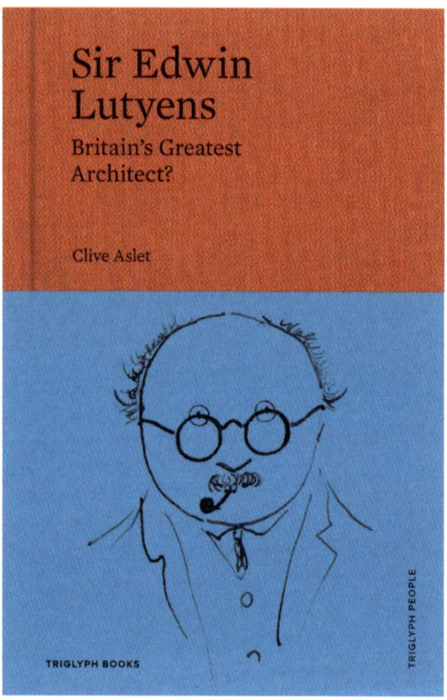

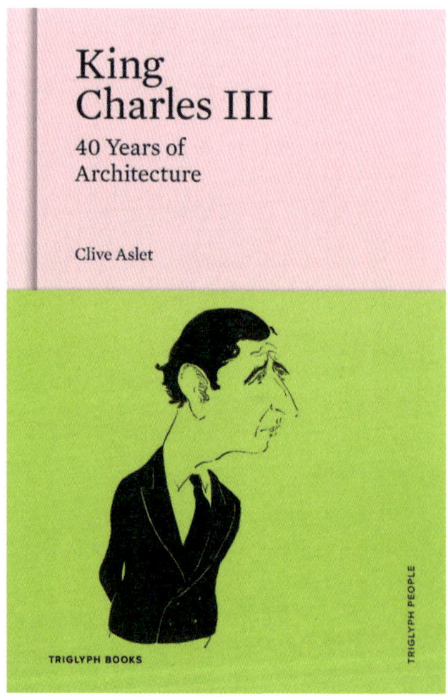

SIR EDWIN LUTYENS: BRITAIN'S GREATEST ARCHITECT?

'As someone who absolutely adores Lutyens and his work I didn't believe there was anything more I could discover about him ... then this beautiful book comes along.' **George Clarke, Architect**

'Lively and scholarly, Aslet's concise biography, elegantly argues for Lutyens's place at the top table of British architecture.'

Loyd Grossman, Broadcaster and Author

'Clive writes with effortless knowledge, bringing the trials and triumphs of Lutyens to life in a way that feels exciting and new.'

Ben Pentreath, *House & Garden* July 2024

'There are compelling reasons to revisit Lutyens, and nobody could do it better than Clive Aslet.' **Alan Powers, *Country Life* May 15, 2024**

'At the opening of this immaculate book, Clive Aslet, one of our most distinguished architectural historians, notes that there have been substantial biographies of Sir Edwin Lutyens, and he does not pretend to emulate them. His achievement, however, is considerable.'

Simon Heffer, *The Spectator* May 18, 2024

'Books can be polemic, books can be challenging, and sometimes books can just tell a good story. Clive Aslet's short biography of Lutyens tells a very good story – not entirely unknown but still packed with enough surprises to keep one reading to the very end.'

Dr Stephen Games, *Booklaunch* Issue 20, July 2024

KING CHARLES III:
40 YEARS OF ARCHITECTURE

'Until now there has not been a proper study made of the King's contribution to the built environment. This brilliant book takes us through all of it.'

Jools Holland, OBE DL,
Composer, Pianist, Bandleader and Broadcaster

'Here is a book and a half, a quite glorious book and a half. The King's interest in architecture has always been stirringly exemplary, and as Aslet most poetically puts it, it is thanks to our noble King that 'Harmony is back on her throne."

Lucinda Lambton, Writer, Photographer and Broadcaster

'This is the only book since *The Vision of Britain* that effortlessly charts King Charles III's passage from Prince to King through his passion for architecture and the built environment. Aslet's unique insight and access to the people who were closely involved makes this the most credible account of the past 40 years.' **Alireza Sagharchi, Architect**

'Nicely paced and elegantly executed. It is also beautifully produced.'
Keith Miller, *Times Literary Supplement*, August 8, 2025

'Aslet has tracked our King's long engagement with building and landscape in a survey that manages to be lively and learned at the same time... He does a bang-up job of tracing the life of a King who's always been "big on architecture."'

Douglas J. Johnston, *Winnipeg Free Press*, Oct 25, 2025

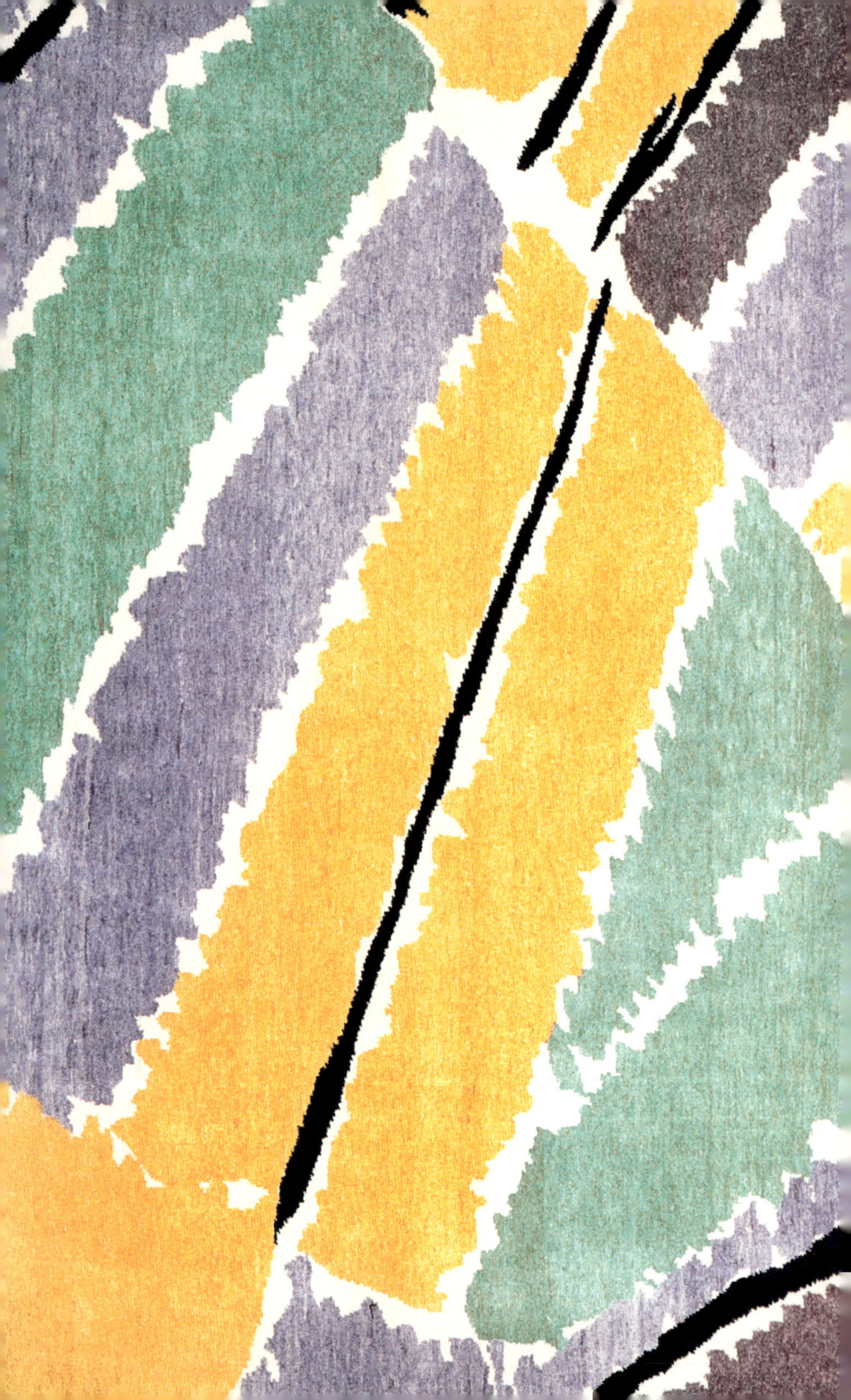